Bak's Sand Pile

Strategies for a Catastrophic World

Ted G. Lewis

Professor of Computer Science
Naval Postgraduate School

AGILE PRESS

An imprint of Agile Research and Technology, Inc.

Published in the United States by Agile Press,

an imprint of

Agile Research and Technology, Inc.

Williams, CA

Printed in the United States of America

First printing, March 2011

ISBN 978-0-9830745-0-2

Cover design by Melissa "Missy" Lieurance and Charles Hamper

info@agilepress.com

www.agile-rt.com

TABLE OF CONTENTS

PREFACE

Why write another book on catastrophes? There are two main reasons: 1) the number and intensity of disasters appear to be increasing, and 2) the literature on natural and human-caused disaster is spread across many disciplines and lacks a unifying theory. The first reason—disaster creep—is clearly a major concern to modern society. We need to understand the cause, and hopefully the remedy, for the malaise. Until we understand catastrophes, we won't be able to do much about them. The number and intensity of disasters will increase until we understand why they happen at all.

The second reason—the search for a unifying theory—concerns modern society's ability to survive over the next 100 years. Terrorism, hurricanes, oil spills, electrical blackouts, transportation system collapses, and political and social upheaval all threaten modern society. Do these catastrophes have anything in common? It seems as though the challenges are getting bigger as well as more frequent, across many disciplines. Are there commonalities underlying these collapses, disasters, and catastrophes? A unifying theory is a step toward understanding the connections between and among complex modern systems.

I propose a unifying theory that explains how accidents, disasters, and catastrophes are intensified by the way modern society has evolved into a collection of highly connected, optimized, and cost-efficient systems. Everything has been optimized—principally by eliminating surge capacity that allows a given system to deal with any overload it experiences. Add to this optimization of capacity the fact that modern just-in-time systems have squeezed out any tolerance for error, and you have the ingredients of what the Danish physicist Per Bak called *self-organized criticality*. This has brought modern society to the brink, and it is our own fault. Modern systems weren't designed to be resilient, self-correcting, and secure, but rather to be low-cost, efficient, and optimized for profitability. As a consequence, the critical infrastructures supporting modern civilization have evolved over the centuries into fragile, error-prone systems. We have reaped the benefits of short-term efficiency, but now we are suffering from it. Efficient, optimal, and cost-effective systems are why $#^! happens.

Many of our modern energy, transportation, health care, telecommunications, and political systems are highly vulnerable to small changes that propagate and develop into major disasters. Think of these systems as garments vulnerable to unraveling by tugging on a single thread. In this case, unraveling means collapsing the financial, energy, communication, and political systems we depend on.

Before we can overcome this tendency to unravel, increase our resiliency, and secure our support infrastructure, we need to understand what causes system failure. A comprehensive unifying theory of catastrophes can guide the development of adequate policy and strategy across multiple disciplines and multiple support systems. This unifying theory is outlined in chapter One, and applied to the many systems that we depend on every day—energy, power, Internet, government, and business—in subsequent chapters. These are all areas that fall within the sphere of homeland security. As it draws on, develops, and innovates extant ideas and visions from a range of disciplines, this book is envisaged as a contribution to the cumulative and emergent, but also nascent understanding of what homeland security really entails.

Bak's Sand Pile is a metaphor for how non-linear, complex systems behave. Per Bak was a creative scientist with an unconventional idea—why not turn the world upside down? Instead of treating catastrophes as outliers, why not treat catastrophes as the norm, and stability as the outlier? In Bak's universe, everyday stability is simply the prelude to the main event—unexpected and extreme collapse. Only through collapses and catastrophes does the world evolve. Life is a series of passages from catastrophe to catastrophe with inconsequential periods of calm in between. We need to learn to navigate stormy seas, because they are the new normal.

If we accept Bak's viewpoint, then how can we mitigate inevitable collapses? We cannot prevent all catastrophes, nor should we try to because they are the key to progress. We can, however, limit their consequences. Small power outages are better than massive power outages; mild political turmoil is preferable to major upheaval; small communication failures are less objectionable than huge failures; and deflected terrorist attacks are more manageable than 9/11-sized attacks. How do we mitigate these risks? The answer lies deep in *Bak's Sand Pile*.

This book is the result of collaboration with the creative and conscientious members of the editorial and production teams at Agile Press, who made the prose more readable and the graphics gorgeous. It has also involved numerous Center for Homeland Defense and Security students, who made this book relevant to the real world. I would also like to thank the 'stars' of this book for their cooperation: Chao Tang, Kurt Wiesenfeld, Nassim Nicholas Taleb, Charles Perrow, Luis Amaral, Martin Meyer, Jerry Williams, Albert Hyde, Donald Turcotte, Bruce Malamud, Mitchel Resnick, Albert-Laszlo Barabasi, Injong Rhee, Minsu Shin, Seongik Hong, Kyunghan Lee, Song Chong, Dirk Brockman, Dennis Derryberry, Hank Eskin, Lars Hufnagel, Yanqing Hu, Rebecca Cann, Mark Stoneking, Allan Wilson, A. Clauset, M. Young, K. S. Gleditsch, Ben Carreras, Ian Dobson, David Newman, Massoud Amin, Scott Brusaw, Julie Brusaw, Marc Maiffret, Ryan Permeh, Ron Minnich, Don Rudish, Frank Bass, Craig Reynolds, and Luís Bettencourt.

1

BAK'S PARADOX

Per Bak   Chao Tang   Kurt Wiesenfeld

"Equilibrium is death. Change is catastrophic. We must adapt because we can't predict." ✓
– Per Bak1

Sand Piles

Imagine a beachcomber pouring grains of sand on a flat stretch of beach. As the beachcomber dumps more grains onto the cone-shaped pile it eventually reaches a critical point—an extreme state of *self-organized criticality*. At that point, a chunk of sand breaks away and cascades down the side of the cone. The process repeats itself when another slow build up of sand is followed by a sudden release of a section of the cone, followed by yet another build up and so on. Don't let the apparent simplicity of this child's play fool you. The sand pile experiment is an example of a simple system that has complex behaviors—what I call 'simple-but-complex systems.' ✓

Systems like this disguise a deep process of great significance. As it turns out, the size and timing of these simple avalanches is impossible to predict. Building sand piles may be simple, but even though they are relatively simple systems, predicting when the inevitable landslides will occur or how big they will be is in fact impossible. This form of

1 http://www.paulagordonshow.com

•   15

complexity can be found in many real-world phenomena that I describe more fully in this book.

Per Bak, Chao Tang, and Kurt Wiesenfeld (BTW) used the analogy of a sand pile to illustrate a fundamental principle of many complex systems—a principle they called *self-organized criticality, SOC*. Systems exhibiting SOC tend to self-organize into a critical state and, once in this state, any change to the system results in chain reactions that may impact a widespread number of elements in the system. So once the sand pile has reached a critical state, the addition of a single grain of sand may have no consequence or it may lead to avalanches of unpredictable sizes—even extreme avalanches that almost completely destroy the sand pile. The three researchers came up with this concept while working together in the late 1980s at Brookhaven (Bak, Tang & Wiesenfeld 1987). It was to become known as the *Bak-Tang-Wiesenfeld (BTW) experiment* or, more popularly, the *sand pile experiment.*

The extraordinary thing is that the BTW experiment explains many naturally occurring and human-caused phenomena of keen interest today. For example, sand piles are excellent models of financial collapses, fires, earthquakes, hurricanes, power outages, oil spills, terrorist attacks, and political upheaval. But Bak took his idea several steps further. He speculated that SOC explains life itself. According to Bak, Darwin's evolutionary theory of life on earth depends on SOC. Without it, none of us would be here today!

Kurt Wiesenfeld, now a Professor of Physics at Georgia Tech said, "I wouldn't myself use the term 'experiment' because what we did was numerical simulations, and among physicists this is considered much closer to theory." The BTW experiment was performed by a computer. Imagine a checkerboard with numbers placed randomly in squares. At some point the total value of the randomly placed numbers in a particular square exceeds some critical value, spilling over to adjacent squares. The overflow to adjacent squares may trigger an additional overflow to more adjacent squares, etc., leading to a sequence of overloads and spills. This was the effect that led the BTW team to use the sand pile metaphor. These virtual avalanches displaced an unpredictable amount of virtual sand at unpredictable time intervals. Many avalanches were small, some were medium-sized, and a few were large. The exact size of the avalanches was unpredictable, and virtual sand pile landslides of various sizes happened without warning.

The cause of these avalanches is completely explained by Newton's laws of physics, and physicist Bak thoroughly understood these laws. In fact, Newton's laws are rather simple in this case, but were nevertheless unable to explain when or how much of the pile would collapse next. Not even Isaac Newton himself would be able to calculate the size and timing of BTW's landslides! This simple experiment is both deterministic (grains are subject to gravity) and probabilistic (timing is random). Sand piles are clearly more complex than they appear. So, too, is life: both simple and complex, just like Bak's sand pile.

Life Isn't Fair

Individual parts of a sand pile behave rather badly—they appear to randomly break away and cascade down the side of the cone-shaped pile without warning. Although individual avalanches aren't predictable in the small, they are predictable in the large. By this I mean that while we cannot determine when the next avalanche will occur, nor can we calculate its size, we can calculate the *probability* of an avalanche of a certain size. For example, we know that approximately 40,000 people in the United States die in traffic accidents every year, and yet we have no way of predicting which person will die next. According to the National Safety Council, the probability of dying on your commute to work tomorrow is 1 in 6,500 annually, or 1 in 84 over your lifetime, but nobody can predict the exact date of his or her demise.[2] Thus, the likelihood of an

---

2   http://www.nsc.org/Pages/Home.aspx

automobile fatality is predictable in the large, but unpredictable in the small. Traffic fatality statistics describe the behavior of the traffic-driver system, but fail to predict individual behaviors of drivers. So it is with simple-yet-complex systems such as sand piles—we cannot predict the behavior of individual grains of sand, but we can model the statistical behavior of the entire sand pile system.

Predictable unpredictability is a characteristic of most complex systems—they exhibit predictable properties in the large, even though their inner dynamics are often unpredictable or too complicated to predict. This seems to be a contradiction, but in fact, the general form of randomness is captured by *probability distributions*. These distributions are obtained by observing a large number of events. A stream of individual grains disappears into the sand pile only to turn up later in an avalanche. In between their appearances we lose track of the individual grains, but their aggregate effect is an inevitable avalanche. Similarly, a stream of commuters disappears into traffic only to turn up later in an accident. In between, we have no idea what each individual driver does, but we can still estimate the likelihood of a fatality. Thus we turn to probability theory to answer the questions that the great Isaac Newton could not answer—what is the probability distribution of when the next avalanche or catastrophe will occur, and how big it will be?

The BTW experimenters simulated thousands of avalanches and counted the number of times avalanches of all sizes broke away and cascaded down the side of the simulated pile of sand. These counts were placed into bins from the smallest to the largest possible avalanche size, and then normalized to add up to 100%. Plotting the normalized counts in this way yields an estimate of the probability of an avalanche of a particular size or larger. At one extreme, they found that there is a *high* probability that a small avalanche will eventually occur. At the other extreme, there is a *very small* chance that a catastrophic avalanche will occur.

The curve obtained by counting avalanches in this way is called an *exceedence probability curve*. It represents the likelihood that an event such as an avalanche, earthquake, airplane accident, or terrorist attack will occur with an associated damage of a certain size or larger. Exceedence curves are also used by the insurance industry to set premiums based on risk (Grossi & Kunreuther 2005). I use them in this book to characterize resilience in complex systems and understand the nature of catastrophes. In the next chapter, I show that exceedence probability curves like the one obtained by Bak, Tank, and Weisenfeld flawlessly model disastrous fires, earthquakes, terrorist attacks, and other catastrophic events.

Bak wasn't an insurance actuary, so he characterized exceedence probability in terms that a physicist understands. The shape of the sand pile curve is a *power law*, the rate of decline of which is determined by an exponent, q.[3] Power laws are lop-sided, meaning that a small avalanche is much more likely to occur than a large avalanche. As the exponent increases, the power law more rapidly declines from high to low probability, making the distribution increasingly lopsided. Bak's avalanches obeyed a simple power law with exponent equal to one, but a power law can have an exponent different than one. Figure 1.1 shows a typical power law.

Most of us are not physicists, so we only need to know that the larger the exponent is for a system, the more frequent the events are at the low end of the consequence scale represented in Figure 1.1 by the horizontal axis. Conversely, smaller exponents mean flatter power laws, or power laws with 'fat,' 'heavy,' or 'long' tails. Typically, curves with an exponent less than one are considered 'fat' or 'long-tailed,' while curves with exponents greater than one are considered short-tailed distributions. Whether a power law has a large or small exponent, q is of great significance; hence, the reason I make such a fuss about its numerical value.

---

3   Power laws are of the form $y = 1/x^q$, where $x > 0$ and $q > 0$.

By the way, the consequence scale or horizontal axis can be anything of interest. It can be damages due to a hurricane, casualties in a war, ticket sales of the top 100 movies of all time, the elapsed time between terrorist attacks, or the decline in industrial production as shown in Figure 1.1a, or the length of the recession as shown in Figure 1.1b.

Figure 1.1. Power law models of the U.S. economy compared to Bak's sand pile.

a. Economic decline (represented by the percent of decline in industrial production) 1854 – 2001 as an exceedence probability. Consequence is defined as the percentage drop in industrial production.[4] The solid line is a power law approximation to the actual data with exponent 1.67.

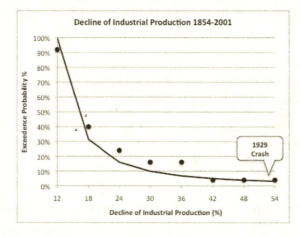

b. Exceedence probability of length of economic declines 1854 - 2001. Length of time is the number of months elapsed between peak economic activity and trough or lowest point of economic activity. The solid line represents sand pile exceedence probability with an exponent of 1.70.

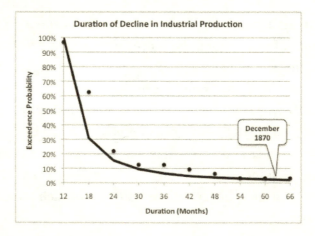

4   http://www.nber.org/cycles.html

Figure 1.1 shows that economic activity obeys a power law just like the BTW experiment, but with different exponent values. For example, Figure 1.1a shows that the exceedence probability of a recession (typically defined as two successive quarters of industrial decline) of a certain size or larger in the United States during the last 150 years obeys a power law with exponent equal to 1.67. Figure 1.1b shows that the exceedence probability of length of recessions obeys a power law with exponent equal to 1.7. Sand piles and catastrophic economic events behave alike, but with different exponents. Economic activity is more likely to be punctuated by small changes and short durations, bursts, because the power laws of Figure 1.1 are lop-sided.

The interesting fact is that even though these events are radically different, they all obey a power law! Power laws are very common in the real world. In fact, they have many names. Zipf's Law, Pareto's Law, scale-free, fractal, and self-similar systems are a few other names given to the mathematical model describing the same phenomenon—power laws. An interesting thing about power laws is that *they are not Bell-shaped Normal Distributions*, the staple of any introduction to statistics and probability. Unlike symmetric Normal Distributions, power law distributions are asymmetric. Extreme events are highly rare, while modest events are rather common.

What does the power law tell us? In the case of avalanches, Bak's power law says that small avalanches occur much more often than large avalanches. In fact, extremely large avalanches are extremely rare. This is a fortunate fact of nature: the most common disasters are small while major disasters—catastrophes—are rare! Events that obey a long-tailed (flatter, small exponent) power law are more disruptive and dangerous than events that obey a short-tailed (sharper, large exponent) power law. So we should hope that life is not only unfair, but drastically unfair, with sharply declining power laws for earthquakes, floods, fires, terrorist attacks, market crashes, and epidemics. In terms of major events such as hurricanes, earthquakes, economic meltdowns, terrorist attacks, and other disasters, sharply declining exceedence probability curves—and the power laws describing them—are better.

If the horizontal axis is *time* instead of damage or size, a sharply declining power law means many small events are clustered in time, while a few events are widely spaced out in time. That is, events are bursty. Flatter curves mean big events are more likely to be evenly spaced in time, even if they are spaced further apart. These are not so bursty. Figure 1.1b illustrates this concept. Small economic declines are much more closely spaced together in time than large ones. Recessions are bursty, while depressions are episodic.

The Other Shoe Drops

In the next chapter I expand on the utility of power laws and show that they model extreme events of all sorts much better than traditional methods, such as averaging. However, let us first examine the second part of Bak's radical theory of reality. Bak postulated that power laws are the consequence of the build-up of complexity in systems due to various forms of self-organization. Self-organization is an emergent process of complex systems whereby simplicity is gradually replaced by complexity. The process is considered 'self-organizing' because to the outside observer, the emergence of complexity is intrinsic; it is contained within the system itself. In most systems, however, self-organizing requires energy to transform or rearrange the inner workings of the system. Tectonic movements 'organize' earth's crust until an earthquake occurs; regulatory forces shape the electric power grid or telecommunications systems of an entire nation until a catastrophe occurs; and political energy is poured into governments and societies, fueling socio-economic self-organization that generally leads to financial ruin, war, and social change.

Bak categorized the process of turning energy into complexity as *self-organization,* and the ultimate pinnacle of complexity as *self-organized criticality,* SOC. Ultimate SOC is the state of a system on the verge of collapse due to its own complexity. SOC shows up in the shape of the power law characterizing a system's behavior. Systems with high SOC have long-tailed exceedence probability curves, which suggests that they suffer larger consequences. Thus, there is a connection between SOC, resiliency, and the power law 'signature' of such systems. But what is SOC, really? How does it work, and why does it often lead to a disastrous end? To get a better handle on what SOC is and how it works within complex systems, consider the pitfalls of fatal attraction among rabbits!

Figure 1.2. The build-up of criticality in an imaginary red/blue rabbit population leads to extinction.

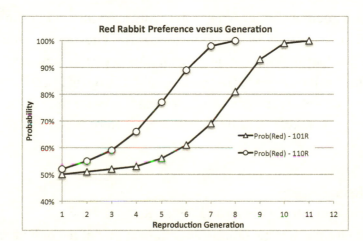

Fatal Attractors

Consider a simple example of an evolutionary system consisting of an initial population of 100 red rabbits and 100 blue rabbits. Red rabbits breed with blue rabbits to produce offspring, and vice versa. I'll assume parents reproduce only 2 offspring once in their lifetime and then die off. Furthermore, breeding rabbits produce offspring rabbits in proportion to the fraction of red rabbits currently in the population at the time reproduction takes place. Thus, initially, 100/200 or 50% of offspring are red rabbits, and the other 50% of the first-generation offspring are blue. Like most rabbits, my hypothetical red-blue rabbit population repeats a reproductive cycle forever or until it runs out of either red, blue, or both kinds of rabbits.

Extinction of either red or blue rabbits means extinction of the entire population, because it takes two to tango. The question is, how many red rabbits does the population contain after a certain amount of time has passed? Is it possible for red or blue rabbits to go extinct? Extinction of either red or blue rabbits would be a catastrophe for this rabbit world, so finding an answer is critically important. Here is how this system works:

Rabbit Reproduction
1. Start with R Red Rabbits and B Blue Rabbits
2. Produce the next generation until the number of red or blue rabbits reaches zero:
    a. The probability of a red offspring, Pr(R) is equal to the number of red rabbits divided by the total number of rabbits.
    b. Produce 2 offspring: Pr(R) of them are red and the rest are blue
    c. Let the parents die off. Cuddle the offspring.

This simple system appears to be stable and self-organized, but not anywhere near self-organized criticality. Rabbit world should produce both red and blue rabbits for an eternity without bound. Starting with an equal number of red and blue rabbits means that an equal number of red and blue rabbits are produced on each new generation, because both parents are replaced by their offspring. There is nothing complex about this 'complex system.' Or is there?

Now suppose at some point the number of breeding red rabbits reach 101 and the number of breeding blue rabbits is 100 (perhaps one blue rabbit encountered a wolf). Using the rule that says the probability of producing a red offspring is equal to the ratio of red-to-total rabbits, we get Pr(R) = 101/201 = 50.3%. Now the system slightly favors producing more red rabbits than blues from this point on. Since it takes both red and blue rabbit pairs to produce more rabbits, the next generation of offspring comes from 100 of the 101 reds and 100 of the 100 blues. But, 50.3 % of the 200 offspring (101, rounding up to a whole rabbit) are red, and 99 are blue. Therefore, the next generation consists of 101 red rabbits and 99 blue rabbits, because their parents have died off. Intuitively, after many generations, we should expect 50.3% of the population to consist of red rabbits. But this doesn't happen.

This system evolves by constantly adjusting the probability of red offspring according to the current mix of red-to-total rabbits. Figure 1.2 shows how a small deviation from 50% escalates until it eventually reaches 100%. At this point, only red rabbits are reproduced; that is, this system reaches a critical point where only red rabbits are reproduced. And since it takes a red and a blue rabbit to make another rabbit, the system reaches a terminal state where no additional rabbits of any color are produced. This terminal state is called an attractor, because the system is attracted to it like a magnet to iron. Critical point and attractor are different terms for the same thing. So now self-organized criticality is defined as a property of evolving systems that have a critical point as an attractor.

Figure 1.2 shows how a slightly imbalanced rabbit system evolves over a number of generations starting with 101 and 110 red rabbits, respectively. This rabbit world is imbalanced because at some point there are slightly more red rabbits than blue. Even a very small deviation in the probability of producing a red offspring sets into motion a chain reaction ending in the extinction of the entire rabbit species. In Figure 1.2 the probability of producing more red rabbits increases in an S-shaped fashion. When it reaches 100%, the rabbit population breeds to extinction! The entire population eventually dies out unless something intervenes to change things. This simple but complex system turns energy (reproduction) into self-organization (breeding red and blue rabbits) that increases until it reaches a critical point (100% red rabbits) and collapses.

Almost all real-world systems contain similar minor imbalances. Such biases are called *preferential attachments* in the scientific literature. Preferential attachment is one of the major sources of SOC. I will illustrate preferential attachment through a number of examples later, but the key point here is to observe that systems near their critical point often contain small variations or biases that grow and consume the entire system. In the rabbit example, preferential attachment acts like a magnet to pull red rabbit reproduction closer and closer to 100%. This increases SOC, which causes the system to collapse even though the imbalance in reproduction probability starts out as a relatively minor event. In this trivial example, the rabbit population collapses because there are no more blue rabbits to breed with the red ones.

Like many complex systems, the simple rabbit population is fragile. Even a very slight change in the number of red rabbits leads to the catastrophic demise of the entire rabbit world! Subtle non-linear properties like this are common to many simple systems—this is one reason why such simple systems are considered complex. It also explains why it is difficult or impossible to predict sizes and timings associated with the collapse of complex systems.

My rabbit example isn't very convincing. In fact, it is so contrived that it might be used as a reason to put this book aside as the ravings of an academic. But my rabbit example is not far from reality. In fact, the universe and everything in it was created by a self-organizing process very similar to rabbit preferential attachment. We owe our very existence to a cosmic imbalance that led to a catastrophic event called the Big Bang.

Asymmetry of the Big Bang

Per Bak would have been gratified to learn that the most recent explanation of the Big Bang theory may be an application of preferential attachment and criticality. The theory postulates a universe initially made of a highly concentrated, very hot ball of densely packed matter and antimatter particles. *Antimatter destroys matter* when the two collide, creating energy in the process. So, if the cosmic ball of matter and antimatter had initially contained an equal number of matter and antimatter particles, they would have destroyed each other and there would be no universe today. Obviously, this didn't happen!

The Big Bang is a mirror of the Red/Blue rabbit universe—an equal number of red and blue rabbits leads to an enduring race of rabbits. A slight imbalance led to their extinction. On the contrary, an equal number of matter and antimatter particles would have lead to an extinction of the universe, whereas a slight asymmetry led to its existence. Cosmologists believe that a slight preference for matter emerged around 10^{-43} seconds into creation; for some reason, matter particles outnumbered the antimatter particles. But instead of leading to extinction, the asymmetry led to a universe with much more matter than antimatter—clearly a more pleasant outcome than extinction. The Big Bang was successful because of its imperfection. In fact, it would have fizzled without preferential attachment!

The asymmetry was very slight, about one part per billion. But preferential attachment took over, accelerating the inequality between matter and antimatter as the discrepancy grew larger. Again, the analogy with the imaginary rabbit world is inescapable. The number of red rabbits grew faster than the number of blues, until all offspring were red. Similarly, the amount of matter grew faster than the amount of antimatter, until nearly all particles were matter. In fact, the rate increased as time passed because more matter begat even more matter. Thus, Figure 1.2 is also a reasonable model for the growth of matter in the universe, although the analogy can only be stretched so far—we haven't yet reached the end of the universe!

Asymmetry in the balance between matter and antimatter led to an attractor that is today's evolving universe. What happens when the critical point is reached? Was the creation of our world an exercise in self-organization? One could easily argue that it was.

The Most American Dane

Subsequent to publication in 1996 of Bak's book, *How Nature Works: The Science of Self-Organized Criticality*, the sand pile experiment received the attention of many writers in many diverse fields of study. The build-up of SOC and its unpredictable release of energy was used as a metaphor by Al Gore in his 1992 book, *Earth in the Balance: Ecology and the Human Spirit*. Could the impending climatic disaster awaiting humankind be just like a sand pile edging ever closer to collapse? Apparently Al Gore thought so.

Mark Buchanan, in his book *Ubiquity: Why Catastrophes Happen*, (Buchanan 2000), may have been the first popular science writer to note the generality of SOC and its connection with catastrophes. He describes a number of diverse and unrelated systems that exhibit self-organized criticality, suggesting that SOC isn't just a property of sand piles. I will describe some of these systems in greater detail in later chapters;

needless to say, I agree with him, or I wouldn't have written this book. Buchanan used complexity theory to explain the start of WWI, forest fires, and extinctions. My goal is to stretch both Buchanan's and Bak's ideas even further to explain technical, socio-economic, and political events shaping today's seemingly chaotic world.

Nassim Nicholas Taleb describes a miniature Tower of Babel he built by dropping Rio de Janeiro beach sand onto a pile of sand in his popular book *Fooled By Randomness* (Taleb 2004). Eventually SOC gets the best of his tower and it collapses in what Taleb describes as a *non-linearity*. Non-linear extreme events are called Black Swans in Taleb's sequel, *The Black Swan* (Taleb 2007). Taleb's metaphorical Extremistan is a place where highly unlikely extreme events seem to happen with more frequency than they reasonably should. I will take you on a deeper tour of Taleb's world in the next chapter. As it turns out, Taleb's Extremistan has a lot in common with Bak's sand pile.

Joshua Ramo's "concept of world disorder" equates SOC with the "age of the unthinkable" (Ramo 2009). He devotes an entire chapter to the sand pile metaphor, claiming that Bak "could have been speaking about the Middle East, relations between the United States and China, the oil market, disease, nuclear proliferation, cyber warfare or a dozen other problems of global affairs and security" (Ramo 2009:59-60) Ramo's use of Bak's ideas expanded the theory beyond the technical, physical, and biological sciences, deeper into the socio-political realm. Is global terrorism perhaps a kind of SOC? I think so, and provide supporting evidence in the chapter on Boids, Termites, and Politicians.

Over a period of several decades, Bak's theories have continued to gain scientific respectability and more recently have been used to explain behaviors outside of the science and technology community. It would seem that Bak's fame was on solid ground in 1987, and his ideas would soon be used to explain why complex systems of all kinds eventually fail, recover, and fail again. SOC was poised to become widely accepted by Bak's peers. But this didn't happen. What went wrong? Chao Tang, who is currently Professor of Biochemistry and Biophysics at the University of California-San Francisco, insightfully describes Per Bak, perhaps explaining why the sand pile analogy hasn't yet revolutionized the scientific or socio-economic world:

> Per was a very straightforward person, unconventional, unorthodox, and anti-establishment. He liked to be controversial, and more often than not, he would embarrass the speakers in seminars and conferences by asking them simple questions and insisting to have simple answers. He had many friends, and also many 'enemies.' To many he may not have appeared to be a 'polite' person. But he could actually be very sweet. He was a great cook—he cooked for me twice at his home (once steak and once fish), and those were among my best dining experiences. (Tang in e-mail to author, June 2010)

Kurt Wiesenfeld is now a professor of physics at the Georgia Institute of Technology. Even decades after their post-doc time together, his admiration for Bak holds strong. He recalls:

> He was one of those larger-than-life people one often hears about and only very occasionally meets. Per was outgoing, loud, and if I had only a little interaction with him I probably wouldn't have liked him. But he wears extremely well. I will relate one story to illustrate. I visited Per at Brookhaven in the winter of 1985. At the time I was at UC Santa Cruz doing a one-year post-doc stint, and was looking for another post-doc job. I saw a fair amount of loud talking/arguing that day, and was amazed during private conversations that virtually everyone there made excuses (it seemed to me) for Per's aggressive manner. After working there myself, I understand it. He generated a lot of affection among those who got to know him (and, it seemed to me, a fair number of enemies among the rest). The point is that he might make a rude joke about someone's ideas, but was just as likely to make the same sort of joke about himself. And that was an endearing trait. (Wiesenfeld in e-mail to author, August 2010)

Perhaps Bak was too loud and abrasive. Perhaps he was a man ahead of his time. Or perhaps his peers recognized and then quickly forgot him like so many other pioneers of the unconventional. Bak was highly critical of the scientific establishment, and they of him. He especially disliked "big science," criticizing it for wasting money while ignoring the small-project geniuses. Bak championed the underfunded lone genius. In his mind, creativity and intelligence were more important than large grants. Or was Bak simply too outrageous? Predrag Cvitanovic, also a professor of physics at the Georgia Institute of Technology, said

> Bak was the most American of Danes. Danes eschew confrontation, but [Bak] was arrogant and loved to fight with his colleagues in academia. We all have stories of how we first met him, usually remembered by some outrageous statement or insult. (Wikipedia entry on Bak)[5]

I asked Tang what he thought of SOC, nearly 25 years after the BTW experiment. He responded that,

> I think it is fair to say that the discovery of SOC was really a joint work of three of us, with critical inputs from Sue Coppersmith. I am of course biased, but I think the discovery opened the door to a new way of thinking about complex systems and the emergence of scaling. The original sand pile model (and the many subsequent models) is simplified and idealized. While simplified models played absolutely essential roles in many fields of physics, including statistical mechanics, it remains to be seen how general and how widely applicable the SOC model is in explaining natural phenomena. I have no doubt that it can be applied to some natural systems and the SOC mechanism is behind the observed 'critical' behavior in these systems. But it is not clear that it is as universal and as widely applicable as Per had hoped. In any case, I think it is a great idea and I believe it will prove to be a useful model. (Tang in e-mail to author June 2010)

Wiesenfeld's response to the same question:

> Besides teaching, raising two daughters, and coping with marriage, my current research projects are in various areas but have in common the emergence of coherent dynamical behavior between interacting

---

5   http://en.wikipedia.org/wiki/Per_Bak

'elements'. I'm sure being a co-creator of SOC has changed my life, but I can't really tell just how. For example, I'm pretty nearly award-free, and never had a juicy job offer. But I'm pretty sure the attention (and large number of technical literature citations) took off a lot of the early-career pressure that young faculty are under when it comes to getting tenure. (Wisenfeld in e-mail to author, August 2010)

Bak may have upset the scientific community, but the people closest to him continue to admire and respect him decades later. In fact, his ideas have grown in stature as the years have passed, much like the value of a deceased artist's masterpiece. The more I examine Bak's sand pile, the more it seems to explain things—why we experience catastrophic events, and what we might do to reduce the consequences due to failures of modern complex systems. I continue to find truth in Bak's sand pile decades after the BTW experiment was first performed. I hope you do too.

Act Three: Punctuated Reality

The Bak-Tang-Wiesenfeld sand pile experiment was so compelling and easy to understand that many writers, researchers, and politicians took it and ran without deeper analysis. Most readers of Bak's book never reached the last chapter where he greatly expanded his theory of SOC. According to Bak, the inevitable impact of SOC on complex systems is long periods of relative calm infrequently punctuated by catastrophes. But why the long periods of relative calm and the sudden collapses? Bak's theory not only provides an explanation for this, but also claims that the pattern is a necessary evil—without it, we would not be here today.

Bak took his theory to the extreme. He argued that reality is more than a series of mild events punctuated by rare disasters. Instead, the existential clock stands still until something happens. And when something does happen, history jumps ahead in time. 'Progress' isn't smooth, but sporadic; it jumps forward in fits and starts. Put differently: reality is punctuated rather than smooth.

Bak goes further. Infrequent collapses, he claims, are necessary to advance evolution and change a system's state from low to higher levels of complexity. In Bak's vivid imagination, time stands still until a system's critical point is reached, a failure occurs, and the system rebuilds itself at a higher level of sophistication. Self-organized criticality not only exists, it is what makes punctuated reality possible, thus overcoming entropy, the tendency of all systems to decay into disorder. What emerges as a result, is something better, more elaborate, and more evolved. Without this emergence, intelligent life would not have evolved from relatively inert elements, and humans would not have evolved societies capable of supporting enormously complex structures such as cities, elaborate reasoning systems, and high culture, including literature, music, and mathematics.

Punctuated reality is a feedback system as shown in Figure 1.3. The vertical *normal accident* loop is what we experience most of the time. We spend our lives reacting to what Perrow called *normal accidents* (Perrow 1999), illustrated here by the Exxon Valdez oil spill in 1989 and the Oklahoma City Bombing of 1995. Each accident produces a relatively modest response—oil tankers are now required to be double-hulled and terrorists receive the death penalty under the Antiterrorism Act of 1996. I consider these relatively frequent adaptations to deadly, but rather mild catastrophes 'normal.' While they are usually precipitated by a disaster, they are responsible for relatively small changes, labeled 'optimized self-organization' in Figure 1.3. These incidents often contribute to an increase in self-organized criticality by increasing the complexity of rules, increasing efficiencies, optimizing, hardening, and ratcheting up SOC.

Figure 1.3. The two major feedback loops of punctuated reality.

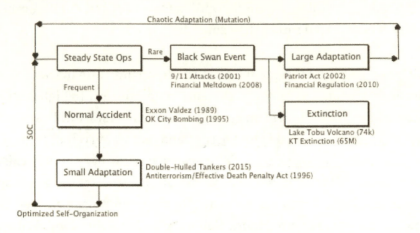

Society responds to Perrow's normal accidents by making small adaptations, typically to optimize or remedy their perceived cause or causes. These adaptations are fed back into the system in order to improve it. Self-organization can take many forms (which I will discuss later) but in many cases so-called improvements actually drive the system closer to its critical point. A system becomes more fragile as it approaches its critical point—a property Bak found intriguing, because it appears to contradict common sense. The paradox inherent to Bak's claim is that improvements often lead to disaster.

Systems are not born in a critical state; rather, they evolve into it. Along the way, most dynamical systems are in constant flux—adjusting, improving, optimizing, and evolving far from criticality. Nonetheless, change brings on risk, and risk is handmaiden to disaster. Perrow suggested that accidents like the Three Mile Island nuclear power plant disaster are caused by many small fractures or failures building up into bigger failures. He recognized that disaster is the end-result of interactions internal to complex, highly connected systems. Normal accidents, like preferential attachment, are the result of a series of adjustments over a period of time that end up in an *attractor* state. According to Perrow, accidents are normal—to be expected—because of system complexity and connectivity. I will return to Perrow's theory in more detail in chapter three.

The horizontal feedback loop of Figure 1.3 is more serious. I call this the *Black Swan* loop, in reference to Taleb's book of the same name and characterization of Black Swans as rare, extreme, and unpredictable outliers. Such extreme events are responsible for extinctions or large adaptations in nature; they are abnormal accidents. The terrorist attacks of 9/11 and the financial meltdown of 2008 are two such examples. They are in a class of their own mainly because of their unimaginably low probability, unimaginably high consequence, and unimaginably vast ripple-effect on the United States and world. The chaotic adaptation following 9/11 was perhaps as consequential as the attack itself.

Black Swans are capable of wiping out entire species. For example, the Lake Tobu volcano nearly wiped out the entire human race some 74,000 years ago. Archeologists claim that fewer than 15,000 humans survived this catastrophe, and according to the prevailing archeological theory we are all descendants of roughly 1,000 surviving females capable of reproducing. The Lake Tobu 'volcanic winter' sent the few remaining humans northward out of Africa into the Middle East and Europe. Humanity may have barely avoided extinction but we adapted and reappeared as a mutated and improved species. In fact, human intellect and capability exploded subsequent to this near-extinction event, known as a genetic *bottleneck*.

Similarly, it is commonly believed that the *KT Event* (Cretaceous-Tertiary Mass Extinction event) exterminated the dinosaurs 65 million years earlier. Scientists speculate that 70% of all life on Earth was exterminated by an asteroid striking the Yucatan region adjacent to the Gulf of Mexico. Once again, a pattern emerges: disaster precipitates adaptation through some sort of mutation or change, followed by reemergence of a new species on Earth. In both cases—Lake Tobu and the KT Event—the biological system suffered a Black Swan event that resulted in chaotic adaptations. These adaptations accelerated evolution and migration, ultimately producing fitter species.

The significance of Black Swans is that they lead to large adaptations. The Patriot Act of 2002 following the terrorism of 9/11 reduced personal freedom in the United States, and the Iraq and Afghanistan campaigns have been elements of the longest and most costly war in American history. Similarly, the financial regulation following the meltdown of 2008 precipitated the most extensive changes in free market capitalism since the 1930s. Their effect on capitalism has not fully played out, but it will most likely create chaos for some time following the crash. These adaptations send waves in all directions. Their effects are felt for years. Black Swans deserve a deeper analysis, which I provide in the next chapter.

Bak's Big Idea

The two feedback loops of Figure 1.3 are related. The normal accident loop sets up conditions for a Black Swan feedback loop. Black Swans drive change, which in turn drives 'progress.' Here is how it works. The normal accident loop is a high-frequency feedback loop that continuously adjusts SOC. SOC increases because of incremental, but continuous, optimizations and other expediencies designed to improve daily life. Machines are made to be more efficient, computers become cheaper and faster, regulations and laws are adjusted to take into consideration more subtle variations. Energy systems are constantly optimized to squeeze more efficiency from them, and financial systems are optimized to squeeze out more profit. Political expediency is optimized to gain more power—politicians pander to voters and lobbyists. Transportation systems are 'improved' to make them perform better at lower cost. The list is very long!

The normal accident feedback loop increases self-organized criticality as a byproduct of these optimizations. Each pass through the loop increases SOC and brings a system closer to the edge of disaster. Eventually the optimized system reaches its critical point so that, when a relatively insignificant event occurs, its effect is magnified. Oil exploration is improved so that drilling 5,000 feet under the Gulf of Mexico is not only economical but also more efficient and profitable than ever before. Perhaps corners are cut in terms of safety, or the technology is pushed to its limits. Suddenly, when a small explosion occurs on a 'normal' oilrig, the entire Gulf is flooded with millions of barrels of oil. Electric power grids run near their limit and suddenly, when something insignificant happens in Ohio, the lights go out in New York. When mortgage-backed securities are optimized through packaging and repackaging of derivatives, the failure of an insignificant loan company in Southern California trips a firestorm of financial failures. When intelligence and law-enforcement agencies in the USA 'accidentally' fail to prevent penetration of airport security in Boston, the Twin Towers and Pentagon are successfully attacked, triggering a series of consequences that lead to global warfare and adaptation around the globe. An unknown virus in China ignites a global disease, and so on. Ever-expanding SOC can be found in diverse systems whether they are physical, biological, virtual, political, or economic.

Bak's big idea goes beyond tipping point theory. It defines tipping points as critical points—system attractors—that pull a system in a certain direction. But after the inevitable collapse of a critical system there is a period of adjustment and adaptation that sets the stage for the next round of increasing SOC followed by subsequent collapse. Financial systems collapse, adapt, create another bubble, collapse again, and so forth. Massive change awaits us on the other side of the tipping point. The cycle seems to repeat forever or, in very rare instances, lead to extinction.

This model of the world suggests a paradox. Our natural inclination is to optimize and improve efficiency in every possible modern system. In fact, this benefits society by delivering goods and services to large populations at the lowest prices. It spurs development and efficient use of resources, but it also increases SOC. By doing the 'right thing,' we set ourselves up for the 'big thing.' Improvements lead to criticality, and criticality leads to catastrophe. Complex systems benefit humanity, and yet they contain the seeds of disaster. Progress stands still until catastrophe strikes, but without catastrophe there can be no advancement. The longer we postpone the inevitable collapse, the bigger it is. This is Bak's Paradox. This is our paradox—the 'main challenge' I will address in the remainder of this book.

2

THE CASINOS
OF EXTREMISTAN

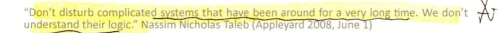

"Don't disturb complicated systems that have been around for a very long time. We don't understand their logic." Nassim Nicholas Taleb (Appleyard 2008, June 1)

The Prophet of Boom and Doom

Modern decision-makers, long-range planners, and policy wonks face challenges never before confronted. Enormous ecological disasters such as the Gulf Oil Spill of 2010, terrorist attacks of global consequence, biological and climatic events that impact everyone on the planet, economic meltdowns that spread like pandemics, and disruptive technological change—they all defy the planning scenarios of the world's best futurists, especially given that the occurrence of these events seems to be increasing. Figure 2.1 illustrates the problem: unpredictable natural disasters are on the rise. The number of yearly disaster declarations have increased by nearly ten-fold since 1950, and the trend is an upward one. Of course, the FEMA (Federal Emergency Management Agency) trend may in part be due to better reporting, and a greater tendency for governors to ask for aid due to the lure of financial assistance from the federal government. It is also likely that the number of incidents is simply increasing.

More generally, an increased frequency of hurricanes, earthquakes, power outages, traffic accidents, terrorist attacks, environmental accidents, social discontent, and political chaos make 'business as usual' irrelevant and inadequate in our daily lives. The trend seems to be toward less predictability, not more. As I argued in the previous chapter, the only certainty is uncertainty. Extreme events are as unpredictable as a winning hand in a gambling casino. Thus the 'new normal' is the unpredictable and extreme abnormality of Extremistan, a metaphorical world described by Nassim Nicholas Taleb (Taleb 2005; 2007). Extremistan is characterized by rare and unpredictable, high-consequence events—the so-called *Black Swans*. Taleb contrasts Extremistan with Mediocristan, his metaphorical world of predictable events and everyday averages.

Taleb is a Lebanese-born writer, scholar, essayist, epistemologist, statistician, risk engineer and trader. He made several fortunes by exploiting financial disasters (including the 2008 financial meltdown), and from writing about the unpredictability of these disasters. Taleb's genius lies in noting that the price of a commodity gradually rises (boom) until it suddenly drops (doom), and when it drops, the correction is catastrophic—not predictable and gradual. He translated big drops into big profits. Bryan Appleyard called him the "prophet of boom and doom," because of his ability to exploit extreme events (Appleyard 2008). His best selling book, *The Black Swan*, published in 31 languages, sold over 2 million copies from 2007 through 2010. Taleb has street-cred, largely because his anticipation of collapses in financial markets in the late 1980s and again in the late 1990s predated the 2008 financial meltdown by several years.

Taleb believes it is impossible to understand current events using traditional statistical methods, but he believes that doom (Black Swan) always follows the boom. Even when we look back at disastrous events through an historical lens, we distort the facts to make them fit our current (incorrect) worldview. Rational or 'book-learned' knowledge is not only inadequate, but often misleading. Instead, knowledge acquired through experience is the only know-how that we can trust. Taleb ranks good intuition above logic when it comes to predicting the next big event. In his view, practice can be turned into knowledge, but not the reverse.

Taleb would disagree with many views expressed in this book, claiming them to be a fool's errand. In his view, building models to explain the world is like "lecturing birds how to fly" (Taleb, 'Fooled by rationalism'). Taleb chronicles how our 500-year naiveté regarding classical probability theory has led us down the primrose path of false security. As a consequence of being brainwashed by centuries of expected utility theory, we have been 'fooled by randomness'—also the title of his 2005 book[1]. This expectation has turned us into outlier-ignoring automatons.

According to Taleb, predicting unusual events is impossible and a waste of time because extreme events obey a separate set of rules. Calculating the average height of all humans says nothing about the height of the tallest basketball players, and averaging the time elapsed between terrorist attacks tells us nothing about when the next attack will occur. Knowing the average value of something reveals nothing about the extreme value of something. And unfortunately, most of us have been taught to act on averages.

I disagree with Taleb and believe we can remedy the current malaise by upgrading from the classical scientific notions of randomness, which are based on averages and the Law of Large Numbers[2], to models based on the power law. As Bak prophesized, the future is punctuated, not

---

1   Expected utility theory (EUT) considers decision making under uncertainty in terms of potential gains and risk aversion (a preference for cautious behavior that minimizes risks, but produces smaller gains). EUT defines risk as 'expected loss,' which is the probability of an event occurring multiplied by the associated cost.

2   The Law of Large Numbers says that the more measurements you take, the closer the average is to the expected value, i.e. the more accurate your estimated value.

smoothed-out as the Law of Large Numbers suggests. In other words, in the world of Extremistan, average values don't count! The randomness, lack of predictability, and extreme events of Extremistan fall into place once the classical Normal Distribution (bell curve) is replaced by power laws. At least, that is the thesis of this book.

My logic is this: modern risk-informed decision-making and policymaking are fundamentally based on classical probability theory. In turn, classical probability theory is based on Pascal's breakthrough in 1654, which created the modern field of probability. But, Pascal assumed a General Brownian Motion (GBM) space-time continuum, a model based on the ubiquitous bell curve. GBM assumes that events, behaviors, and accidents of history are like air molecules in a room, walking the random walk of a drunkard, but never getting too far out of balance. Molecules are equally likely to move left, right, up, or down. Averaged over sufficiently large swaths of time and sufficiently large collections of molecules, GBM gives the illusion of controlled chaos. Extremes are averaged out. While an extreme state is possible, the probability that all molecules will some day collect in one corner of the room is so small that we can ignore it. For the most part of the past 250 years we did.

The GBM model is inadequate to explain Taleb's Extremistan. As Taleb suggests, the old tools may be inadequate. However, in contrast to Taleb, I believe the new tools of complexity theory[3] and power laws are up to the task. We need a new model that distinguishes Extremistan from Mediocristan. Bak foresaw the new model and formulated its principles: lop-sided power laws for describing likelihood; self-organized criticality and punctuated reality for explaining extreme events; and complexity theory for tying it all together.

---

3   Complexity theory deals with systems composed of interconnected parts that exhibit behaviors or properties that are not obvious from the behaviors and properties of the individual parts.

Figure 2.1. FEMA Declared Natural Disasters 1950-2010. Disasters are defined as any natural or man-made incident such as major storms, floods, landslides, earthquakes, fires, tornadoes, hurricanes, and destructive winds, in which States have declared an emergency (see http://www.fema.gov/news/disasters.fema). This plot includes natural disasters only.

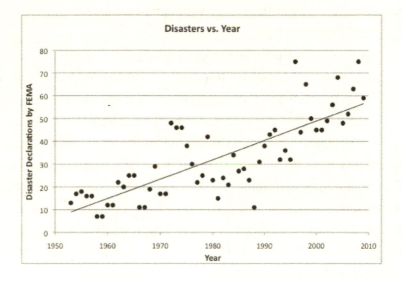

Extremistan vs. Mediocristan

According to Taleb, we live in Extremistan (Taleb 2007), where daily survival means placing bets in the Casinos of Extremistan on the social, economic, physical, virtual[4], and political systems that support modern society. Modern supply chains, communication, transportation, energy, and socio-political systems are complex and unpredictable, just like a casino. They are sand piles, constantly building self-organized criticality as we optimize them for greater performance—and ever-increasing risk. Eventually they collapse.

Extremistan isn't necessarily good or bad—it just is. It obeys a different set of rules than its establishment counterpart, Mediocristan. The bell-shaped Normal Distribution shown in Figure 2.2 rules Mediocristan. It

---

4   The Internet, baby!

is based on GBM and the Law of Large Numbers. Events tend to cluster symmetrically around an average value, thus, the bell-shaped curve, the width of which is determined by the amount of variation from that average, is defined by both average value and variance.

Power laws, on the other hand, represent extremes: highly likely low-consequence events fall on the left and highly unlikely high-consequence events fall on the right, also shown in Figure 2.2. Moreover, many more low-consequence events occur than high-consequence events. This makes power laws lop-sided. Unlike the bell curve, power laws are L-shaped and have no average value or variance. Furthermore, power laws are scale invariant, meaning that no matter which measurement scale is used, the power law curve will look the same. A magnified section of a power law is itself a power law, thus power laws are *self-similar* or *fractal*. They are also described as having long tails because they stretch to the right, indicating a non-zero probability of extreme, albeit rare, events. The longer the tail, the *heavier* or *fatter* the power law. And as I will show below, long-tailed power laws indicate the self-organization that intrigued Bak.

There are deeper differences: the rules of Mediocristan reinforce our long-held belief in stability—that systems may occasionally veer off track but eventually return to a stable state. Events in Mediocristan gravitate toward a mean value, which is rational, bounded, and resilient. Events in Extremistan follow a power law that has no average value and no measure of variability indicating how close or far away events tend to be from the average value. Its long tail stretches out to infinity, and fat-tailed power laws mean extreme events are more likely to occur in Extremistan than in Mediocristan. In what follows, pay attention to the tails of the power laws I describe, because their lengths indicate the presence of extremism!

The Casinos of Extremistan are non-linear and unbounded. Systems may or may not bounce back after a catastrophic incident. They may exhibit the 'butterfly effect,' whereby a small change results in a major non-linear effect. It is more likely that incidents cause permanent damage or precipitate major adjustments as described in the previous chapter. This means that our concepts of risk and resilience are all wrong, largely because they are based on unrealistic assumptions of equally likely random events, with known averages and known variability. Rather than following the bell curve, reality follows a lop-sided power law.

It is amazing that after 350 years of evidence to the contrary, we have only recently begun to acknowledge the mismatch between bell curves and actual experience. As we wake up to punctuated reality, we realize that life is a bigger gamble today than ever before (as demonstrated by Figure 2.1). We suspected that life isn't fair, as I described in the previous chapter, but now we have proof. Power laws, not bell curves, describe punctuated reality. The question is, why are the Casinos of Extremistan ruled by power laws? Why is reality punctuated? There is no simple answer, but we can see the outlines. As modern society becomes more connected through supply chains, the Internet, globalization of business, interdependent financial systems, and coupled business ecosystems, it also becomes more critical in the sense of Bak's sand pile.

The remainder of this chapter is devoted to showing you how the fundamentals of punctuated reality drive world events—events that behave like sand piles and take place in the Casinos of Extremistan, the world in which we live today. My thesis is that Black Swans aren't as unpredictable as we think. I argue that we can indeed approximate when the next 'big one' will occur, and how bad it might be. At the very least it is possible to determine the shape of the power law that describes events in Extremistan. In fact, power laws can describe the size, timing, and location of major events of our time. As it turns out, the odds favor inconsequential events over disastrous events, closely timed events over randomly timed events, and local events versus far-away events. In the Casinos of Extremistan, big ones are rare, bursty, and near one another.

Figure 2.2. Comparison of the bell curve and the power law. Bell curve events cluster around an average value that may lie anywhere in the range of consequence values. On the other hand, power law events are much more likely to occur on the left and rarely occur on the right side of the range of consequence values.

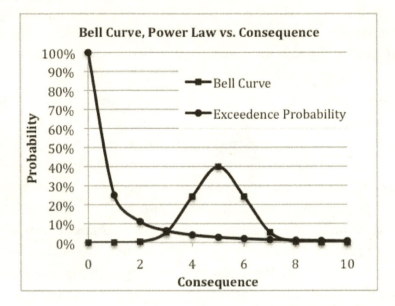

Pascal's Triangle

Prior to 1654, winning large sums of money playing games of chance, winning and losing wars, or dying from an unknown disease was determined by the gods of providence. Only a few charmed gamblers could beat the odds. The rest of us blamed our fortunes on various deities, as Peter L. Bernstein describes in his excellent history of risk, *Against The Gods* (Bernstein 1998). Mere humans were at the mercy of higher powers and luck had little to do with it. But in 1654, the gods of providence lost their mythical allure, as so many other superstitions did during the Age of Enlightenment. Human understanding of chance took a big turn for the better when Antoine Gombaud, Chevalier de Méré (1607-1684) posed a perplexing gambling problem to a brilliant young mathematician named Blaise Pascal (1623-1662). Pascal proceeded not only to solve Gombaud's gambling problem, but he established the branch of mathematics we now call *probability theory*. Pascal essentially quantified what was previously thought to be non-quantifiable. Our contemporary understanding of risk owes its scientific validity to Pascal.

Gombaud's *Problem of the Points* asks, what are the odds of a player winning a game requiring a certain total number of points when players A and B each need an additional number of points to win? For example, players A and B may need to score 3 and 4 points, respectively, to win a game of tennis. Assuming equal tennis skills, as in the famous match between Björn Borg and John Patrick McEnroe in 1980, what are the odds of player B coming from behind and winning the match?

Pascal solved the problem using a mathematical device that still bears his name: *Pascal's Triangle*. But he had to invent probability theory to do it. More importantly, he boldly claimed that chance isn't up to divine providence at all. In fact, chance can be quantified, just as Newton would adeptly and rigorously quantify gravity and its effect on mass some decades later. Chance lost its mystical luster as Pascal reduced it to mathematical logic.

Pascal argued that the probability of player A winning is simply the quotient: (number of outcomes favorable to A)/(total of all outcomes). This can be done quite simply by listing and counting all possible combinations of events and then enumerating those outcomes favorable to A. The enumerated results form a triangular shape, hence the designation of Pascal's Triangle.[5] Plot Pascal's Triangle on an X-Y axis and you get the famous bell-shaped curve, the Normal Distribution in statistics and probability. If tennis player A needs 3 more points and B needs 4 more points to win, then B can come from behind and win as long as B wins 4 points and A wins no more than 2 points. Thus, the total number of all possible outcomes is $2^{(4+2)} = 64$, in the worst case. Pascal's

---

5   Actually Pascal's Triangle was known as the "arithmetic triangle" to the Chinese mathematician Chu Shih-Chieh three hundred years earlier (Boyer 1991).

Triangle gives us the number of outcomes favorable to B: (1+6+15) = 22. Therefore the probability that B comes from behind to win is 22/64 or 34.375%[6].

Pascal was recognized as a mathematical prodigy by the age of 12 (Boyer 1991). By eighteen, he started a company to manufacture and sell the first mechanical calculating machine, an early forerunner of modern computers. He dabbled in hydrostatics in 1648, and was soon on an equal footing with the great mathematicians of his time. 1654 was a big year for Pascal. In addition to inventing probability theory, calculators, and mathematical theorems, he experienced an epiphany that turned his attention to theology. One story is that a near-death carriage accident precipitated his transformation from man of science to devotee of God. Perhaps the real story, related by Boyer, is that Pascal experienced a "religious ecstasy" during a sleepless night in 1654 (Boyer 1991:366). Either way, from that time on, he contributed to the advancement of mathematics only one more time during his life.

Let's apply Pascal's Triangle to a serious modern problem. Suppose law enforcement authorities track a group of people suspected of planning a terrorist attack. The terrorists must 'win five rounds' in order to achieve their goal: 1) they must be trained and armed, 2) get into the country, 3) learn to fly a commercial airliner, 4) hijack an airliner, and 5) successfully crash the hijacked airplane into their target. In terms of the *Problem of the Points*, the terrorists are gambling that they can win five rounds before authorities discover their plot and stop them.

Now suppose law enforcement authorities discover that terrorists have completed two of the five steps needed to complete the terrorist's plan. To head off the attack, the authorities must discover the final three steps or rounds so they can interdict the terrorists before they complete all five steps. Further suppose the terrorists must complete only the last

---

6   The Triangle is obtained by enumerating the favorable outcomes: there is one way for B to win by scoring 4 points in a row; 6+15 ways of scoring 4 points before A scores 3 points.

2 steps to complete their attack. The terrorists must win two rounds and the authorities must win 3 more rounds. What are the odds for successfully thwarting the attack? Pascal's Triangle provides the answer: the authorities have a 31.25% chance of preventing the attack. Odds are 5:16 that the attack will be stopped.

This example is rational and logical. Moreover, it is supported by 350 years of mathematical history. The problem is that it makes assumptions that may not be true. For example, Pascal's Triangle assumes 'winning rounds' are independent and equally likely events. The bell curve is assumed to be symmetric, with an average value in the middle, as shown in Figure 2.2. Pascal's Triangle is elegant, but fails to solve the problem, because it is based on the Normal Distribution, i.e., the bell curve. Terrorists and catastrophe's obey power laws, not bell curves.

Zipf's Disruptive Technology

Everything changed with Zipf's Law and Pareto's 80-20% rule. Zipf and Pareto discarded the notion of a reality ruled by the bell curve, where extremes are averaged out. Zipf and Pareto asked, what if the real world is governed by extremes, instead? Then power laws should be used instead of bell curves. In fact, evidence is mounting that power laws explain many phenomena in the real world better than GBM. Let's examine a few non-GBM phenomena and see if power laws fit better than the bell curve.

George Kingsley Zipf (1902-1952), a Harvard University Professor of German, was one of many early pioneers to realize that many real-world phenomena violate Pascal's Triangle[7]. Rather, some things are

---

7   Jean-Baptiste Estoup (1868-1950) may have discovered Zipf's Law before Zipf! See http://en.wikipedia.org/wiki/Jean-Baptiste_Estoup

asymmetrical and lop-sided, ruled by the power law distribution as shown in Figure 2.2. Zipf illustrated his disruptive idea by showing that the frequency of occurrence of any word is inversely proportional to its rank order. Thus, the most frequent word occurs approximately twice as often as the second most frequent word, three times as often as the third most frequent word, and so on. The distribution of words in prose—known as Zipf's Law—is lop-sided and mathematically compatible with a power law.

Similarly, Vilfredo Pareto (1848-1923), the famous (or notorious, depending on your socio-political view) founder of *mathematical economics*, discovered wealth distribution is lop-sided—only a few people are wealthy while the majority are not. Pareto re-discovered the power law—not an uncommon discovery during the twentieth century. Many people would come to the same conclusion: life isn't fair! In fact, life is often lop-sided and best described by a power law.

Pareto and Zipf observed different phenomena, but their conclusions were founded on the same principle: certain events are more common than others and occur more frequently than expected. This may seem like common sense, but it contradicts the 'common sense' of classical Normal Distribution and GBM. In the mathematics of Pascal, dictionary words would appear with the frequency of tossed coins, and half of the world's population would be wealthier than global average while the other half would be poorer. This is the mathematics of Mediocristan, while the mathematics of Zipf and Pareto are the mathematics of Extremistan.

The power law describes a lopsided, rather than symmetrical, world. Could it be that Bak's power law is also the foundation of Taleb's Extremistan? The data is still mounting, but a sample from just a few unrelated disciplines illustrates my point with ease (Bettencourt, Lobo, Helbing, Kühnert & West 2007; Klieber 1932)—that certain phenomena seem to behave like sand piles. Power laws have been shown to the following throughout the world and at other scales of meas.

- ✓ The size of cities
- ✓ The number of new patents filed
- ✓ Consumption of electricity
- ✓ The number of gasoline stations
- ✓ The length of power and communication cables
- ✓ File size distribution of Internet messages
- ✓ The size of oil reserves in oil fields
- ✓ The standardized price returns on individual stocks
- ✓ The size of sand particles
- ✓ The size of meteorites
- ✓ The number of species per genus
- ✓ The area burnt in forest fires
- ✓ Kleiber's law: the metabolism of animals scales with mass
- ✓ The severity of large casualty losses for certain lines of business such as general liability, commercial auto, and workers compensation.
- ✓ Shoplifting from stores, as well as crime incidents reported from apartment complexes and motels in various cities in the U.S. (Eck, Clarke & Guerette 2007).

Sand Piles and Terrorist Attacks

Power laws describe the obvious: *small* incidents, measurements, accidents, catastrophes, and so forth, occur much more frequently than *big* ones. Big incidents have big consequences, but they are rare. The observed frequencies of accidents and terrorist attacks aren't equally random at all. Instead, they obey the lop-sided power law.

For example, a simulation of the terrorist attack scenario presented earlier produces a power law that relates the likelihood of an event with a certain size or consequence. Once we know the relationship between size of an event and its likelihood, we can begin to understand risk— the expected consequences of events in the Casinos of Extremistan. How does this work? Recall the hypothetical scenario whereby a group of terrorists must successfully complete five tasks—training and equipping, entering the country, learning to fly, hijacking an airliner, and flying it into a building—to do their dastardly deed. Each of the tasks has an associated, and possibly different, probability of success. Now, to make the example more interesting, further assume there are four targets and the terrorists must hijack four airliners and fly each of them into a building. This creates an array of possible consequences: none of the attempts succeed (zero consequences), one succeeds (25% consequences), two (50% consequences), three (75% consequences), or all four succeed (100% consequences). By converting consequences to a percentage, we can compare one kind of event with others.

Instead of trying to estimate probabilities of partial or complete success, as Pascal would do, suppose the terrorist scenario is played 100,000 times inside a computer. Each time the scenario is simulated, random values are independently assigned to probabilities of success, and the expected consequences calculated, binned, and aggregated into an exceedence probability (the probability that consequences will equal or exceed a certain value) as described in chapter 1. One trial simulation produces consequences that add up to 10%, other trial runs yield 89%, 35%, 12%, 55%, 92%, etc, until the computer plays out 100,000 scenarios. The 100,000 consequences are recorded and ranked, producing a curve like the one shown in Figure 2.2. Just as Zipf ranked words according to their frequency of occurrence, the computer has now ranked simulated terrorist attacks according to their consequences. The resulting power law is lop-sided, just like Zipf's Law.

Even more intriguing is the fact that repeated simulation of this scenario produces an exceedence probability just like the one produced by simulation of Bak's sand pile experiment.! Both sand piles and terrorist attacks produce lop-sided results: small consequences are much more likely than large consequences and the distribution has no average value—all the ingredients of Extremistan. Why do terrorists and sand piles share the same probabilities? Is this just a coincidence? What other systems behave this way, and what causes them to behave in similar manner?

The fact that both terrorist attacks and sand pile avalanches generate nearly identical power law curves raises a provocative question: are all catastrophes[8] somehow related? While catastrophic events may be caused by different underlying mechanisms, I claim that their risk profiles (almost[9]) always look the same: they all obey a power law. If this is the case, then perhaps they are caused by similar mechanisms. But perhaps I am getting ahead of myself...

Casinos of Homeland Security

In the context of homeland security, public safety is the gamble and the casinos are the eighteen critical infrastructure sectors identified by the National Infrastructure Protection Plan (NIPP 2009): food and agriculture, public health, emergency management, communications, energy and power, cyber security, and so forth. Because of the vastness of the United States, funding limits, and the probabilistic nature of hazards, national security policy is based on balancing risk and reward. But as the country cannot afford to protect everything, it must focus on

---

8   Here and throughout the book I define catastrophe as does Taleb: a high impact, rare and
     extreme event with large consequences.

9   Automobile fatalities seem to be an exception (Massie, Campbell & Williams 1995).

the highest risk assets. Like any gambler, we weigh the risks and take our chances.

Rational people make decisions based on perceived risk and reward every day (Starr 1969; Fischhoff, Slovic, Lichtenstein, Read & Combs 1978; Slovic 1987). The Department of Homeland Security (DHS) has employed a risk/reward strategy called *risk-informed decision-making* for purposes of resource allocation. Fundamentally, this strategy attempts to assign a risk estimate[10] to individual assets, and then prioritize them according to this estimate. Resources are allocated to the highest-risk assets first, and then to lower risk assets next, until resources run out. The government spends more money on high-risk bridges and tunnels, power stations, commuter stations, and import/export ports than on low-risk assets. But how does DHS calculate risk, and does this estimated risk accurately model reality?

Note that this strategy does *not* incorporate a return-on-investment calculation, so it is impossible to optimize allocation so that money is invested in assets with the biggest payoff in terms of reduction of risk. That is, 'biggest risk' does not equal 'biggest payoff' because mitigation of risk in one sector may be much more costly than in another sector. All risk reductions are not equally effective. For example, if an investment of one million dollars in bridge A reduces its risk of collapse due to an earthquake by 40%, but investing one million dollars in bridge B reduces its risk of collapse by 60%, which is the best investment? Things get even more complicated when comparing physical risks with cyber risks, or when the per-unit cost of risk reduction differs between a bridge and an Internet service provider.

In addition, DHS risk-informed decision-making ignores system-wide effects and resiliency. The low-consequence failure of a tripped power line ignores the system-wide effects if the power line failure disables

---

10 Risk is estimated as the product of the probability of a hazard, the vulnerability of a given asset to the hazard, and the consequence (the expected damages, casualties, economic loss, etc.)

the entire power grid as it did in 2003. It is not clear whether single-asset investments are effective on a system-wide basis, because they may not prevent system-wide failures. In fact, if Bak's self-organized criticality is present, hardening one asset in a complex system may lead to bigger, rather than smaller, failures. For example, in the electrical power grid sector, an *increase in reliability* of individual components has been shown to *increase the consequences* of cascade failures (Newman, Carreras, Lynch & Dobson 2008). This goes against intuition, but it is completely logical in Bak's sand pile universe. And it underscores why homeland security investments should focus on the whole sand pile, not just individual grains of sand or isolated avalanches.

Currently the DHS risk-informed decision-making strategy is based on Pascal's Triangle (Cheesebrough, Stenzler, Langbehn & Hanson 2009). For example, the U.S. Coast Guard's Maritime Security Risk Assessment Model (MSRAM) risk assessment tool has powerful features for estimating threat, vulnerability, and consequence, thus automating the calculation of risk. However, it is single-asset focused and cannot evaluate the impact of a single asset failure on entire systems. MSRAM can identify weaknesses in the New York–Elizabeth port, but it cannot tell us the global impact of port failure on the global shipping system. Suez

I analyzed MSRAM's database of 17,500 risk assessments of ports and assets within ports[11] as of 2009 and found that estimates of vulnerability obey a near-perfect bell curve with a mean of 24%. This bell curve was as perfect as if produced by monkeys throwing darts at the 24% mark on a plot of the Normal Distribution! The more monkeys assigned to the job, the more accurate the aggregated result, but the average value would still be 24%. Such vulnerability estimates are from Mediocristan because they obey a bell curve.

---

11 Port assets are anything from loading docks to cranes to the information technology systems used to log and track shipments.

Coast guard subject matter experts input consequence estimates into MSRAM ranging from a few million dollars to billions of dollars. Such big numbers might lead one to believe that U.S. ports are at risk. A risk-informed decision process dictates that money should be spent on the highest at-risk ports, so shouldn't we be spending billions on ports? In fact, the Coast Guard is pursuing a high-risk strategy resulting in large investments to secure major ports. But when MSRAM consequence data are binned to obtain the exceedence probability curve the reader has come to love, it becomes clear that ports are *not* high-risk assets.[12] Indeed, my analysis places U.S. ports in the 'low-risk' category. Taxpayer's money can better be spent on higher-risk systems.

SOC Equals Risk

We know that many of our Casinos of Homeland Security (critical infrastructure sectors) have reached their self-organized criticality (Dobson, Carreras, Lynch & Newman 2007; Malamud & Turcotte 2006). The overly connected hubs in the public switched telecommunications network, near-capacity tie lines in the power grid, congestion on highways, lack of surge capacity in hospitals, and viruses worming their way through the Internet are examples of self-organized systems near their critical points. The existence of SOC in these critical systems means we should be searching for a new security strategy. Instead of focusing on single-asset risk reduction, homeland security should focus on reduction of self-organized criticality; that is, a better strategy would focus on reducing the causes of criticality in complete systems rather than focusing on individual assets.

Several mechanisms can reduce self-organized criticality. Of course, the problem can be solved at the engineering level by an addition of surge capacity, operating systems below capacity, and restructuring networks to back them away from SOC. Each of these solutions has corresponding

---

12 Power law exponent was 1.7, so risk declines as consequence rises.

costs, however. A more global solution is to change regulatory policy—the rules regulating infrastructures across the entire nation. Re-design of regulation is a better approach because it spreads the economic burden across entire industries. Sub-SOC systems are more resilient because their power law exponents are larger, which means they withstand failures with lower consequences. But entire industries must cooperate or individual owners and operators will end up being punished for 'doing the right thing.'

One example is the electric power grid. After decades of operating at capacity, it has evolved into a state of self-organized criticality, compounded by incremental patching of its transmission network (Dobson, Carreras, Lynch & Newman 2007). An engineering solution to this problem is to harden substations, increase capacities of transmission lines, and replace worn equipment. Indeed, this is being done by utilities, but power outages continue because simply hardening existing infrastructure isn't effective. Instead, regulatory policies are needed to motivate the utilities to build out more transmission capacity and promote local distributed generation (reducing the need for transmission capacity), among other things. The objective of these policies must be to reduce the sector's system-wide criticality. I take up this topic in more detail in the chapter on 'Blackout USA.'

A similar criticality exists in the communications sector due to the rise of highly concentrated switching hubs in the national network (National Security Telecommunications Advisory Committee 2003), which is also detailed in a later chapter. These so-called *telecom hotels*—buildings that house multi-vendor switching equipment for information technology and communications industry owners and operators—are a direct consequence of the 1996 Telecommunications Act. This relatively new regulation advocates *peering*, the process of sharing networks among competitors, which in turn promotes co-location of switching equipment. Peering saves money and optimizes communications efficiency, but it also creates a target for catastrophe. The law needs to be changed before a cataclysmic failure results in a national telecommunications blackout.

As I have mentioned above, similar self-organized criticalities exist in other infrastructure sectors—financial systems tend to self-organize into criticality, public health/hospital systems have inadequate surge capacity, the World Wide Web/Internet is notoriously near its critical point with respect to denial of service attacks, worms, and cyber threats, and so on. Unfortunately, these vital infrastructures have not been thoroughly studied from this new perspective. This work needs to be done. If the goal is to reduce risk and improve resilience, the strategy of the DHS must shift from classical risk reduction to SOC-reduction. The former aptly applies to isolated assets, but complex system risk and resiliency is a function of SOC, not risk. In other words, SOC reduction should be the objective. I will illustrate this property of complex systems throughout the remainder of this book, but this is the bottom line: the fragility and vulnerability of complex systems derives from more than individual asset fragility and vulnerability. We must also consider system-wide properties that lead to SOC. System analysis differs from component analysis mainly because a system is a complex set of interconnected components whose behavior is more than the sum of the behaviors of its parts.

Table 2.1. Exceedence probability exponents for hazards with low-risk and high-risk profiles (Hanson 2007; Kuhn 1997; Liu, Gopikrishnan, Cizeau, Meyer, Peng & Stanley 1999; Song, Weicheng, Binghong, & Jianjun 2001; Song, Zhang, Chen, Fan 2003; Tseng, Lee & Li 2009).

	Asset/Sector	Consequence	Exponent
Low Risk	S&P500 (1974-1999)	$Volatility	3.1-2.7
	Large Fires in Cities	$Loss	2.1
	Airline Accidents	Deaths	1.6
	Tornadoes	Deaths	1.4
	Terrorism	Deaths	1.4
	Floods	Deaths	1.35
	Forest Fires in China	Land Area	1.25
	East/West Power Grid	Megawatts	1
	Earthquakes	Energy, Area	1
	Asteroids	Energy	1
	Pacific Hurricanes	Energy	1
High Risk	Hurricanes	$Loss	0.98
	Public Switched Telephone	Customer-Minutes	.91
	Forest Fires	Land Area	.66
	Hurricanes	Deaths	.58
	Earthquakes	$Loss	.41
	Earthquakes	Deaths	.41
	Wars	Deaths	.41
	Whooping Cough	Deaths	.26
	Measles	Deaths	.26
	Small Fires in Cities	$Loss	.07

Extremes of Extremistan

Threats to systems are called *hazards.* For example, hurricanes and earthquakes are hazards, as well as terrorists and bank robbers. Table 2.1 lists a number of familiar hazards and the exponent of the power law that describes the hazard's exceedence probability obtained from historical data. Interestingly, each of these hazards obeys a power law. But the shape of each hazard's power law—as determined by its exponent—may differ. If the exponent is relatively large, the exceedence probability drops off quickly. If it is relatively small, the exceedence probability curve is long-tailed, meaning that extreme high-consequence events are more likely to happen. This is the difference that separates hazards into categories, and makes the linkage to Bak's sand pile so intriguing.

Table 2.1 separates hazards into either low-risk or high-risk categories, depending on the power law exponent of their exceedence probability curves. Hazards with a power law exponent greater than or equal to one are considered low-risk, while hazards with a power law exponent less than one are considered high-risk. Higher exponents mean higher resiliency[13], so if we want to increase a system's resiliency we must increase the value of its power law exponent.

To relate risk, power law exponent, and resilience to one another, I use an insurance industry definition of risk. Instead of expected loss, the insurance industry defines risk as the probable maximum loss, PML (Grossi & Kunreuther 2005). It is easy to calculate: simply multiply consequence by exceedence probability. This is how I obtained the risk profiles in Figures 3 and 4. PML risk is a system property, not merely the risk associated with a single asset. It represents aggregate risk and, indirectly through the power law, the resilience of an entire system. This approach allows us to analyze the impact of small failures in a large system—on the resilience of the entire system. For example, telecommunication, power, energy, transportation, and other complex systems can be characterized by their resilience (power law exponent) and PML risk.

To see how this works, consider the high-low risk profiles of the hazards shown in Figure 2.3. The two curves illustrate how risk monotonically increases as consequence increases (high-risk) or decreases with

---

13 My definition of resilience is very rudimentary: it is the ability of a system to withstand an attack. High resilience means low consequence.

consequence after initially increasing (low-risk). This convenient way of classifying extreme events in Extremistan is easy to understand and apply. Hazards with resilience exponents below 1.0 are high-risk, while hazards with exponents above 1.0 are low risk. This classification scheme has important implications for risk-informed decision-making.

To illustrate the application of this theory to a physical infrastructure, consider results for the telecommunications sector circa 1990 (Kuhn 1997). Data collected by Kuhn and analyzed by the author were used to construct the exceedence probability curve, which was then plugged into the PML risk equation to obtain the high-risk curve of Figure 2.4. Consequence is defined as millions of customer-minutes lost due to all kinds of events such as lightning strikes, accidents, etc. As you can see, the telecommunications system studied by Kuhn exhibits high-risk self-organized criticality. Fortunately, the 2010 version of telecommunications is very different than the 1990s version, principally due to the 1996 Telecommunications Act. Unfortunately, the ·contemporary telecommunications industry is suffering from a different malady—self-organized criticality. I describe this malady in detail in the chapter titled, 'Can You Hear Me Now?'

The shape of these curves has an interesting bearing on strategy. Risk-informed decision-making recommends prioritizing investments according to risk: buy down high-risk assets starting with the highest risk. In Table 2.1, risk is highest when consequences are small—hazards with low-risk profiles such as airline accidents, floods, terrorism, and large fires in cities. Conversely, risk increases with consequence for hazards with high-risk profiles, such as hurricanes, earthquakes, wars, whooping cough, and measles. When viewed from the lop-sided power law perspective, risk-informed decision-making takes on a meaning different from the one being practiced today by homeland security analysts. Instead of prioritizing according to expected loss, which is the product of threat, vulnerability, and consequence, the Casinos of Extremistan analyst should prioritize by probable maximum loss, PML risk.

When it comes to protecting citizens, strategists have a choice between investing in prevention or response. Prevention means spending money to eliminate the hazard, typically by hardening the system. Response means spending money to respond to and repair the system after it is damaged. Prevention is preferred if you are certain that disaster is inevitable—it can be considered a waste of money otherwise—and response is often more costly in terms of lives lost and recovery after the fact than prevention. Which strategy is most appropriate in Extremistan?

Should a *prevention strategy* be applied to hazards with high-risk profiles that tend to occur infrequently, precisely because they are rare? Similarly, a *response policy* might be appropriate for frequently occurring hazards with low-risk profiles, because PML risk is minimal for small consequence incidents. Perhaps an 80-20% rule should be applied: invest 80% in prevention and 20% in response for hazards with high-risk profiles; and invest the opposite—80% in response and 20% in prevention—for hazards with low-risk profiles. This dual-mode strategy avoids the dangers of putting all resource eggs in one basket.

This is the conundrum of homeland security. The cost of prevention is high, and the public is unlikely to pay for it—until something bad happens. Response is often considered 'too little, too late' by the public, especially when lives are at stake. Thus, emergency management, public safety, public health, first responders of all sorts, and their policy managers are in a bind. They are damned if they do, and damned if they don't.

Figure 2.3. PML risk versus consequence for hypothetical low- and high-risk hazards. High-resilience hazards decrease PML risk as consequence increases. Low-resilience hazards do the opposite, as PML risk increases with consequence.

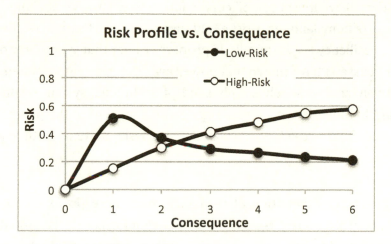

Figure 2.4. PML risk versus consequence for low- and high-risk exceedence probability curves. The low-risk curve corresponding to a power law with a large exponent (1.5) is hypothetical, while the high-risk curve (0.85) was obtained by analyzing telecommunications outages reported by Kuhn (Kuhn 1997).

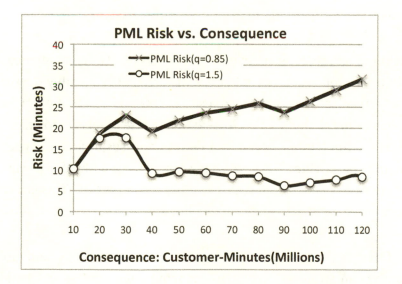

A Resilience-Informed Policy

Now that I have morphed bell curves into power laws, what should the strategy of homeland security be? My suggestion is to focus on resiliency, where resiliency is a system-wide property rather than a property of an isolated asset. I have shown that power laws describe entire systems as effectively as deceptively simple sand piles. Indeed, system resiliency is handily rolled into a single number: the exponent of the power law obtained from exceedence probability analysis. Systems with higher exponents are more resilient.

The operational definition of resilience given here (exponent of the power law) gives analysts a simple resilience-informed decision-making metric that addresses entire systems, rather than single assets. It also applies to interdependency analysis across sectors, structural strengths and weaknesses of complex systems such as the electrical power grid, financial systems, telecommunication networks, and transportation systems. Most significantly, the metric captures the structural and intrinsic strength/weakness of interdependent sectors.

As it turns out, there is an inverse relationship between resiliency and SOC. In subsequent chapters I argue that resiliency steadily decreases as self-organized criticality increases. Furthermore, I will continue to emphasize my claim that SOC increases because of increased efficiency and adaptations to economic, regulatory, and social forces. Typically, resilience is sacrificed for efficiency, profits, or both. If we want to become more resilient and secure, we must reverse SOC. This is a claim I must prove in the remainder of this book.

The foregoing argues for a change in national strategy and policy. Mediocristan strategy focuses on reducing vulnerability and building consequence mitigation capacity—more fire-fighting equipment, more training for law enforcement personnel, better risk analysis, and stockpiling of food, water, and vaccines, to name a few examples. It also requires better coordination, collaboration, and information sharing among disparate agencies in order to prepare and respond to inevitable incidents.

Extremistan strategy, on the other hand, focuses more on intelligence support, asset hardening, redundancy, surge capacity, and perhaps a reduction of operational efficiency in sectors such as energy, transportation, and telecommunications. The Casinos of Extremistan work better when they are *less* efficient, *less* profitable, and *less* centralized. This is Bak's Paradox.

The Extremistan strategy *anticipates* the unexpected and unpredictable high-impact event. Black Swans are the rule, not the exception. Rare, high-impact incidents are eventually going to happen, but as SOC increases, the resulting catastrophes are much bigger, costlier, and fearsome than emergencies in Mediocristan. Thus, SOC reduction becomes the best defense.

In 2006, 70% of the 197 pages in the NIPP contained the word "risk," while 21% contained the words "resilience," "resilient," or "resiliency." Three years later, 73% and 45%, respectively, contained these key words [NIPP 2009]. The 'resiliency words' appeared over twice as often in the 2009 strategy document than in the 2006 document. DHS is slowly moving away from Pascal's Triangle toward a 'resiliency-informed' decision-making strategy. Unfortunately, the 2009 NIPP does not provide an operational definition of resiliency, and it ignores the reality that nearly all infrastructure assets are part of larger, more complex systems.

The likelihood of major hazards such as hurricanes, earthquakes, terrorist attacks, wars, diseases, and fires—expressed in terms of an exceedence probability—not only obeys a power law, but *exceedence probability analysis identifies which systems are high- and low-risk systems*. Significantly, categorization of systems into low- and high-risk gives policymakers a new tool when making decisions about funding prevention and response. Recognizing the problem is the first step towards fixing it.

3

Normal
Accidents

"Complex interactions are those of unfamiliar sequences, or unplanned and unexpected sequences, and either not visible or not immediately comprehensible." Charles Perrow (1999)

Why $#^! Happens

I met Charles 'Chick' Perrow in his Stanford office to talk about his latest passion, energy policy and global warming. It was the last day of his 'west coast sabbatical,' so we only had an hour to talk. Chick spends winter and spring at Stanford and the rest of the year at Yale University. I spotted his trademark curly hair from the hallway as I approached his Encina Hall office. Here is the pioneer of catastrophe theory before there was a catastrophe theory, I thought as I entered his office. Global warming threatens to be the ultimate catastrophe, according to Perrow, unless we do something about CO_2 emissions. The government's first priority must be to eliminate carbon from the atmosphere before it is too late. I will have more to say about energy policy in a subsequent chapter. My purpose in visiting the professor goes all the way back to the

1970s, when the world was suffering from the first major energy crisis and the first significant ecological disasters and near-disasters.

Perrow was perhaps the first person to look deeply into catastrophic events and ask, why do some events turn into catastrophes while others don't? The Three Mile Island (TMI-2) nuclear reactor accident in 1979 sent him on a two-decade search for the answer. On the surface, the TMI-2 accident was highly improbable and unexpected. It started when a cup of water leaked out of the secondary cooling system, which increased moisture in the instrumentation, which in turn abruptly changed air pressure, signaling two pumps to stop, triggering a wind-down of a turbine, which caused a build-up of heat, tripping a cooling water release, streaming cooling water into a blocked pipe, and finally misleading an operator into making the wrong decision. The temperature continued to rise until the reactor melted down—all because of a cup of water!

TMI-2 happened because five small events that could easily have been rectified weren't. One insignificant incident led to another, which led to yet another incident, and so forth, snowballing into something big. According to Perrow, TMI-2 was both normal and an accident. He considered such disasters normal accidents because they were incidents that anyone would expect to occur during normal operation. Nothing out of the ordinary. And yet they spread and magnified the consequences as the TMI-2 nuclear reactor system continued to degrade. For some reason, normal accidents spread and magnify instead of ceasing and dying out like most small incidents.

The TMI-2 catastrophe was like so many others that start out as insignificant accidents and end up as a 'big one.' Complex nuclear power plants fail just like Bak's sand pile. Most of the time the failures are insignificant, but on rare occasions power plants totally collapse just like the rare massive landslide in a sand pile. Perrow's normal accidents provided an explanation for system collapses even before Bak formulated his sand pile theory.

Perrow devoted a decade to studying the big ones, including the TMI-2 nuclear power plant disaster; the 1984 release of deadly gas from the Union Carbide plant in Bhopal, India, which injured over 200,000 people and killed 4,000; the Chernobyl, Ukraine, nuclear power plant fire and radioactive release that exposed 600,000 people to radiation and caused the evacuation of 336,000 people; and the space shuttle Challenger disaster in 1986. The TMI-2 disaster inspired Perrow to discover *normal accident theory*. His central idea came from observing that disasters typically are caused by, "... the interconnectedness of the system, and the occasions for baffling interactions." (Perrow 1999:15). Complex systems are complex because of these "baffling interactions." Perrow's work was done in the late 1970s and early 1980s, but in 2010 he said,

> It was Three Mile Island that just happened to fit with an observation I was starting to work upon: as organizations became bigger, and absorbed more and more of other organizations and society, they could bump into each other in unexpected ways because of connections we did not anticipate. When I looked at the testimony of TMI-2 operators I discovered that it was the unanticipated interactions that bewildered them; things that were not connected linearly kept bumping into each other because, as with organizations growing bigger and absorbing more functions, the complex technical systems no longer had discrete simple parts, but multipurpose parts. (Perrow in e-mail to author, December 27, 2010)

The key phrases in Perrow's theory of disasters are 'interconnectedness,' along with 'baffling interactions' that are 'bumping into each other.' Perrow may have postulated his theory before complexity theory took root, but his intuition was right on target. Today we would lay the blame for many disasters at the feet of 'connectivity' and 'complexity.' In fact, the main ingredient that makes systems complex turns out to be their connectedness. If we want to understand Bak's sand piles and the many systems that behave like cascading sand piles, we first must understand 'connectedness.'

What exactly is *normal accident theory* (NAT)? According to Perrow, the difference between an *incident* and an *accident* is the difference between failures of a single component, or what he called a *part* or *unit*, and the failure of an entire system. Incidents are bad things that happen to parts of a system. Accidents are bad things that collapse the entire system. Most often, a normal accident is the result of a chain reaction—a series of incidents that magnify and spread throughout a complex system. In other words, normal accident theory distinguishes mundane component failures from dramatic, system-wide failures, and the primary property that distinguishes a system from its parts and units is *complexity* and *coupling*. According to Perrow, normal accidents are caused by a pattern of complex coupling among the parts and units of a system.

Simple failures occur often and most of them are so insignificant they are quickly remedied and ignored. Such incidents are frequent and low-impact. A few rare failures don't stop with the malfunction of just one unit or part; rather, they spread to adjacent parts and units like dominos toppling one another. Perrow's dominos, however, topple one row, then two rows, three rows, etc., as falling dominos branch out along parallel rows. This branching process magnifies consequences and often reaches all parts of a system. These are called *normal accidents* because they lead to complete system failure. Generally, normal accidents are the cumulative result of incidents that not only spread more widely but that have much more serious consequences. TMI-2 started with a small, insignificant leak in a seal, and ended up as the largest nuclear power plant meltdown in U.S. history.

The disaster at Bhopal added an additional dimension to Perrow's pioneering theory: that really catastrophic disasters are really rare.

> Bhopal taught me something quite different: just as it takes the unexpected, and really quite rare, interaction of multiple failures [to] cause a system failure, for that failure to be catastrophic requires a rare combination of conditions. We had had 40 years of chemical plants

with toxic potential, but why only one Bhopal? (Perrow in e-mail to author, December 27, 2010)

Power laws were not in the lexicon during the 1980s, but Perrow intuitively understood them. NAT combined complexity theory and the lop-sided randomness of Extremistan into one 'grand theory of catastrophes' decades before complexity theory was a part of our vocabulary. It was the first attempt to understand the physics of catastrophes. Perrow wrote:

> Occasionally, two or more failures, none of them devastating in themselves in isolation, come together in unexpected ways and defeat the safety devices—the definition of a 'normal accident' or system accident. If the system is also tightly coupled, these failures can cascade faster than any safety device or operator can cope with them, or they can even be incomprehensible to those responsible for doing the coping. If the accident brings down a significant part of the system, and the system has catastrophic potential, we will have a catastrophe. That, in brief, is Normal Accident Theory. (Perrow 1999: 356-357)

To recap, Perrow's definition of NAT incorporates three key ingredients: 1) occasionally two or more failures come together in an unexpected way, 2) failures cascade faster if the system is tightly coupled, and 3) systems prone to NAT have "*catastrophic potential.*" The first ingredient is another way of expressing the power law—the law that describes lop-sided unpredictability. The second is a new ingredient, as it introduces the idea of coupling or connectedness to which I devote the remainder of this chapter. The third is simply an elegant way of expressing self-organized criticality. Recall from the previous two chapters that self-organized criticality, SOC, is a complex system's way of edging nearer to its criticality over time. For a number of reasons, SOC builds up, increasing a system's potential for collapse. "Catastrophic potential" is Perrow's way of expressing SOC. Without this invisible ingredient, TMI-2 would not have melted down.

Coupling or connecting one part of a system to another provides pathways for failures to follow as a fault spreads throughout a system. In complex systems theory, coupling is called *connectivity* or linkage. A system is considered a networked system, or simply a *network*, when parts of the system are connected to one another by *links*. Thus, Perrow's theory adds something new (old) to our understanding of why $#^! happens. His theory includes complex network theory, an elegant theory well understood by experts in other fields, but rarely applied to the study of disasters and catastrophes. Modern complex network theory explains normal accident theory. At a deep level, complex systems like TMI-2 are collections of simple components linked together in subtle but critical ways. It is this connectivity that distinguishes simple systems from complex systems.

Figure 3.1. A simple network. Connectivity (coupling) is shown as links between pairs of nodes.

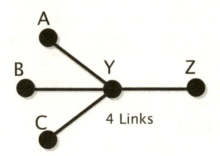

Connecting the Dots

Network theory is an overly sophisticated phrase for an extremely simple idea. Take the network shown in Figure 3.1 as an example. This network can represent almost anything—cities and roads on a map, a diagram of a pipeline system, a route map of part of a commuter rail system, or the molecular structure of a drug. Networks are even used to model online social networks such as Facebook.com or LinkedIn.com. Networks are abstractions, but don't let abstraction scare you—network theory is very simple. In fact, that is its beauty—it is an abstraction that gets at the underlying structure of many kinds of systems, hence its power and flexibility.

Suppose Figure 3.1 represents the supplier-customer relationship between companies A, B, C, Y, and Z. In network terminology, these are *nodes*. Companies A, B, and C supply parts to company Y, which in turn combines them into a product and sells the assembled product to company Z. This network represents a simple supply chain for some product. Node Y is called the *hub* because it has the most connections (four), suppliers A, B, and C are *source nodes*, and node Z is a *sink node*. In this supply chain, products flow from suppliers to manufacturer, which sells the assembled part to its customer. The product flows are represented by links, shown here as lines connecting pairs of nodes. But this network also models a road map, corporate organization chart, molecular structure, or friends connected to one another through Facebook.com. What is so complicated about such networks?

Network models are useful for studying accidental behaviors of coupled systems. *Coupling*—or links in the terminology of networks—is exactly what Perrow says is responsible for normal accidents. For example, if supplier B fails to deliver a part to company Y, then Y cannot deliver to customer Z. The failure in one node propagates to other nodes, causing domino-like collapse of much of the network. In Figure 3.1 failure of the hub (node Y) affects four other nodes. So failures propagate more widely through highly connected nodes—more than through less connected nodes. Indeed, extensive chain reactions can easily fan out and spread throughout a network containing only a few highly connected nodes. Hubs are more critical than other nodes simply because they are more connected. This partially explains why normal accidents spread and magnify their impact as they propagate through a complex connected system.

When networks fail because of coupling, we say they *cascade*. Cascades are uncharacteristically common in electric power grids, but also in traffic networks (congestion), financial systems (interconnected banks and investment companies), Internet communities (Facebook, LinkedIn, Twitter), and other familiar systems we depend on every day. The financial meltdown of 2008 is a classical example of a cascading, highly connected network of financial institutions—much more complex than Figure 3.1, but therefore also more vulnerable to normal accidents.

Figure 3.2. Representative network model of the financial meltdown of 2008. Nodes represent companies and countries. Links represent business relations and financial transactions. The links shown here are illustrative only.

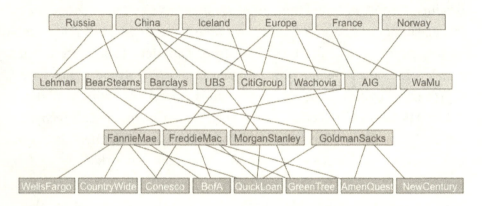

Financial Meltdown 2008

Almost everyone agrees that the financial system of the United States (and of most other developed nations) is a complex connected system. Money, stocks, bonds, contracts, etc. flow from one company (node) to others through transactions (links). Financial systems are supply chains like Figure 3.1 above, only much more complex. Like the supply chain example, these interconnected and coupled financial systems propagate failures along links to adjacent financial institutions. Highly connected institutions spread disaster more widely than less connected institutions. In fact, highly connected banks, insurance, and investment houses act like force multipliers if and when they collapse.

Clearly, such networks often contain Perrow's catastrophic potential, or SOC, as the financial meltdown of 2008 illustrated. In this case, SOC is in the 'wiring diagram' of the network; that is, the topology of the network—how nodes are linked together—is responsible for its fragility. Links provide the paths through which failures travel. If the financial network is wired just right (or wrong), failure can reach every node in the system. In fact, this is one explanation of the 2008 meltdown. The crash of 2008 is a textbook example of Perrow's NAT, and illustrates how the networked financial sector succumbed to its own form of SOC. The culprit was the network's 'wiring diagram.' SOC was embedded in the complex web of financial institutions formed by the network's links.

It is quite easy to think of portions of the global banking and financial industry as a network of connected institutions, as shown in Figure 3.2. Institutions are represented as nodes and the transactions that couple them together are represented as links. This model fits Perrow's coupling and interdependency hypothesis almost perfectly. A perturbation in one institution propagates to other connected institutions via transaction links. For example, failure in one business (node) can drag down adjacent nodes because all the links associated with a failed node are removed, affecting the nodes connected to the links. In Figure 3.2, the failure of Lehman Brothers removes links to Fannie Mae and Russia. If enough links are removed from Fannie Mae, it too collapses, and so on. Although the network in Figure 3.2 is only an approximation of the real network (which was much more complicated), it is a reasonable model of reality. For instance, Goldman Sacks was connected to AIG through a $13 billion transaction that 'failed' in 2009.

Many books have been written about the collapse of 2008 and there are many explanations for why it happened. My purpose here is to illustrate NAT, rather than explain in detail how the financial system of Wall Street works. So I will keep it simple. In grossly simplified terms, the links in

Figure 3.2 represent the flow of derivatives. Mortgage Backed Securities (MBS) derivatives were bundled together and sold as Collateralized Debt Obligations (CDO). CDOs were insured against default by other financial institutions, like AIG, as Credit Default Swaps (CDS). If a CDO failed, the CDS paid out to cover the loss. Finally, because the demand was so high, innovative derivatives called *synthetic* CDOs—synthetic because they were based on paper rather than physical assets such as houses and buildings—were sold into an eager market of risk-takers around the globe. Like grains of sand in a sand pile, these financial instruments were dependent on each other for mutual support: MBS -> CDO -> CDS -> synthetic CDO. When one 'grain' was pulled from the pile, the entire structure collapsed.

In 2007, Goldman Sachs created a $2 billion synthetic collateralized debt obligation (sCDO) called ABACUS, based on 90 bonds derived from subprime mortgages made over the previous eighteen months (subprime mortgages refer to mortgages given to people with lower credit ratings and therefore carrying higher risk). Because they were higher risk, the return rate was higher than, say, AAA-rated bonds. As long as homeowners made their mortgage payments, the CDO was a better-than-average investment. But if homeowners defaulted, the CDO would become worthless, or at least worth a fraction of the initial investment. The CDO and sCDO markets hinged on the ability and willingness of mortgage holders to pay their monthly mortgages.

To hedge their bets, Goldman Sachs bought insurance from AIG in the form of CDSs. This obligated AIG to pay Goldman Sachs $13 billion should the ABACUS CDOs default. As it turned out, Goldman Sachs collected on the AIG CDS in 2009 after the 2008 collapse of the CDO market. This aftershock sent chaotic adaptations in all directions following the crash. So far, the 2008 meltdown fits Bak's punctuated reality model almost perfectly.

Prior to its collapse in 2008-2009, this complex system had at least four levels of financial institutions, all dependent on lower level 'feeder nodes.' Feeder nodes made loans and sold them to the nodes directly above them, which in turn packaged mortgage-backed securities into derivatives and sold them to upper level nodes. Eventually, the derivatives and credit default swaps were sold to non-U.S. investors at the top level of this supply chain network. This complex network system worked well for over a decade. But then an incident comparable to the cup of water leaking out of the TMI-2 reactor started a chain-reaction that led to a massive normal accident. Why did this system work so well for decades only to end in disaster? What was the incident that triggered the meltdown, and why did it lead to the worst financial catastrophe since the crash of 1929?

The financial meltdown perfectly illustrates of the concepts described in previous chapters. I have merely replaced Bak's sand pile with a network. In place of friction among grains of sand, the financial network is held together by links. As the number of links increased over time, the financial network evolved toward a self-organized criticality. In this case, criticality emerged because of 'overly connected' institutions. An insignificant failure in one of the feeder institutions at the bottom of the 4-level system was able to spread along links to other institutions, which were directly and indirectly connected to virtually all others. At some point in the evolution of this network, a labyrinth-like web of links had so thoroughly connected nodes to other nodes that failure in one node would propagate to all others. Like the BTW experiment, the sand pile of financial connections eventually collapsed.

Not all highly linked networks collapse. In fact, most of the time only portions of a network fail when one node fails. Collapses can only propagate to nodes that are connected directly or indirectly to all other nodes. In other words, the capacity to collapse—Perrow's catastrophe potential—depends on the 'wiring diagram.' If links form a path from the failed node to all others, the entire network collapses. If not, only a portion of the network collapses. Most of the time, small portions of the financial network collapse, recover, collapse again, recover, etc.

And it may not come as a surprise to you that the sizes of these partial collapses obey a power law.

Small bankruptcies have little overall effect unless they propagate along connections and spread to most other institutions. The potential catastrophe lies in connectivity among institutions. More connections mean that it is more likely that at least one node is connected to all other nodes. The chance of catastrophic failure increases as the density of links increases. So if the 'no propagation of failure assumption' turns out to be false, the entire web of interconnected banks and investment houses becomes a house of cards. In 2008, the 'no propagation' assumption turned out to be false. Instead of a partial collapse, the web of connections had become so dense that even the most insignificant failure contained the seeds of destruction for the entire system.

Over time, the network became self-organized by adding links and constantly rewiring them. As the network evolved toward SOC, the number of links between levels increased as well as the number of nodes. The closer the network came to its maximum capacity—all nodes connected to all others—the closer it came to its critical point. The built-up network eventually collapsed, not because a large financial institution like Lehman Brothers was too big to fail, but because it was too heavily connected. In fact, one can argue that Lehman Brothers was both big and connected, but its connectivity is what made it critical. The financial network contained nodes that were 'too connected to fail.'

SOC continued to build throughout much of the early 2000's until mid-2007, when local loan companies in Orange County, California, began to fold. Quick Loan, AmeriQuest, New Century, and other feeders at the bottom of the network shown in Figure 3.2 were too small and insignificant to crash the entire financial system themselves, but once the system reached its critical point, these small players became key players. In this case, 'criticality' means that these small players were connected to bigger players, which in turn were connected to even bigger institutions, and so forth, until a failure of the least significant institutions propagated to all institutions.

This explanation of the crash of 2008 is unconventional and suggests a hidden force, SOC, invisibly working under everyone's radar. In fact, SOC was building for decades prior to the collapse, which may have been unpredictable but was nevertheless inevitable. Indeed, the impending meltdown was apparent enough that several clever investors benefitted from the collapse by hedging, as Goldman Sachs did. These clever investors bet against the system and won. How did they know? The few investors that bet against the system and won were either lucky or understood SOC. I doubt that they called it SOC, but perhaps they realized that the build up in the derivatives market was reaching its point of diminishing returns. Or perhaps they guessed correctly that the financial system was fragile and near its 'oversold' tipping point.

For example, the hero of David Faber's best-selling book, *And Then The Roof Caved In*, Kyle Bass, questioned the prevailing assumption that housing prices would continue to go up forever and cheap money would continue to fuel the mortgage market without limit (Faber 2009). Kyle Bass started his own 'anti-mortgage derivatives' hedge fund and walked away with billions. Even Goldman Sachs bet against the mortgage derivatives market with its ABACUS fund.

The inevitable financial meltdown was a network meltdown. It behaved just like Bak's sand pile. So, networks and sand piles have something in common: they both collapse unexpectedly in accordance with a power law. Through numerous examples and a simulation, I hope to convince you that Bak's sand pile shares general principles with many natural and human-caused catastrophes. An understanding of these principles may not make you as clever as Kyle Bass, but it will make you aware of how complex systems such as the financial market can unexpectedly spin out of control.

The basis of my argument is that the fundamental principle of SOC applies equally well to networks and Perrow's normal accident theory as it does to sand piles. In fact, networks are more general and expressive than sand piles. The question is, how does SOC manifest itself in networks—especially the financial network described here—and how do we measure it? By understanding the properties of networks that lead to SOC, the savvy investor can observe the build up to a critical point in network systems and avoid the catastrophes. In the next section, I intend to back up this bold claim.

Figure 3.3 Amaral-Meyer network and the exceedence probability plot derived from simulating its collapse.

(a). Network near its critical point. Nodes and links are added until reaching a critical point whereby most nodes fail because of a single node failure in the lowest level. The magnified insert looks a lot like the network in Figure 3.2—and it should!

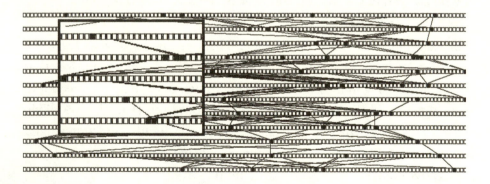

(b). Exceedence probability obtained by simulating single node failures in the network of (a) obeys a power law with resilience exponent of 1.0. The solid bars plot exceedence probability. The risk profile curve shown as a jagged line above the exceedence probability curve is PML risk as described in the previous chapter (the product of exceedence probability and consequence). The vertical axis is exceedence probability and the horizontal axis is the percentage of collapsed nodes resulting from a propagation of a single node failure at the lowest level.

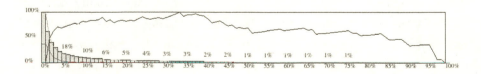

The Amaral-Meyer Network

The financial sector model shown in Figure 3.2 is very similar to a biological extinction model proposed in 1999 by Luis Amaral and Martin Meyer, two physicists working in an entirely unrelated field (Amaral & Meyer 1999). The scientists were trying to model Darwinian extinctions in nature by relating their unique network model to fossil records spanning millions of years. Incredibly, collapses of the Amaral-Meyer network match the exceedence probability power law of extinctions deduced from fossil records! Even more curiously, the Amaral and Meyer model explains why complex network systems such as the U.S. financial system eventually fail. Their model is simple, and yet complex.

Here is how the Amaral-Meyer network model of extinction works. Consider a tiered ecological or *'food network'* consisting of niches, represented by nodes in Figure 3.3a, and links, represented by lines connecting pairs of nodes. Niches are shown as black nodes if they are occupied by a surviving species. Links are shown as lines connecting pairs of black nodes. The idea is to study what happens when nodes are removed, along with their links.

Amaral and Meyer imagined a world in which species at each level of the ecological system occasionally and randomly mutate and fill an empty node or slot above, below, or on either side of themselves at the same level. Mutations occur with small probability and tend to increase the population of occupied nodes, as long as they can link to at least one occupied node immediately below them. Linking establishes a food chain, supporting nodes above, but not below or at the same level. If a node is unable to establish a link or if the link is broken because the lower-level node becomes extinct, the upper-level node also becomes extinct. Thus, species go 'out of business' when they no longer have supporting species one level below themselves.

A curious thing happens when a lower-level node randomly goes extinct and all of its links are removed. This incident propagates to all of the nodes connected to the removed node. If all links are removed from a node in a level above the extinction, it too becomes extinct. The failure is propagated up to the next level by repeatedly removing links to higher-level nodes, etc. Sometimes only one node goes extinct; sometimes a handful goes extinct. In very rare cases, all of the nodes go extinct, because the incident propagates to all surrounding nodes. When most or all of the network collapses because of a single incident, we follow Perrow's lead and call it a normal accident. But such normal accidents are rare and unexpected. In fact, their size obeys a power law.

For the purposes discussed here, Amaral and Meyer's mutations correspond with new financial institutions and extinctions correspond with business failures or bankruptcies. New nodes are constantly being created and old nodes are being removed, so what eventually happens in the long run? The number of nodes steadily increases as mutations fill out niches and expand across all levels. Growth then levels off and remains level for a long period of time, dictated by the rate of extinctions and the rate of mutations. The number of nodes fluctuates up and down, by relatively small amounts. Then the unexpected happens: suddenly and unpredictably, the network collapses. The size of each collapse is measured in terms of the fraction of all nodes. Thus, collapse of size 50% equates to removal of one half of the nodes, shown in Figure 3.3b. Similarly, the elapsed time between major drops in percentage of nodes is shown in Figure 3.3c. Like the BTW experiment, the size and timing of collapses are unpredictable, but both size and elapsed time between major drops obey a power law. The Amaral-Meyer network is a network equivalent of Bak's sand pile. SOC increases along with both density of links and the ways in which the links establish connections among nodes. Therefore, SOC is derived from both link density and network topology.

In terms of a financial meltdown, the difference between an isolated bankruptcy incident and a complete system collapse or meltdown is SOC. At some point, the financial system reaches a state of self-organized criticality such that the failure of a certain company propagates to all other companies through a series of links. When the links are dense (many per node) criticality is reached sooner than when they are sparse (few links per node).

Second, the 'wiring diagram' of a network is defined by *degree of connectivity* of individual nodes; that is, nodes with many connections via links are more critical than nodes with fewer connections. This makes sense if you equate 'importance' with number of transaction links. Highly connected nodes—hubs—have a much greater impact on the network when they are removed than less connected nodes. It therefore makes sense to protect the highly connected hubs. Or does it?

In the simulations of the Amaral-Meyer network shown in Figure 3.3, it turns out that protecting highly connected nodes—those that are 'too connected to fail'—leads to slightly smaller normal accidents. So should the hub institutions be bailed out and not allowed to fail? Bailouts of the 'too big to fail' banks following the 2008 meltdown was a controversial strategy, but was it the best strategy?

Instead of protecting the hubs, suppose these highly connected hubs are periodically removed by 'thinning the herd'—removing nodes before they become too connected. In this strategy, instead of randomly removing a node at the lowest level of the Amaral-Meyer network, hubs are purposely removed; that is, banks are not allowed to become too connected. Simulations show that collapses are dramatically smaller!

Why? Because removing bank nodes before they become too connected reduces SOC.

In terms of the 2008 financial meltdown, limiting the number of connections to nodes mitigates financial catastrophes. Instead of worrying about banks and other financial institutions becoming 'too big to fail,' they should be prevented from becoming 'too connected to fail.' A policy of *link de-percolation* would curb ultimate meltdowns and keeping SOC under control by preventing a node from getting too many links. In the scientific literature, this type of link build-up is a form of self-organized criticality called *bond percolation*. Various kinds of percolation are responsible for many forms of self-organized criticality, as I will explain further in upcoming chapters.

The Amaral-Meyer network illustrates several concepts that explain many kinds of normal accidents. First, SOC increases with connectivity. Connectivity can be of two forms—link density (percolation) and hub size (too much connectivity at a node). Both forms of SOC magnify the consequence of even a seemingly insignificant event. This clue is very useful when predicting the next big one. If we want to avoid Black Swan events, complex network systems must avoid too many links and large hubs.

Predicting the Next Big One

We can learn another important lesson regarding catastrophes by measuring the elapsed time between collapses in the Amaral-Meyer simulation. This might be useful for predicting the next big collapse or at least the frequency of big collapses. In the following, I define a 'big one' as an extinction of 20% or more nodes following an extinction of a single node at the lowest level. I chose this number because a 20% drop in the stock market is cause for panic.

Figure 3.3c was obtained using the same technique I have been using to calculate the exceedence probability curve. The only difference is the x-axis. Instead of measuring the size of a collapse, the x-axis of Figure 3.3c measures the elapsed time between collapses in excess of 20% of the nodes. The distribution of elapsed time between collapses of 20% or more produces a power law, too! Each time a major collapse occurs, we put it in a bin arrayed along the x-axis of Figure 3.3c. After recording thousands of simulated incidents, count the number of elapsed times between collapses and normalize them into a probability distribution. A power law is produced—in this case the exponent of the power law is 0.65.

What does this mean? The distribution of time intervals between successive collapses is lop-sided. Small time intervals are more common than long time intervals. Since the intervals separate successive collapses from one another, the lop-sided shape of the power law says collapses are *bursty*; that is, they occur in closely spaced groups or clusters, separated by relatively long periods of stability. Accidents happen in threes and fours rather than singletons evenly spaced in time.

The bursty behavior of catastrophes makes sense because SOC takes time. After each major collapse, the system resets to a lower level of self-organized criticality and is far from its critical point. SOC slowly builds up over time until reaching a critical point, another collapse occurs, and the process repeats. Complex systems that suffer from SOC are generally *bursty*, meaning that they operate with little or no indication of instability for relatively long periods of time, collapse, and then run flawlessly for a relatively long time until the next big one happens again.

Are the collapse and bursty properties described here unique to Amaral-Meyer networks or do they hold for real-world systems? As it turns out, bursts in both time and space are two more properties of the Casinos of Extremistan. In fact, this kind of bursty behavior has a name: *Lévy flight*. Events in Extremistan obey power laws in both time and space. I devote an entire chapter later in this book to Lévy flight. Meanwhile, suppose we compare the Amaral-Meyer network with historical data. Does the real-world economy obey a power law? You probably already know the answer.

Economic Meltdowns

What does the foregoing say about the general economy? Was the 2008 meltdown pathological, or should we expect it to happen again? If such catastrophes are inevitable, then what is the future of the economy? As I have shown here, the power law that describes Bak's sand pile applies equally to the economy. Both size of meltdown—measured by decline in industrial production—and time interval between major meltdowns follow a power law (see Figure 1.2 in chapter 1).

Economic decline, as measured by decline in industrial production, obeys a power law with exponent greater than one. In the previous chapter I showed that power laws with an exponent greater than one correspond with low-risk hazards because probable maximum loss actually decreases with increasing consequence. Risk initially rises, but goes down as consequence escalates. Because the decline in the power law is steep enough to dampen out increases in consequence, economic risk is low.

For example, the probability of a decline in excess of 20% is approximately 30%. But a major decline, such as the 45% correction in the Dow Jones Industrial Average in 2008-2009 has an exceedence probability of only 4%! The 2008 financial meltdown was rare, but clearly not impossible. An exceedence probability of 4% is roughly equivalent to odds of the next comparable meltdown happening again within the next 24 years. For example, the 2008 collapse occurred twenty-one years after Black Monday, October 19, 1987, when the Dow Jones Industrial Average dropped 22%. Power laws work!

As discussed in the previous chapter, Nassim Nicholas Taleb made several fortunes betting on financial collapses. I consider him a 'Super Bear' because he bets against bull markets. In hindsight, his strategy is quite simple: sit on the sidelines while SOC builds over the period of time considered a 'bull market,' and when 'irrational exuberance' reaches a peak, short the market. These Bears do very little during an upswing but then swing into action when a financial Black Swan occurs. They have learned to ride bursty markets like a surfer in Santa Cruz.

Figure 1.2b in chapter 1 records the bursty behavior of the economy over the past 150 years. Unpredictable drops in industrial production are clustered together in time. For example, everyone knows about Black Friday, when the U.S. stock market crashed and led to the Great Depression, but few remember the subsequent reverberations. Industrial production dropped 53% in 1929, but dropped precipitously again in 1937 (32.5%) and 1945 (35.5%). Production suffered dramatically in 1893 and 1895 (17% and 11%, respectively), and again suffered bursty declines in 1980 and 1981.

The dotted line in Figure 1.2b in chapter 1 is for comparison only. It is a sand pile power law with exponent of 1.0, which suggests that economic activity is slightly burstier than sand piles. Figure 3.3c in the present chapter shows elapsed time results for the Amaral-Meyer network simulation. It is far less bursty because its exponent is less than one. So, the Amaral-Meyer model of time between financial collapses in excess of 20% predicts less bursty behavior. It also suggests a greater length of time between subsequent dips in the economy.

It is impossible to predict exactly when a financial meltdown will happen or how big it will be, but anyone can deduce the following from the Perrow and Amaral-Meyer models:

1. The big ones are inevitable as long as SOC is allowed to build up.
2. Big ones are bursty—they occur in pairs, triples, etc.

3. The Amaral-Meyer network is a fitting model for understanding financial collapses and behaves much like Bak's sand pile.

4. Big ones precipitate a period of chaotic adaptation, such as financial regulation, following the sudden, dramatic meltdown—further confirmation of Bak's theory of punctuated reality.

The Amaral-Meyer network may model many other natural and human-made complex systems that unexpectedly fail after a long period of stability. Typically these systems crash following a small, unassuming incident that upsets the system's equilibrium, rendering it unstable. The timing and size of consequence cannot be predicted ahead of time with great accuracy, but timing and size do follow a power law. Eventually the Amaral-Meyer network self-organizes into a state of criticality and collapses. It confirms the validity of Bak's sand pile experiment and the theory of punctuated reality. It is not only a beautiful illustration of SOC, but also unlocks some additional secrets of complex systems.

CALIFORNIA ON FIRE

California wildfires in October 2007 were so enormous that they could easily be seen from space. Note the East-to-West direction of the smoke.[1]

Santa Ana Winds

California holds the dubious record for the most numerous natural disasters among all states of the Union. Earthquakes and forest fires are its predominant hazards, costing taxpayers billions of dollars per year and often taking lives. Data collected by the National Oceanic and Atmospheric Administration (NOAA) shows that twenty of the 36 U.S. earthquakes resulting in at least $1 million in damages during the twentieth century occurred in California. Since 2000, 9 of the 25 worst fires in the U.S. happened in the Golden State. In 2008, 1.6 million acres (2,500 square miles) of California went up in flames, prompting Kelly Houston of the Governor's Office of Emergency Services to declare the major 2008 fire, "the largest single fire event in the history for California" ('California wildfires' 2008) The state's 2008 Redbook reported total

---

1   http://www.nasa.gov/vision/earth/lookingatearth/socal_wildfires_oct07.html

consequences in excess of $150 million from all hazards including arson, campfires, lightning, smoking, etc.

California's climate is moderated by Pacific Ocean winds that cool the state during the summer and warm it during the winter months, but the months of September and October are challenging as the winds reverse themselves, flowing from the Sierra Mountains out to sea. These warm winds are called *Santa Ana Winds* in the south and *Chinook Winds* in the north. Santa Ana winds make October the warmest month of the year, frequently pushing temperatures into triple digits. October is also California's 'fire season.'

Lightning and careless campers, hikers, and sportsmen often cause fires that are quickly extinguished. But once in a while these small fires explode, growing exponentially as they burn everything from mountain to ocean. Since Californians love nature, many houses are built adjacent to forests, producing inevitable casualties. The October 2007 wildfires were no exception. During the period spanning late October to early November, seventeen Californians lost their lives, and 140 were injured in the massive fires that raged across the lower half of the state.

California wildfires affect more than vegetation and animals—they take critical infrastructure systems with them. The October 2007 wildfires destroyed 3,000 homes, displaced nearly one million people, burned over half a million acres, destroyed or disabled portions of the power grid and telephone systems, and damaged water resources.

But California's unusually extreme fires are caused not only by arson, careless campers, or Santa Ana winds. Arsonists and campers may start fires, but self-organized criticality makes them extreme. In fact, mega-fires, as they are called, can be avoided by a careful application of Bak's theory of self-organization. As it turns out, the intensity of forest fires is largely a matter of *punctuated reality*—a reality under our control. This reality can be managed if we simply reduce a particular form of self-organization called *percolation*.

Figure 4.1. Exceedence probability of California fires in 2007 indicating that they were high-risk (because the exponent with a value of 0.6 is less than one). The steadily increasing risk profile is shown as a dotted line.

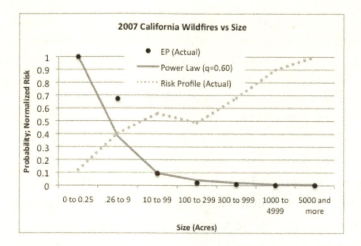

Percolated Forests

California forests belong in the Casinos of Extremistan because the likelihood and size of fires obey Extremistan's lop-sided power law, shown in Figure 4.1. Most fires are small and cause little damage, but some fires are large and disastrous. Even fewer fires are so rare and yet so damaging that they are Black Swans. These *mega-fires* appear to be getting worse. As Figure 4.1 shows, forest fire activity in California is already self-organized into a high-risk system because risk increases with size of fire. The major source of this risk is what forest rangers call *understory*—the build-up of vegetation on the floor of the forest that fuels inevitable destruction.

Unfortunately, mega-fires are increasing because policymakers don't understand Bak's sand pile. Policies favoring pristine forests of unsustainable density have increased forest self-organized criticality to the point where arsonists, campers, droughts, and lightning strikes do far more damage then they should. According to forest management experts Jerry Williams and Albert Hyde,

> Many of our land management laws, policies, and plans are at odds with the thinning, prescribed burning, and selective cutting needed to mitigate the mega-fire threat. And policy strategies that might use high-intensity wildfires to clean up the fuels and solve the problem are not always consistent with the ecologies involved. In many places, we find ourselves between a rock and a hard place. (Williams & Hyde 2009)

Forests, mega-fires, and the management of forests form a complex system that begs for an application of Bak's sand pile theory. In fact, forest systems are perfect examples of self-organized criticality. Depending on how a forest is managed, it can become more, rather than less, vulnerable to mega-fires, and this is the issue facing California forests. But the insight needed to explain why mega-fires happen came from the author of the standard textbook on *Geodynamics*—not forest management—and his bright graduate students. To unravel the connection between forest management and complexity theory, you need to understand percolation theory. In this context, percolation has a technical definition: filling an empty space with randomly placed particles or obstructions much like snowflakes covering the ground in winter.

After writing *Geodynamics* with Gerald Shubert in 1982, Donald Turcotte switched his interest from tectonics to *fractals* and *chaos theory*. Together with Cornell University postdoctoral research associate Bruce Malamud, Turcotte proposed a simple but elegant model of forest fires that explains how percolation leads to SOC, which in turn leads to mega-fires (Malamud, Morein, & Turcotte 1998). Malamud was perhaps an ideal match for Turcotte because he had logged time operating the Stanford Linear Accelerator (SLAC), done a tour in Niger, West Africa for the Peace Corps, and attended Reed College—a forested campus in Portland Oregon (attended a decade earlier by Steve Jobs of Apple Computer).

Malamud is currently a lecturer in the Department of Geography, King's College, London.

For purposes of explaining forest fires, percolation is simply the process of randomly planting trees. Turcotte and Malamud simulated the growth of a forest as a process of tree percolation. They called the self-organized criticality of forests the 'Yellowstone effect' because of a policy implemented by Yellowstone National Park prior to 1972 of suppressing fires, which resulted in a large accumulation of dead trees and understory. This policy was abandoned after a mega-fire in 1980 that destroyed 800,000 acres of forest in Yellowstone. The Yellowstone effect is to forests what grains of sand are to sand piles.

Here is how a simulated forest of percolated trees works. Let a forest be represented by a rectangular grid of squares as shown in Figure 4.2[2]. At each step of the simulation plant trees in randomly selected squares. Repeat this random process, forever. Tree density increases as the empty squares fill up, see Figure 4.2b. The longer we wait, the denser the forest—that is, unless some or all of the trees are wiped out by a fire.

Now suppose a bolt of lightning periodically strikes a randomly selected square. (if the fire is started by an arsonist, use a match instead of lightning, as Malamud did). If the square is empty, nothing happens. If the square contains a tree, the tree and all of its adjacent trees burn down. Burnt trees are erased from the simulated forest, returning it to a blank square. Immediately adjacent trees and all their adjacent trees are removed, see Figure 4.2c. The fire spreads from tree to tree until there are no more adjacent trees. Thus, consequence is equal to the burned area as measured by the number of trees destroyed after each lightning strike.

---

2   Malamud used a 128 x 128 grid, but I used a much smaller grid of 64 x 64.

Forest Fire Simulation

1. Repeat forever:

    a. Percolate: plant a tree in an empty, randomly selected square.

    b. Strike: Periodically strike a randomly selected square, and if it is occupied, burn down the tree.

    c. Spread the Fire: Burn down all adjacent trees and their adjacent trees until there are no more adjacent trees.

Clearly the area burned each time a lightning bolt or match ignites a tree increases as the density of trees increase; that is, high-density percolation leads to mega-fires. Thus, high-density equates with SOC. To reduce SOC, either purposely start small controlled fires or clear out the understory.

Figure 4.2. Malamud and Turcotte's forest fire simulation illustrates SOC.

a. Sparse forest with shaded (green) squares representing trees.

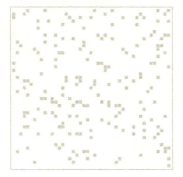

b. Dense forest showing increased percolation of trees—understory has increased the forest's self-organized criticality.

c. Less dense forest showing burned trees after lightning strikes ignited and burned the darker-shaded (red) squares.

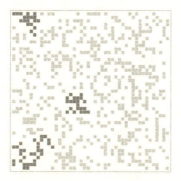

Figure 4.3. Exceedence probability curves for the forest fire simulation.

a. Exceedence probability for frequent fires (periodic strike interval: 10 steps), exponent equals 0.93, so this forest's criticality is high-risk. Light colored (green) bars representing exceedence probability were obtained by simulation; dark colored (blue) bars are probability; straight line (red) is a power law approximation of the exceedence probability.

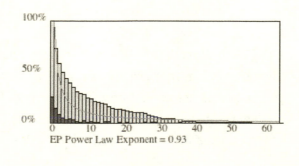

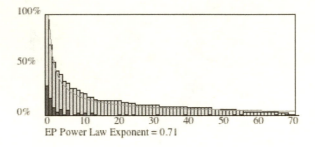

EP Power Law Exponent = 0.71

Self-Organized Fires

Malamud's simple three-step simulation is repeated until enough simulation data is collected to draw the exceedence probability curve as shown in Figure 4.3. In the original simulation, Malamud, Morein, and Turcotte analyzed the frequency-area plot instead of exceedence probability. Their power law mirrors my power law because power laws are all self-similar. I calculated the exceedence probability curve as shown in Figure 4.3 for two periodic strike rates—once every ten and twenty time steps. Notice the effect of periodic strike rate on the exponent of the exceedence probability curves. Infrequent strikes lead to bigger mega-fires than frequent ones! A forest's resiliency is directly related to this exponent—higher exponents mean more resilience. What determines the exponent value, and therefore, the resiliency of the forest?

Figure 4.3 is the key to understanding SOC and its relevance to forest fires. The forest in Figure 4.3a is more resilient than the forest in Figure 4.3b because lighting strikes are *more frequent*. Intuitively, fewer fires should mean less damage, but in this case intuition is dead wrong. In fact, fewer fires mean bigger fires. Moreover, policies that reduce the frequency of fires contribute to mega-fires—the opposite of the result most of us want. What is going on?

Here is what is going on: percolation increases the number and size of tree clusters. Fires get bigger the longer we wait to burn a patch of forest because percolated patches are bigger. If the goal is to reduce the likelihood and severity of mega-fires, it pays to encourage smaller fires more often! This counter-intuitive fact is one reason why modern forest management techniques are increasing mega-fires rather than decreasing them. In fact, consequences increase in proportion to the square root of strike frequency because (rectangular) cluster size increases as the square root of planting time.

If the goal is to reduce risk and therefore avoid major catastrophic forest fires in California (and elsewhere, because this is a general result), it is essential to periodically thin forests in order to reverse percolation. Williams and Hyde explain,

> On some mega-fires, recent understory thinning and/or prescribed understory burning had occurred within the mega-fire perimeter. On these areas, burn severity and resistance-to-control was much lower, compared to adjacent un-treated stands. In one case, a mega-fire was contained after running into a very large treated area whose understory that had been routinely burned at 3-5 year intervals. These observations indicate that understory thinning and prescribed burning ... can have a positive difference, in terms of overall forest resilience and fire protection; even under drought and extreme weather conditions conducive to fire. (Williams & Hyde 2009).

In other words, Malamud's model works! Percolation is another source of self-organized criticality. It is easy to relate percolation of a forest to intensity of fires, but percolation is actually a general concept. It will crop up again in unexpected places. For example, diseases spread faster in dense populations, which is a form of percolation. Thinning people out by quarantine is similar to thinning understory. Similarly, density of financial transactions among banks and investment firms is a form of percolation called *link percolation*. Reducing the number of links in such a business eco-system reduces SOC. So percolation applies to many different kinds of complex systems—forests, banks, and people.

One further note before I expand on these concepts. Not everyone agrees that Malamud's simple model is an example of self-organized criticality. For example, Grassberger, Pruessner and Jensen (Grassberger 2002; Pruessner & Jensen 2002) have shown that power laws describing forest fire percolation do not scale. Recall that the power law is a fractal and as such is self-similar, which is another way of saying that it scales. For example, the power law may be truncated under certain conditions, such as faster growth rate than lightning strike rate, or the size of the box enclosing the forest. Regardless of these technical details, my point is that the build up of criticality in a percolated forest and its release in the form of depleted clusters of trees obey a power law.

People Percolation

Forest fires are more likely to succumb to disaster when trees are planted too closely together. Similarly, people succumb to contagious diseases when they are packed too closely together. Clustering large populations by packing people into cities, airports, and sports arenas is a form of people percolation. It is also responsible for the rapid spread of communicable diseases throughout dense 'human forests.' The only difference is that human forests are social networks rather than acres of trees.

Pandemics have killed more people than all wars combined. The Black Death (1300-1700AD) exterminated 100 million people; the Spanish Flu (1918-1920AD) killed 50-100 million; the Plague of Justinian (540-590AD) exterminated 40-50 million; the Third Pandemic of Bubonic Plague (1850-1950AD) killed perhaps 12 million; the Antonine Plague of the Roman Empire (165-180AD) was responsible for the deaths of 5 million; and more recently, the Asian Flu (1956-1958AD) killed 4 million worldwide. Understanding the dynamics of disease is critical to the survival of nations, and perhaps the entire world. Of course, the germ theory and modern medicine have done much to control epidemics, but prevention is a never-ending arms race between modern pharmaceuticals and adaptable viruses—a war that can never be won.

Epidemics can, however, be mitigated by controlling SOC in social networks. Quarantine strategies are one obvious way of reducing SOC because quarantining is essentially a winnowing process, akin to clearing out understock in a forest. Reducing infectiousness—the probability of contracting a disease even when coming into contact with an infected person—is another SOC-reducing tactic. The ring vaccination strategy practiced by world health organizations has been very effective at reducing SOC and wiping out major diseases, such as smallpox.

I modified Malamud's forest fire simulation and adapted it to model the spread of diseases through percolated populations. Instead of always infecting adjacent squares in the 'human forest,' suppose adjacent squares (people) are infected and die with a certain probability (called infectiousness) or otherwise escape death. *Infectiousness* is defined as the probability that a perfectly healthy person will contract the disease from an infected person and die, also known as the mortality rate. For example, smallpox has an infectiousness of approximately 20-30%, meaning that a typical human has a 20-30% probability of contracting smallpox from another infected human and dying as a result. The likelihood of death can be reduced through vaccination, but it must be applied within a very narrow window of three to six days following contraction of the virus.

I reran Malamud's forest fire simulation with an infectiousness value of 30%. Instead of spreading the disease to adjacent squares, this time the simulation spreads with probability of 30%. That is, 30% of the time adjacent 'trees' contract the disease, pass it on, and expire. Instead of an exceedence probability exponent of 0.70 (high-risk), this time I obtained an exponent of 1.3 (low-risk). By lowering infectiousness from 100% to 30%, self-organized criticality reduces the resilience of the human forest into the 'safe zone.'

Suppose *pandemic* is defined as 25% or more of the population becoming ill due to the spread of some kind of disease. What is the probability of a pandemic? If we use the exceedence probability curve of Figure 4.3b, the likelihood of pandemic is 10.5%, but if we assume infectiousness is 30% instead of 100%, the likelihood of a pandemic outbreak is only 1.5%. The probability of a pandemic is reduced more than ten-fold simply by reducing infectiousness.

Clearly inoculation against any highly contagious disease is an effective strategy, but what if large populations are either too massive to inoculate or there isn't enough time? It would take perhaps 40,000 trained medical professionals approximately three days to inoculate the eight million inhabitants of Manhattan Island against an outbreak of smallpox. But due to the sophistication of the technique, there are perhaps far fewer than 40,000 people in the entire United States able to administer smallpox vaccinations. After three days have passed, it is too late to stop the pandemic.

An alternative to inoculation is to lower SOC by separating people, limiting contact, quarantine, etc. This dramatically reduces the likelihood of pandemic without inoculation. Thinning the crowd, so to speak, from 85% density to 50% virtually eliminates pandemic! By reducing SOC, highly infectious diseases can't spread, regardless of their infectiousness. So two strategies work to reduce risk: inoculation and depercolation. *Inoculation is a form of hardening that reduces vulnerability while depercolation is a form of resiliency that reduces consequence.* Keep these two concepts in mind as I expand on these simple ideas.

Figure 4.4. Conversion of Malamud's checkerboard forest into a mobile social network by linking adjacent occupied squares.

a. Checkerboard forest: Occupied squares are shaded.

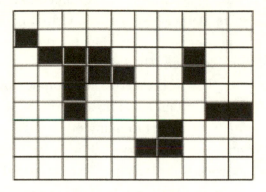

b. Equivalent social network: Adjacent shaded squares (nodes) are linked.

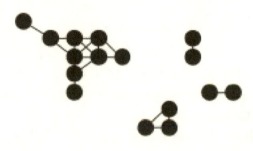

Networked Percolation

People aren't trees in a forest. But like trees in a forest, people are adjacent to other people. For example, the members of your immediate family, co-workers, and friends are adjacent to you in the sense that you come into contact with one another on a regular basis. These relationships form what is called a social network. People are the nodes and relationships are the links. Adjacency is represented by a link between nodes. Thus, Malamud's forest can be converted into a social network by replacing adjacency with a link, as in Figure 4.4. Contagion spreads through the links of a social network exactly like fire spreads to adjacent trees in a forest.

Figure 4.4b is obtained from Figure 4.4a by inserting a link between pairs of occupied squares adjacent to one another. This does two things: 1) it converts the two-dimensional checkerboard into a network, and 2) it converts spatial adjacency into virtual adjacency so that the network no longer needs to be physical—it can be a virtual map of adjacency. For example, social networks are formed all the time over the Internet, regardless of physical location. The Internet converts social networks from the forest metaphor to the network metaphor by 'virtualizing' the model. This is an important generalization, because it extends the usefulness of the network model to many other systems. Specifically, propagation of contagions across national boundaries via air travel is more of a social network effect than an adjacent spatial effect; that is, social networks are mainly responsible for the spread of diseases—a topic that I explore in detail in the next chapter.

The models of Figure 4.4 illustrate a key ingredient of Perrow's normal accident theory, which I described in detail in chapter three. Recall that normal accident theory explains how small failures spread through a system's components, magnify as they spread, and sometimes become major disasters. The main cause of system disaster is *coupling*, represented by links that propagate faults. Recall that normal accident theory directly relates SOC to the density of links in a coupled complex system, just as SOC is caused by increased density of trees in a percolated forest.

Transforming Malamud's forest into a network in this way adds an important feature to Bak's punctuated reality model because networks transcend geographical limits—the network model incorporates mobility. Specifically, the network of Figure 4.4b extends to air travel as well as telephone, and Internet connectivity. Social networks may be physical or virtual. Communicable diseases are transmitted by physical contact. Internet viruses, on the other hand, are just as virulent, even though they are virtual. And as I will demonstrate later in this book, Internet viruses may turn out to be a bigger problem than human diseases.

SOC in Social Networks

Figure 4.4b is an abstraction of a *social network*—a network that shows people's connections regardless of their proximity. For my purposes here, a link represents physical contact through fixed or mobile means. But in general, a link can be virtual. Thus, a human epidemic may be spread across national boundaries because people, birds, insects or other disease vectors move from place to place. These mobile contacts create social networks, which in turn establish pathways for contagion.

Dynamic social network creation through mobility is indeed the story of many viral attacks on populations around the world. Consider the West Nile Virus (WNV), for example. It started in Uganda in the late 1930s, spread to Egypt, Europe, and eventually to Australia and the United States. In this case, epidemiologists speculate that birds hitching rides on intercontinental airliners spread the WNV molecules around the globe.

Self-organization in networks explains the dynamics of disease. As I have emphasized previously, two factors contribute to SOC: *link density* (how many total links there are as a fraction of the maximum number possible) and *node connectivity* (how many links there are connecting individual nodes). Scientists use a measure called *spectral radius* to capture both of these network properties. Don't be concerned with how spectral radius is calculated because I will do the calculations for you! It is simply a number that measures SOC in networks. A higher spectral radius means that more SOC exists, so now you know that higher spectral radius also means higher risk.

I will use a random network as a standard to judge other networks. A random network is simply a network, the links of which are randomly connected to nodes. It is easy to construct a random network: simply select a pair of nodes at random, connect them with a link, and repeat the process until all links have been incorporated. The spectral radius of a random network is equal to the average number of connections. For example, a random network with 100 nodes and 110 links contains 220 connections, so its spectral radius is 220/100 or 2.2. I will use random networks with equivalent number of nodes and links as a standard to evaluate all other networks. If the spectral radius of another network with 100 nodes is higher than 2.2, it must contain some SOC.

For example, the network in Figure 4.4b has a spectral radius of 3.64, which means that it has already built up some self-organized criticality because 3.64 is greater than the equivalent random network with a spectral radius of 2.2. The difference in spectral radius of any network and its random equivalent is due to two things: the density of links and the lop-sided wiring of links. By lop-sided wiring I mean that some nodes are connected by more links than an average node. In Figure 4.4b, the hub is connected by 5 links, which is far above the average of 2.2 links per node. This lop-sided allocation is largely responsible for SOC in Figure 4.4b. Recall that resiliency is inversely proportional to SOC, so resiliency is also inversely proportional to spectral radius. Therefore, spectral radius is also a measure of the fragility of a network. Higher spectral radius indicates weakness of some sort. It is this weakness that I explore next.

Cascades and epidemics spread faster and infect more people in a social network with high spectral radius. This makes sense because link density and node connectivity—both of which increase the numerical value of spectral radius—corresponds with more contact. If the spectral radius is big enough, epidemics not only spread faster, they become *persistent*—that is, they never completely go away, but return over and over again. Persistence is troublesome in human populations, but even more troublesome in virtual populations, the Internet. But I am getting ahead of myself again.

Researchers at Carnegie-Mellon University showed that an epidemic will recur if the product of spectral radius times infectiousness is greater than the rate of people either dying or being vaccinated (Wang, Chakrabarti, Wang & Faloutsos 2003). For example, a disease with infectiousness of

30% will persist forever in the network of Figure 4.4b, because 30% multiplied by 3.64 is greater than 100%. If such a disease invades the simple network of Figure 4.4b, it will never go away! In order to put an end to the persistent recurrence of the contagion, either infectiousness has to decrease to less than 27%, or spectral radius has to decrease to 3.3. This is so because (.27)(3.64) and (.30)(3.3) are less than 100%.

Persistent epidemics can be eliminated from social networks by either reducing infectiousness, or reducing spectral radius. Assuming that nothing can be done about infectiousness, reduction of spectral radius is the only remaining option. For example, the shaded hub node of Figure 4.4b has five connections even though the average is 2.25 links. This anomaly increases spectral radius. Reducing the number of links on this 'super-spreader' node reduces the network's spectral radius and, therefore, its ability to support a persistent epidemic.

Network models help us get to the heart of complexity so that we can begin to understand Bak's sand pile. What I have described tells us that complexity can often be modeled as a network. Self-organized criticality increases with the increase in spectral radius, which summarizes the network's connectivity in a single number. Therefore, criticality increases when connectivity increases through percolation (by adding links to hubs) and link density (adding links overall). This form of SOC leads to catastrophes in forests, social networks, and many other systems that I will describe later. Punctuated reality is rooted in network connectivity and the inherent instability of networked systems that grows with maturation. This factor is clearly what causes mega-fires and, as I repeat throughout this book, is the key factor in cascades and epidemics.

Figure 4.5. A termite network consisting of wood chips shown as dots, and termites shown as dots with legs. Chips are linked to one another if they have been picked up and dropped next to one another by a wandering termite. Links are stretched when a node is moved, unless it gets too long. Long links are cut and discarded.

a. One Termite and 400 random wood chips in a small termite world.

b. One termite partially organizing 400 wood chips in 1.8 million steps

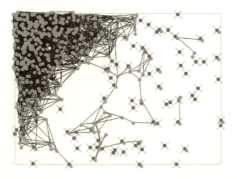

c. Swarm of 100 termites herding 400 chips in 400,000 steps.

Social Termites

Understanding abstract networks is important because so many systems in our world are networks: roads, pipelines, electrical power grids, the Internet, food supply chains, energy supply chains, drinking water, ecosystems, international travel systems, and social networks. When it comes to social networks, a deeper understanding of ants and termites may hold the answer to why complex systems organize themselves into criticality. What do termites know that we don't?

Consider the hypothetical termite world proposed many decades ago by Mitchel Resnick (Resnick 1994). Resnick is a pioneer of complex systems theory with a whimsical way of describing simple systems that are really complex. Even his title is whimsical: LEGO Professor of Learning Research and Head of the Lifelong Kindergarten Group at the MIT Media Laboratory. Resnick is famous for whimsical experiments with virtual turtles, termites, and traffic jams. He inspired me to turn his artificial termites into spiders—termites with a special talent for weaving webs.

Resnick's termite world is a flat rectangular space littered with wood chips and wandering worker termites (see Figure 4.5). Termites aren't very smart, but they like wood chips. So Resnick simulated the behavior of software termites as they staggered around with nothing on their minds but fetching the next chip. To make the simulation interesting suppose one or more termites and hundreds of chips are randomly scattered around as shown in Figure 4.5a. Termites are generally blind, so they ceaselessly wander through the field of chips, grabbing nearby chips one at a time and dropping them when encountering another chip. In this termite world, each blind and butter-fingered termite drops one chip to pick up another chip as it wanders randomly through the field of chips.

I added a feature to Resnick's model: links. My termites connect dropped chips with picked-up chips. The link between pairs of chips stretches up to a point and then snaps as the termite hauls the picked-up chip away from the recently dropped chip. My termites act like spiders, spinning a web of links as they roam around dropping and picking up chips. At least they are more social than Resnick's termites because linking chips together in this manner creates a social network. Consider the resulting network a 'society of wood chips,' much like a human social network.

The simple-minded beasts repeat their chip foraging forever:

Termite Walk

1. Scatter N chips at random; set maximum length of links.

2. Repeat for every termite, forever:

   a. Random walk: Take a step of size STEP in any direction.

   b. If a chip is encountered pick it up,

      i. If carrying a chip already, drop it.

   c. Connect the dropped and picked-up chips together with a link.

   d. Remove long links.

Resnick observed that even this simple system is complex. After many iterations of pick-up by a single termite, a pattern emerges as chips begin to pile up in one or more regions of the square universe shown in Figure 4.5b. In fact, these piles are like Bak's sand piles in reverse: instead of collapsing, they accumulate and grow into a single pile of chips, see Figure 4.5c. As the chips become more concentrated and linked together, the system edges closer to its critical point. Without knowing it, a single termite creates a system with ever-increasing SOC. If a swarm of 100 termites do the same, an even more organized network of woodchips emerges. The network of Figure 4.5c is much closer to its critical point than the network of Figure 4.5b. Given enough time, the termites build an interesting network structure with SOC. Curiously, they create a complex system from the cloth of simple components without any coaching from the outside world.

Consider what eventually happens over time: a distinct pattern begins to emerge after a single termite has wandered around a field of 400 chips for 1.8 million steps, as shown in Figure 4.5b.[3] Remarkably, the random wandering of a simple termite creates a web with complex (network) structure. If we add more termites we get a complex self-organized system, faster. There is no cooperation among the swarming termites in Figure 4.5c, and no central command. And yet a swarm of 100 termites collates 400 chips into a single pile after only 400,000 steps!

The termite world may be simple, but it is also complex. Simple actions, such as a random walk, produce a complex pattern, dramatically illustrated in Figure 4.5. As it turns out, the termites increase the chip network's SOC as they herd the chips closer together. The internal structure of the chip network matures from low (random) criticality, to medium, and finally to a critical state. How do we know this?

The evolved chip network of Figure 4.5b is more susceptible to the spread of contagious epidemics than the network of Figure 4.5c, because Figure 4.5b is 1.8 million iterations old and Figure 4.5c is only 400,000 iterations old. Figure 4.5b is over four times older than Figure 4.5c, therefore the older network's spectral radius should be higher— it is more evolved (Malamud, Morein & Turcotte 1998). Suppose this conjecture is tested (or calculated) by simulating a cascade failure or epidemic. Simulation of thousands of epidemics produces an exceedence probability similar to the power law curves described in the Casinos of Extremistan. The exceedence probability is then used to calculate the likelihood of a pandemic. For example, assuming an infectiousness of 10%, the probability of an epidemic affecting 25% (100) nodes or more in Figure 4.5b is 4.7% versus 0.56% in Figure 4.5c. Susceptibility to pandemic is ten times greater in the older and more highly organized network than the younger and less organized network. Clearly the older network is less resilient.

---

3   In this simulation, termites take pixel-sized steps: 20 pixels in any direction, and pick up chips when they come within 15 pixels of a nearby chip. They also wait 5 time steps before picking up another chip. Links snap if they exceed 100 pixels in length.

Generally termites organize chips into clusters, but they also innocently organize the network into a state of criticality. Mature networks are more critical than younger networks. In fact, this property has been observed in real systems: the century-old electric power grids found in most industrialized nations are more critical than the younger Internet and telecommunications networks (Dobson, Carreras, Lynch & Newman 2007). This profound observation has major implications for all kinds of systems.

Young and old complex network systems are alike in one respect: economic, social, and political forces shape them. Telecommunications networks, for example, have evolved into criticality because of the 1996 Telecommunications Act, and the eastern power grid of the United States was shaped by the 1992 EPACT, an energy policy act that partially deregulated the industry. Power grids are especially susceptible to *NIMBY* ('Not In My Back Yard') social pressure that has made it difficult to build out additional transmission capacity because of environmental concerns. I discuss how EPACT shaped today's power grids in the chapter on 'Blackout USA.'

Before I get into the details of specific systems, consider what termites show us: complex systems tend to become more structured or organized as they age, and old or highly evolved systems contain more SOC. Unless energy is expended to avoid this build up of SOC, it will increase and eventually the system will reach its critical point. This observation is profound because it says that complex systems defy entropy! Energy goes into a system to overcome losses due to entropy, of course, but some of that energy goes towards super-structure, a form of excess organization that Per Bak identified as SOC. This is not a refutation of the Second Law of Thermodynamics, but rather an extension that seems to apply only to living things—termites and humans alike. According to the Second Law of Thermodynamics, it is impossible to build a perpetual motion machine because in every energy transaction, energy is lost to entropy. Entropy, of course, is a form of noise, friction, or disorder. If everything else I have written about in this book is a mystery, remember this, dear reader: *self-organization is a property of all 'intelligent systems' that evolve into increasingly complex structure, most typically as a result of some form of optimization, efficiency, defense, survivability, or plain ordinary 'growth.'*

Figure 4.6. Three general network structures: random, cluster, and scale-free.

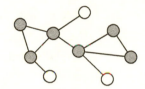 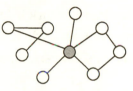

A - Random   B - Cluster   C - Scale-free

Categorizing Complex Networks

As networks mature they typically become more susceptible to cascade failure unless we expend time or energy to reverse SOC. Termites and people behave alike in one general respect—both species construct systems with complex internal structures. But some systems are more complex than others, perhaps because some architects are more intelligent than others! Is there a hierarchy among systems that relates their intrinsic structure to complexity? In fact, scientists have classified complex networks into three major categories as shown in Figure 4.6. Networks evolve from *random* to *clustered* and eventually *scale-free networks*. Built into this evolution is also an increase in SOC. Of course there are gradations between these categories, as most systems exhibit some properties of each category.

As a gross generalization, random networks have no structure, clustered networks have local structure, while scale-free networks are distinguished by a major global property—hubs. In addition, the spectral radius of each category of network increases from random (low), clustered (medium), and scale-free (high). Thus, each category corresponds to greater SOC.

A purely random network is one in which any pair of nodes are equally likely to be connected. Figure 4.6a, for example, contains nine nodes and ten links. Links connect to nodes at both ends, so there are 20 possible connections. Therefore, the average number of connections in this random network is 20/9 or 2.22. This is also the spectral radius of the random network. Random networks rarely occur in the wild, but they are a useful benchmark against which real systems can be compared.

Figure 4.6b is slightly more evolved, because it has two nodes with four connections, and, moreover, it contains clusters. A cluster is a group of triangular sub-networks, shaded in Figure 4.6b. As the number of triangular sub-networks around a node increases, the cluster coefficient of the network increases. The cluster coefficient of the cluster network in Figure 4.6b is 41% (several nodes—the shaded ones—are part of a triangular sub-network), while the coefficient in Figure 4.6a is zero (there are no triangular sub-networks).

Cluster networks are slightly more susceptible to cascade failures and epidemics than random networks because their spectral radius is slightly higher. For example, the cluster network's spectral radius is 2.66, versus 2.28 for the random network. This means cluster networks are slightly less resilient than random networks. To illustrate this point, using a node infectiousness of 20%, the network in Figure 4.6a has a resilience exponent of 0.56 while the resilience exponent of the cluster network in Figure 4.6b is 0.51. Plugging these exponents into the power law describing these networks and calculating the likelihood that 25% or more of the nodes will fail in an epidemic, I get 16% and 19%, respectively. In other words, there is a 16% chance that 25% of the nodes in the random network will succumb to an epidemic compared to a 19% chance in the clustered network. Clustering is a form of SOC that reduces resilience, but as it turns out, it has only a minor effect on network resilience.

Figure 4.6c illustrates the extreme opposite of a random network. Scale-free networks contain many nodes with one or a few connections, and one or two nodes with the lion's share of connections. They typically contain a hub with several times more connections than the average node. In other words, scale-free networks are lop-sided. The example in Figure 4.6c contains a hub with six links, indicated as a shaded node. This lop-sidedness is a form of SOC that yields an even higher spectral radius than the other networks in Figure 4.6. All three networks contain the same number of nodes and links, but the spectral radius of the scale-free network is 2.84, which is 1.28 times the average. Therefore, the scale-free network is the least resilient category of network. Figure 4.6c has a resilience exponent of 0.46, which is the lowest of all three. Of all networks, scale-free networks are the most vulnerable to epidemics.

Left unattended, wood termites build scale-free networks. Starting from a random network structure, termites herd wood chips into a cluster network, and over time, into a scale-free network. Termites are not the only animals to do this. Humans also create scale-free networks. The Internet is perhaps the best example of a scale-free network, but the eastern power grid and many other critical infrastructure systems are scale-free as well (Dobson, Carreras, Lynch, & Newman 2007). The western power grid of the U.S. is closer to a cluster network, perhaps because it is younger.

I don't want to offend power engineers, but termites are apparently as good as humans when it comes to constructing networks such as the electric power grid. Power engineers should not be offended, however, because power grids are just as susceptible to SOC as any other complex system. Indeed, electric power grids demonstrate the basic concept of self-organization. As complex systems evolve and age, they tend to rewire themselves into clustered or even scale-free networks! I explain this tendency in more detail in the chapter called 'Blackout USA.'

Hub Envy

The main reason that networks evolve into scale-free networks with dominant hubs goes back to the beginning—the Big Bang. In chapter one, I explained how matter out-paced anti-matter during the first 10^{-43} seconds of existence, and how this slight preference for matter eventually led to dominance of matter over anti-matter. I suppose if anti-matter had won out, we would have called it matter, but this is semantics (and we wouldn't be here to have that discussion in the first place). Regardless of which one dominated, the point is that one form of matter grew faster than the other. Recall that this is referred to as 'preferential attachment' in science, 'increasing returns' in economics, and 'network effects' in hi-tech circles. *Preferential attachment* is typically at work in wood chip networks as well as in Internet and power grid networks. As termites compress the chips into smaller space they gain a preference for nearby chips. This preference grows as chips are piled together, because the bigger piles attract more termites. Bigger piles beget even bigger piles!

Preference starts out small—only a very slight edge is needed to start the accelerating preference. A small, random group of chips can start the process. The small pile accidentally gets bigger than the others and then snowballs into accelerated growth. Snowballing is an appropriate term for what happens next because closely packed chips get packed even tighter because they are closer. It takes longer for termites to haul isolated chips to another chip so that they can be linked. Meanwhile, other termites have linked perhaps dozens of densely packed chips together. Once a chip gets dragged into a cluster of chips, it rarely escapes.

Table 4.1. A sample of scale-free network systems and corresponding exponent of the power law of the system's underlying network.

System	Exponent
Avian Flu Social Network	1.2
Washington DC Water	1.7
Gulf Oil Pipeline System	1.8
Mid-Atlantic Power Grid	1.8
SE Penn Transit System	1.8
Top 30 U.S. Telecom Routes	1.9
9-11 Terrorist Attacker Cell	1.9
World Wide Web Out	2.1
Actors in same movie	2.3
Japanese Business Transactions	2.4
Sexual Contacts	3.4

Super-Spreaders

Scale-free network systems are near their critical points—their point of collapse. Why? Intuitively, scale-free networks with large hubs are prone to rapid propagation of faults, because hubs are *super-spreaders*: nodes that accelerate and magnify the spread of faults. The distance between two nodes is equal to the number of hops between them. A hub is closer to all other nodes than any other node in the network and also has many more links. Therefore, when the hub is contaminated, it rapidly spreads the anomaly to many others. It makes sense—hubs spread disaster farther and wider than any other node in the network.

Carrier hotels in the telephone communication network are super-spreaders, as are large Internet Service Providers (ISPs), vital substations in the eastern power grid, and the largest transportation hubs in the international airline route system. If the goal is to reduce SOC, reducing hub connectivity (links) will have the greatest impact for the least effort. Does this observation suggest a way out of SOC?

Plotting the fraction of nodes with k links yields a power law distribution for scale-free networks (see Table 4.1 for examples). This is why such networks are called 'scale-free'—power laws are a byproduct of scale-free structure. The exponent of a scale-free network link distribution is typically greater than one. This means that there are many more nodes with few connections than nodes with many connections. Like most things described in this book, scale-free networks are lop-sided. Higher exponent values mean more lop-sidedness, which of course means that the hub is a bigger super-spreader. You may think that scale-free network systems are rare, but after more than two decades of research into all sorts of systems, researchers have discovered that scale-free networks are rather common. This is unfortunate, because scale-free structure is a form of SOC that reduces resilience. Thus, many critical systems are fragile, simply because they are scale free.

Table 4.2 lists a few common network systems along with their spectral radius and the equivalent random network benchmark. High spectral radius relative to an equivalent random network's spectral radius indicates the existence of SOC. For example, the Gulf Oil (underwater) pipeline and 9/11 Terrorist Cell networks are the most fragile, while the San Francisco Water and Power network and Tier-1 Internet Service Providers are the least fragile networks listed in Table 4.2. Thus, the degree of SOC can be measured down to the decimal point!

Coupling and network structure explains why normal accidents happen and why extreme events happen in Extremistan. This structure relates to SOC, which relates to fragility in complex systems. In the next few chapters I examine some of these systems in more detail, hopefully convincing you that unless we do something to reduce SOC, the fate of Bak's sand pile awaits many vital systems on which our everyday lives depend.

Table 4.2. Real systems and corresponding spectral radius (SOC) of the system's underlying network compared with an equivalent random network (Benchmark).

System	Spectral Radius	Benchmark
Washington DC Water	3.35	2.33
Gulf Oil Pipeline System	4.11	2.28
Mid-Atlantic Power Grid	3.25	2.44
SE Penn Transit System	3.34	2.25
Top 30 U.S. Telecom Routes	4.70	3.33
9-11 Terrorist Attacker Cell	8.63	4.84
Tier-1 Internet ISPs	4.86	4.00
Washington State Ferry Routes	3.83	2.87
San Francisco Water and Power	2.63	2.21

5

LEVY FLIGHTS

Paul Pierre Lévy (1886-1971) was a French mathematician and educator who studied a type of random walk found in nature, which was subsequently named after him. The length of hops in these so-called Lévy flights obeys a power law.

A Global Romp

The man stopped by the Fushan produce district on his way home from work to pick up fresh ingredients for dinner. His wife and four children waiting at home always looked forward to his legendary specialty—a mixture of chicken, civet "cat", snake, and stir-fried vegetables. Unfortunately, the recipe became internationally infamous after its first victim died a few days later. The palm civet, a tree-dwelling animal with a raccoon-like face and a cat-like body was responsible. An investigation by public health experts from around the globe traced the cause of death to the infected civet, which carried the previously unknown virus called Severe Acute Respiratory Syndrome (SARS) (Xu et al. 2004). In November 2002, Victim One, the man's wife, and four other relatives became the first casualties of the first global epidemic of the twenty-first century.

The Fushan incident didn't end in China because SARS turns out to be quite contagious. The contagion also benefited from a fact of modern life: millions of people travel by air every day to all points of the globe, and they take their viruses with them. A combination of population density and long-distance air travel turned a trickle into a flash flood.

Victim One and his fellow citizens in Guangdong Province in South China inadvertently created a social network that would eventually wrap around the world. This social network is shown in Figure 5.1. Notice that it covers a vast part of the world. The small group of people living in Guangdong Province—who had contracted the SARS virus from bats and then passed it on to civet cats, which returned the favor by contaminating more humans—spread SARS to other countries in a globetrotting Lévy flight.

A restaurant stir-fry cook living in Heyuan, 560 miles from Fushan, checked into the local hospital with flu-like symptoms and then became so ill that he was transferred to Guangzhou two days later. His physician Liu Jianlun accompanied him on the 100-mile ride, never suspecting what he was up against. SARS spreads by human contact, through sneezing and coughing. The disease hit physicians and health care workers hardest.

Doctor Liu Jianlun was soon called away to attend a wedding in Kowloon, 102 miles from Heyuan. He checked into room 911 of the Kowloon Metropole Hotel and, while waiting for the lift on the ninth floor, infected six or seven people who were also waiting. Next to him were three Canadians, a man and a woman from Hong Kong, and an American businessman. The lift and room 911 became the epicenter of a global contagion (see Figure 5.1). Later when the details of how SARS spread from this address to the whole world, Metropole management would change the room number from 911 to lucky 913.[1] According to

---

1   "9" is considered the luckiest number in China, perhaps because its pronunciation is phonetically close to 'long-lasting.'

inquiries put to the Metropole by members of the press, room number 911 never existed!

On Feb. 21, 2003 Liu Jianlun fell ill and checked out of his room and went to the Kwong Wah Hospital in Hong Kong. By March 4, 2003 he was dead. Two of the Canadians waiting for the lift checked out of the hotel and spent the night with their son in Hong Kong. Later they flew home to Canada and infected their immediate family members. In fact, everyone waiting for the lift with Jianlun became ill and hospitalized in various countries, including China, Vietnam, Singapore and Canada. Additionally, three women from Singapore who stayed on the 9th floor returned home and fell ill. Johnny Cheng, for example, carried the disease to Hanoi and died after spreading the contagion further.

Doctor Carlo Urbani, an infectious diseases specialist working for the World Health Organization in Hanoi, attended Johnny Cheng. Urbani noticed the spread of flu-like symptoms among hospital workers and initially suspected it was avian influenza, but later realized it was something new. Unfortunately, he had already contracted the new disease. On March 11 he flew to Bangkok to attend a medical conference, and died there on March 29, 2003.

Eventually Liu Jianlun's social network quickly spread SARS around the globe, infecting 8,422 and killing 916 people in 29 countries before it dissipated and faded by June 2003. Guests panicked and cleared out of the 487-room Hotel Metropole when its role as SARS hub was announced on March 19, 2003. Even though the contagion began on November 16, 2002, the People's Republic of China delayed notifying the World Health Organization until February 10, 2003—three months, 806 cases, and 34 deaths later. After considerable international criticism, the country's Health Minister apologized for delays in reporting. Chinese medical officials began reporting the status of the SARS regularly on April 2, 2003.

Within months following reports out of China, the epidemic was nearly over. Like a traffic jam at the peak of the commuter hour, SARS appeared out of nowhere, spread alarmingly fast, and then—just when it looked like it would never end—it disappeared. What seemed like a global threat to humanity came and went in less than a year. Bursty SARS raised fears of pandemic, but more interestingly, it raised questions regarding the spread of epidemics in a modern world where air travel connects people to one another regardless of where they live. What is the nature of these threats and why did SARS suddenly stop in its tracks?

Figure 5.1. Flight of the deadly SARS: The social network that propagated the deadly SARS virus around the globe (Xu et al. 2004).

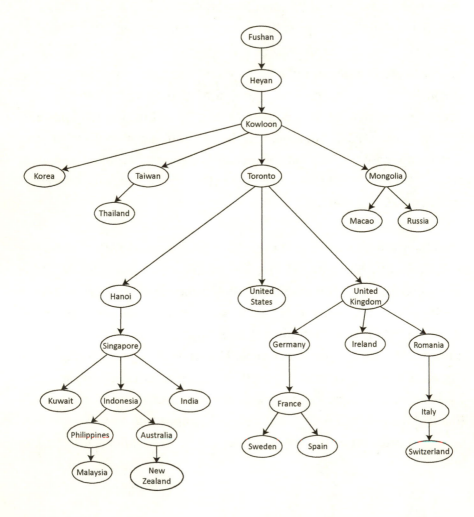

The Lévy Flight Path

The SARS epidemic illustrates another property of the Casinos of Extremistan: the distances between Black Swan events such as SARS, HIV, H1N1 obey a power law. So, too, do the distances between terrorist events, which will be shown below. The movement of epidemics and terrorists is bursty. Bursty events are characterized by a lot of local displacements occasionally punctuated by a big jump in displacement. When the frequency of small and big jumps is recorded on a probability distribution plot, we discover an amazing fact—most events are local, but not all. Once in a while, disastrous events take sizeable jumps as they bounce around the globe. Considered altogether, they form a lop-sided power law due to the fact that most movements are short-distance or local, while a few movements are extremely long-distance.

In 1937, French mathematician Paul Pierre Lévy discovered the Extremistan equivalent of Generalized Brownian Motion (GBM, as outlined in earlier chapters, is the random traversal of particles). Lévy's statistical world deviated from Brown's world in one important way: particles studied by Lévy behaved badly. Their movements were punctuated by an occasional jump that didn't fit the Normal Distribution predicted by the empiricist Brown and explained by Einstein. If Brownian molecules bounce around at random like classical theory predicted, then why did Lévy's particles occasionally jump much farther? Why do Lévy's particles act like they are from Extremistan?

Lévy observed that in some systems, particle movement is *bursty*, not smooth and uniformly random. For example, water dripping from a leaky faucet is bursty. A series of quick drips is typically followed by a long pause of random length, only to be followed by another series of quick drips. If you spent the day recording the elapsed time between drops, and plotted these times on a probability distribution plot like that of Figure 5.3, it would be lop-sided. It turns out that Lévy stumbled onto a general theory that explains the movement of animals, humans, and contagions like SARS. Objects in the Casinos of Extremistan *move* according to the same power laws that dictate the exceedence probability of catastrophes. Most movement is local, but occasionally an object jumps relatively long distances. Displacement between objects in space and time is bursty, just like catastrophic events are bursty in terms of consequences. Once again, Extremistan is a metaphorical land of extremes.

Extremistan is Lumpy

How does Lévy flight explain why objects in the real world cluster together in space? Why is the world lumpy? There are two explanations. Albert-Laszlo Barabasi attributes Lévy flight behaviors to priority-based decision-making. Barabasi maintains that we keep a list of tasks that we need to do in our head. The tail of this "to-do" list grows as tasks pile up on a first-in basis. But according to him, we process these queued-up tasks on a priority basis, with the most urgent task first. Tasks arrive in order, but we process them out of order. High-priority items get done first, and low-priority items get pushed back to the end of the list. This creates another lop-sided power law, because lower-priority tasks wait longer to be processed than higher-priority tasks. Barabasi says, "when individuals execute tasks based on some perceived priority, the timing of the tasks will be heavy tailed, most tasks being rapidly executed, while a few experience very long waiting times" (Barabasi 2005). He provides the mathematics to show that prioritization turns Normal Distributions into power laws.

For example, your action-packed evening plan may include picking up the kids from school, fixing dinner, and watching TV, in that order. But what actually happens is that you answer an unexpected telephone call, unexpectedly give a ride to the neighbor's kids as you collect your own children, and your spouse has dinner waiting for you when you arrive late. And forget watching TV—you are too tired! Your task list grows as events happen in time, but you process them in a different order—the order determined by your self-imposed priority. Some tasks get your attention right away, but a few have to wait for a long time. Even fewer drop off the end of your list and never get processed. The length of time tasks spend on your mental list obeys a power law. And power laws that describe displacements are called 'Lévy flights' or 'Lévy walks.' Your action-packed evening turned out different than you planned—it turned into a miniature Lévy flight.

Why do we care about this curiosity? Power laws were shown to be real-world models of catastrophe in the previous chapters. But they described the magnitude of catastrophes, not their timing or location. Lévy flights, or walks, add a geospatial and temporal dimension to Bak's sand pile theory because they model the geospatial and temporal spread of contagions, ideas, people, and products. Events of a certain size occur with probability given by a power law. By adding Lévy flights to the mix, we can see that events are also distributed in time and space according to a power law!

Figure 5.2. Lévy flight of termites: foraging termites visit each chip at most once.

a. A termite begins shopping in an area with barriers shown as shaded rectangles.

b. Intermediate Lévy flight of the shopping termite.

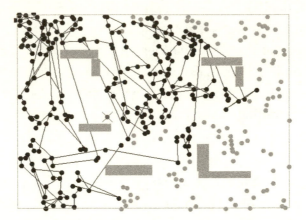

c. Fully explored Lévy flight of the shopping termite.

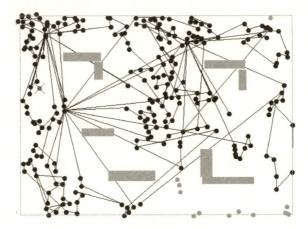

Termites Go Shopping

I admire Barabasi, but I favor my *foraging theory* of Lévy flight over his priority-list theory because non-sentient creatures like ants, bees, and artificial termites also carve out Lévy flights. I doubt that termites keep mental lists. Making lists and processing them in priority order takes too much thought. Foraging, on the other hand, is a mindless activity that any creature with an appetite can handle. It is a behavior common to many animals: ants, bees, sheep, deer, and human shoppers! Deer, for example, seek a pasture for grazing, and then move on as soon as it is depleted. They have evolved over the millennia to travel a considerable distance from depleted meadows to greener pastures as a matter of survival. Weaker animals that stay too long in one place are either eaten by predators or starve. So grazing species 'learned' to take long trips between meals.

Foraging is simple to simulate, so I gave the worker termites described in the previous chapter a new task: wander around as before, but never pick up a chip a second time. Instead, pass over previously encountered chips. Connect the two chips with a link, as before, and repeat the process, forever. In this simulation, links can be as long as necessary to record the path taken as the termites forage. If lengths of the resulting links obey a power law, the foraging termites have walked a Lévy walk! On the other hand, if the length distribution of the links obeys a Normal Distribution, the termites have walked a purely random walk. Are foraging termites from Mediocristan of Extremistan?

Termites randomly stagger around, bumping into chips as they go but only linking up with previously unvisited chips—chips that they have previously encountered get passed over. Eventually every chip in termite world will have been visited once, and only once. Figure 5.2 shows the paths traveled by a termite as it wanders randomly through a terrain containing obstacles as well as chips. I placed a few barriers in the termite world to emphasize that the length of links is not influenced by topology or geography. Lévy walks have nothing to do with landscape and everything to do with depletion of resources (chips) and the unpredictability of termites (randomness).

I let the simulation run for thousands of time steps, and sure enough, the length distribution of links in Figure 5.2 obeys a power law just as Lévy predicted. Why? Termites move on when all neighboring chips have been visited because the rule is to visit each chip only once. Even if the shopping termite stumbles on a chip that it has already visited, it must pass it by. This rule forces termites to find greener pastures elsewhere, much like animals do in nature. As simple as this explanation is, it comes close to modeling what real humans do in the real world. Even more profound, this simple model does a good job of describing complex spatial and temporal systems.

Fly Like A Termite

Do humans shop like termites? Evidence suggests that we do. Researchers Injong Rhee, Minsu Shin, Seongik Hong, Kyunghan Lee, and Song Chong of North Carolina State University strapped GPS tracking devices on students at New York City University and tourists at DisneyWorld and tracked their coordinates as they walked and rode buses and subways over approximately ten acres of terrain (Rhee, Shin, Hong, Lee, & Chong 2008). They not only recorded where the subjects traveled from September 2006 to January 2007, but also how long they stayed at each waypoint. And sure enough, people and termites forage alike. According to the North Carolina State University scientists,

> Biologists have found that the mobility patterns of foraging animals such as spider monkeys, albatrosses, and jackals can be commonly described in what physicists have long called *Lévy Walks* ... to explain atypical particle diffusion not governed by Brownian motion. A Lévy flight or walk is the longest straight line trip from one location to another that a particle makes without a directional change or pause (Rhee, Shin, Hong, Lee, & Chong 2008:1).

People take Lévy walks, and birds and airplanes take Lévy flights. Whether it is a walk or a flight, the length distribution is a power law. People and animals alike take a lot of small steps, and only a few very long steps as we forage. The North Carolina team, for example, found that tourists and shoppers do what most animals do—they move about in straight-line paths, the lengths of which are distributed according to a power law. The power law distribution in this experiment had an exponent equal to 0.3, so it was a very long-tailed, lop-sided, Lévy walk! Humans make occasional large jumps to greener pastures after pauses in between as they forage.

The North Carolina experiment is intriguing on its own, but the phenomenon of punctuated Lévy walks goes much further. Let me explain. In a fascinating study of virtual movement in the online virtual world of Second Life, Professor Michiardi Pietro and graduate student Chi-Anh La found that players of Second Life also walk the Lévy walk as they move about in a virtual world (La & Pietro 2008). The two EURECOM[2] researchers found that, "The statistical distribution of user contacts show that from a qualitative point of view user mobility in Second Life presents similar traits to those of real humans" (La & Pietro 2008:79). Apparently termites, avatars, and humans forage alike in cyberspace. Indeed, there is something universal about Lévy flights. The phenomenon is not limited to animals in real or virtual space. Many other natural and human-made systems do what foraging animals, human or otherwise, do. Here is a sample:

- ✓ Length of airline flights
- ✓ Length of albatross flights
- ✓ Distances traveled by dollar bills
- ✓ Intermittent dripping of faucets
- ✓ Fluctuation of beating hearts
- ✓ Distances traveled by ants, bees, sheep, deer, monkeys, and people
- ✓ Length of brush strokes of some Jackson Pollack paintings!

2 EURECOM is a graduate school and a research center specializing in communication systems, founded in 1991 by Telecom ParisTech (Ecole Nationale Supérieure des Telecommunications, Paris, France) and EPFL (Swiss Federal Institute of Technology in Lausanne).

Figure 5.3. The SARS epidemic is a Lévy flight with power law exponent approximately equal to 1.6.

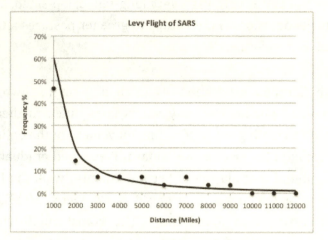

SARS Travels

We already learned that SARS explosively spread to 26 countries around the world and contaminated thousands of people. But what is perhaps most interesting is that it didn't reach every corner. In less than a year, the disease that started with a family of six in China fizzled and vanished from the global scene. At its height, the contagion traumatized public health officials throughout the world because they feared that it would kill millions. In the end, SARS contaminated relatively few countries and then stopped. Why did it stop?

To find out I measured the distances along links of the SARS social network shown in Figure 5.1, and constructed the probability distribution shown in Figure 5.3. I had to make some assumptions, especially regarding the topology of the SARS social network. Which pairs of countries should be linked? When in doubt, I used the dates when SARS victims were discovered and the shortest distance between two infected victims to establish a link and determine its length. As you can see, SARS dutifully obeyed a power law with exponent of approximately 1.6. (Keep this number in mind, because it will pop up again).

Lévy flights are lop-sided and bursty, as they should be, but SARS visited only a small fraction of the entire globe. A truly virulent disease like bubonic plague or smallpox could encircle the globe and reach every country, especially if aided by modern air travel. What was different about SARS and why did it 'attack' the countries it did? Indeed, the SARS epidemic raises two big questions regarding catastrophic pandemics: 1) Why do they reach some parts of the world but not others, and 2) Why do they stop? To answer these difficult questions, suppose we follow the money.

Figure 5.4. Data entry form of www.WheresGeorge.com, **a bank note tracking web site created by Hank Eskin.**

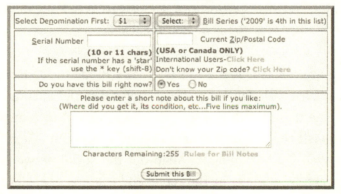

Follow the Money

Professor Dirk Brockmann has spent much of his young career studying the interaction between modern air travel and the spread of contagions—a field called *human mobility*, which he pioneered. His theory is based on the physics of social and air transportation networks—the disease vectors used by microbes to circle the globe. Brockmann and his team of graduate students at Northwestern University, located outside of Chicago, applied the laws of physics to understand Lévy flights in human social networks. Their theory answers one of the questions I posed above.

Brockmann started his quest somewhat by accident while visiting Dennis Derryberry, an old friend living in Vermont who was intrigued by a web site called www.WheresGeorge.com. As the name implies, WheresGeorge.com tracks the movement of dollar bills. It was started as a lark in 1998 by database programmer and business consultant Hank Eskin. "It's a fun diversion," says Eskin. "Some people would call it a useless diversion."[3] But Hank's 'useless diversion' caught on. Decades later, over 140 million bills have been entered by volunteers, and registrations are still going strong as I write this chapter. Moreover, Hank's 'useless diversion' became very useful to Brockmann and Hufnagel, the Northwestern University researchers studying the flight of SARS and other potentially dangerous diseases.

Dollar bills are tracked via their serial numbers and the consumer's ZIP code (see Figure 5.4). Before a participating consumer spends her $1 to $100 bill, she tags it with "www.wheresgeorge.com" to remind future owners to visit the site and update the bill's location. WheresGeorge.com uses Web 2.0 technology to map out the social network created by consumers. By connecting the reported locations of each registered bill, the web server at WheresGeorge.com constructs a social network in much the same manner as my artificial termites build networks out of wood chips. When Brockmann learned of WheresGeorge.com from Derryberry, he realized that,

> For each registered bill one can monitor these movements and study the logs posted by individual finders. Forming an image of millions of these dollar-bill journeys in my head, I was convinced that analyzing the data could reveal essential properties of human mobility—which is, after all, the driving force behind the dispersal of banknotes. (Brockmann 2010:32).

---

3 http://www.wheresgeorge.com/press/nyt/nytimes.html

Where bills are found, people are not far away. Brockmann and Hufnagel set about mining the WheresGeorge.com database to map out the Lévy paths created by the tagged dollar bills. Their goal was to estimate the probability that a bill travels a certain distance in a certain time. That is, they wanted to find a two-dimensional mathematical model of mobility. One dimension is geographical distance traveled, and the other dimension is the time each bill spends in one place. Their analysis of 464,000 transactions produced an answer very similar to the results my termites produced in Figure 5.2 and the SARS epidemic produced in Figure 5.3: dollar bills follow Lévy flights with an exponent of 1.6 (distance) and elapsed time distribution with exponent 0.6 (Brockmann, Hufnagel & Geisel 2006:465). The magical exponent 1.6 appears once again, but not for the last time!

Brockmann is a physicist, so much of his work is described in the highly specialized language of the physicist. He calls human movement *displacement* and the spread of people, objects, and ideas *diffusion*. In the arcane terminology of physics, Lévy flight is called *super diffusion* because it describes a process of scattering similar to General Brownian Motion on steroids. To a physicist, Lévy flights are super diffusive because displacements obey a power law rather than a Normal Distribution. Particles in Extremistan are super diffusive because they spread farther and wider than particles in Mediocristan. Brockmann and his colleagues discovered that human mobility is also super diffusive. In other words, humans walk a lop-sided random walk governed by a power law. Brockmann et al. state,

> ...that dispersal is anomalous in two ways. First, the distribution of traveling distances decays as a power law, indicating that trajectories of bank notes are reminiscence of scale-free random walks known as Lévy flights. Second, the probability of remaining in a small spatially confined region for a time T is dominated by algebraically long tails that attenuate the super diffusive spread. (Brockmann, Hufnagel & Geisel 2006:462)

When I accused Dirk Brockmann of walking a Lévy flight with his own career, he said,

> I am always impressed by people who follow a path that they anticipate for many years in the future. This has never happened to me. I guess I never really worry about my career in the way that some of my colleagues do. What I like are ideas, preferably crazy ones and I would like to see more courage in Science. If anything this is what I convey to my students. We need more risk in science, risk of being wrong. I think science is a bit slow these days because the majority of the community is slowed down by the risk of failure. My goal is to convey to the members of my team and my students that great discoveries almost require failure. That's my passion. (Email from Brockmann to author, July 15, 2010)

I could not agree more—science needs more risk-taking outliers. Then again, if everyone worked outside of the box like Brockmann, there would be no outliers!

Attenuated Pandemics

Brockmann's research helps us understand how diseases spread around the globe—modern air travel creates social networks that support globe-spanning Lévy flights—but his analysis falls short of explaining why some epidemics fail to become pandemics. Why did the bubonic plague kill one-third of the European population in the fourteenth century while SARS died out after killing only hundreds? After all, SARS spread to almost 30 countries with a population in excess of Europe's during the middle ages. The answer: SARS was an *attenuated pandemic*.

There are two basic kinds of epidemics. The first kind, SIR (Susceptible-Infected-Recovered), describes individuals in a population that are initially susceptible to a disease, then infected with a certain probability, and finally either removed (die) or recovered so they are no longer susceptible. SIR describes many biological populations that achieve immunity after recovering from a disease, because the disease eventually dies out, kills its host, or is ineffectual because its infectiousness is too low to sustain a further spreading.

The second kind of disease is known as SIS (Susceptible-Infected-Susceptible). It spreads throughout a population of individuals that are initially susceptible, then infected with a certain probability, and finally recover, only to become susceptible again. An SIS population can die out or sustain a contagion forever, if conditions are right for recurrence of the disease. An SIS contagion that never completely dies out is considered *persistent*. Some Internet viruses are persistent SIS viruses—waxing and waning, but never vanishing completely.

Recall from the previous chapter that a social network will support a persistent SIS virus if the product of infectiousness and spectral radius exceeds the rate of recovery. This is an important result both in the war against Internet viruses and the efforts to eradicate virulent diseases in fixed populations. But the theory falls short of explaining persistence (or lack thereof) of diseases like SARS and H1N1 in a global social network. To explain persistence (or lack thereof) in global diseases we need a spatial theory. As it turns out, Lévy flights are a perfect match, because a Lévy flight creates a spatial network.

Before 2010 there was no explanation of SIS persistence of contagions spread by Lévy flights. Then, a group of researchers studying the spread of H1N1 (led by Yanqing Hu of Beijing Normal University) found the relationship between Lévy flight and SIS spreading (Hu, Luo, Xu, Han & Di 2010). They claimed that an SIS epidemic dies out if the power law exponent is less than or equal to 2! Hu and colleagues say, "the epidemic is liable to disappear if there are more long-distance connections than short ones" (Hu, Luo, Xu, Han & Di 2010:2). Furthermore, epidemic spreading is most speedy when the exponent is exactly 2. Long-distance connections increase the tail of the power law describing Lévy flight. As this tail grows longer, the exponent decreases, so the flights contain longer displacements. Eventually the power law is so lop-sided that there are more long-distance connections than short connections.

Hu and his fellow scientists arrived at their important finding by adding a new element to the Lévy flight theory. Essentially, they assumed that there exists an energy component of contagious diseases that defines a limit on the distance and time that can elapse following contraction of a disease. Hu's social network contains links with weights representing the energy required to transport the contagion along links. Each node of their social network represents a small geographical area, such as a province or county. Each weighted link represents the communication time or quantity of people flowing between adjacent nodes. The amount of energy consumed by a transmission is proportional to the distance traveled along a link. Finally, energy is conserved, which means that longer links take energy away from shorter ones. If this theory applies to all kinds of diseases, then H1N1, SARS and other diseases have limitations—they die out when links are too long.

A definitive answer to the question of why SARS died out remains elusive, but researchers are getting closer. Brockmann's work suggests that social networks established by air travel create Lévy flights with an exponent of 1.6 (less than 2), which may explain why SARS died out. Combining Brockmann's model with Hu's model explains why Lévy flights extend the reach of viruses, but at a cost. As distances increase and contagions require more energy to transmit across social networks formed by air travel, conservation of Hu's energy sets in to limit the virulence of the disease. The contagion gets weaker with distance.

The bad news is that modern air travel has made global Lévy flights a reality. The good news is that social networks with more long links than short ones attenuate potential pandemics. In the case of contagious diseases like SARS, virulence runs out of vigor as displacements increase, which eventually stops the unstoppable. For now, at least, air travel has its limits as a vector of catastrophe.

Human mobility as defined by Brockmann, Hu, and others isn't new. In fact, human mobility may not only explain how global diseases move about, but also how we got here in the first place! Lévy's power laws explain the biggest human mobility of all time—the Great Migration we know as 'Out of Africa.'

Out of Africa

Epidemiology describes how diseases, celebrities, product endorsements, and ideologies spread around the globe. I previously showed how network topology (spectral radius) impacts the spread of calamities in the chapter on normal accidents. Now you know that super diffusion via Lévy flights is yet another influence on the lop-sidedness of Bak's punctuated reality. Topology and Lévy flights both contribute to the spread of epidemics. Together with infectiousness, they provide a comprehensive theory of why contagions persist or stop. It also explains how human mobility works.

Lévy flight mobility is a fundamental trait of animals and humans, so it should explain how humanity spread around the globe, beginning with an East African 'Mitochondrial Eve' 150,000 years ago. Did humans in fact walk the biggest Lévy walk in history? In 1987 population geneticists Rebecca Cann, Mark Stoneking, and Allan Wilson traced the ancestry of everyone alive today to a 'Mitochondrial Eve', a woman who lived somewhere in East Africa between 150,000 to 170,000 years ago (Cann, Stoneking & Wilson 1987). *Mitochondrial DNA*, or *mtDNA* for short, is passed down from mother to daughter, leaving a genetic trail that can be backtracked from present day people to our oldest known ancestors. A similar process has been used to identify the 'Y-Chromosome Adam,' the oldest known male ancestor of us all. Adam and Eve DNA traces are like modern GPS traces—they leave a geo-location trail that scientists can reconstruct by sampling DNA from living people. Essentially, DNA can be used to travel backwards in time, tracing the movement of humans.

As humans migrated from Africa to Asia and Europe, and ultimately to North and South America, small mutations called *haplotypes* randomly appeared in human DNA, which gave rise to slightly different DNA sequences in descendants of Adam and Eve. Haplotypes always pass on a common pattern called *nucleotide polymorphisms*, thus, it is possible to connect the DNA dots to identify and group people into categories called *haplogroups*. Mitochondrial Eve belonged to haplogroup L0, which eventually split into two distinct groups, L1 and L2. Subsequent mutations in the DNA code have created groups with tags such as N, M, M*, etc. Ancient human mobility is traceable across the planet by tracing the mutations: from L0 to L1, L2, L3, N, etc.

Around 80,000 years ago something dramatic happened: a Black Swan event forced L3 humans to migrate out of Africa. The Black Swan might have been an ice age, but it is more likely to have been the explosion of the Mount Toba supervolcano in Sumatra, Indonesia. One of the largest explosions ever recorded, Mount Toba plunged the planet into a 6 to 10 year volcanic winter. The catastrophe reduced the world's population to approximately 1,000 breeding women, creating a bottleneck in human evolution. Today Lake Toba is a resort area enjoyed by Indonesians.

The timing of Mount Toba's explosion matches anthropological records suggesting that a mass exodus of the L3 haplogroup took place approximately 75,000 years ago. The resulting genetic bottleneck may also explain why we all come from Africa. The genetic bottleneck created by the supervolcano reduced humanity to fewer than 10,000-15,000 men, women, and children, all of which were descendants of Mitochondrial Eve. By the way, Mitochondrial Eve never met Y-Chromosome Adam— he lived thousands of years later!

Lévy Walk The Walk

Geneticists have since traced several great waves of human migration moving east, then north into Egypt, Asia, and eventually Europe. Haplogroups N1, M96, and M9 traveled less than 500 miles; M223, M3, and H less than 1,000 miles; and other haplogroups, such as A, B, and C-D, migrated across the Bering Straights into North and South America. They were the outliers, traveling nearly 18,500 miles to their new homes. Keep in mind, these short and extremely long migrations happened in a relatively short span of time.

Like bread crumbs dropped by ancient explorers to find their way back, humanity left their DNA markers along a path from Africa to the far corners of the earth: Eve > L1/L0 > L2 > L3 > N > R, etc. Their Lévy walks were mostly short excursions, but occasionally they were punctuated by big jumps across continents and oceans. So I conjectured that humanity walked the same walk described by Brockmann and his colleagues and asked: does the 150,000 year old Lévy flight made by our ancestors match the human mobility model proposed by Brockmann and colleagues?

To find out, I did a back-of-the-envelope calculation of the distances traveled by each haplogroup. I obtained my data from the *Genographic Project*, a team of renowned scientists from all over the world who study population genetics.[4] Distances were measured from starting points, branch points, and end points in the maps provided by the Genographic Project. The data are very approximate and my calculations are rough, but my analysis of migratory path lengths confirms Brockmann's result. Human migration is a Lévy flight with an exponent of 1.6, the same exponent obtained by Brockmann and Hufnagel! What is the significance of 1.6?

---

4   https://genographic.nationalgeographic.com/genographic/lan/en/atlas.html

Termites foraging among wood chips walk Lévy walks when they avoid previously encountered chips. They find new chips only after taking relatively long jumps (though not too long) because they bounce around at random instead of making a beeline for the next unencountered chip. Consumers carry dollar bills over short and long distances before spending them. But they can't seem to hold onto the dollars too long because they need to buy things. Global contagions such as SARS and H1N1 spread like California wildfires and then suddenly die out when distances become too long. The great human migration out of Africa seems to be a Lévy flight, but it too has limitations, because humans cannot go beyond their supply lines. In all of these cases, we observe that Lévy flights have limitations. At some point, displacements are just too large.

I believe Hu et al. have it right. Lévy flights are limited by the ratio of long-to-short hops. In each case, Lévy flights are limited by distance and the resulting power law inevitably must be lop-sided, such that the exponent is less than 2. And 1.6 is a reasonable number less than 2! Until a better explanation comes along, my explanation for the significance of 1.6 is this: if the exponent is too large, displacements are simply too large. If the exponent were smaller—say, less than 1.0—then the social network is overcome by SOC; that is, catastrophic events are so extreme in high-SOC systems that they collapse before significant progress can be made. High-SOC systems are in a constant state of chaos.

Figure 5.5. Lévy flights in time and space for known al-Qeada attacks from 1993 through 2009.

a. Power law distribution for time intervals between attacks has an exponent of 1.25.

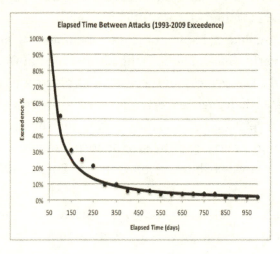

b. Power law distribution for distance between subsequent attacks has an exponent of 1.6.

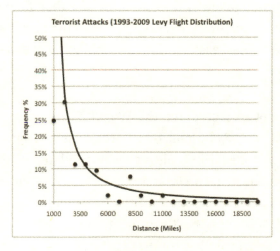

The Arabic word *al-Qaeda* translates to 'the base' in English. The organization was founded in 1988 to fight Russian invaders in Afghanistan, and like a haplogroup, the members of al-Qaeda have traveled the world. But unlike ancient immigrants, al-Qaeda trips are designed to kill. The severity of these attacks obeys a power law with exponent greater than one; hence, terrorism is a low-risk endeavor. This should not be surprising, because the damage done by any military force is proportional to its size, and the size of social networks like al Qaeda follows a power law distribution (Johnson et al 2005; 2006).

Clauset, Young, and Gleditsch (2007) showed that the severity of terrorist attacks obeys a power-law distribution, but with different exponents, even when controlling for the type of weapon used (e.g., firearms, explosives, etc.) or the level of prosperity of the target country. So terrorist attacks follow power laws, but do they follow Lévy flight paths? Does Brockmann's model predict where the next al-Qaeda attack might take place? Once again, a simple compilation of distances tells an intriguing story.

The first attempt to take down the World Trade Center occurred in February 1993, over 8,000 miles from 'the base' in Afghanistan. Eight months later, October 1993, al-Qaeda-inspired terrorists killed U.S. soldiers in Somalia—much closer to the base. The truck bombing of Khobar Towers barracks in Dhahran, Saudi Arabia, killed 19 Americans in June 1996, 1,400 miles from the previous attack. The next four attacks leading up to and including the 9/11 attacks on New York and the Pentagon in Washington D.C. were separated by 1900 miles (Dhahran, Saudi Arabia to Kenya), 8870 miles (Kenya to Seattle), 10545 miles (Seattle to Yemen), and 7040 miles (Yemen to New York). Once again, I have assumed terrorist attacks are sequenced, which may not be true. But even if they are not sequenced, are they really any different than the foraging humans, animals, and viruses described here?

The Lévy flight of attacks continued even after the 9/11 catastrophe. In December 2001, the shoe bomber tried to detonate a bomb on a flight from Paris to Miami; in April 2002 al-Qaeda bombed an historic synagogue in Tunisia; a car bomb explosion outside of a hotel in Karachi killed 14 in May 2002; and a second bombing occurred outside the American consulate in Karachi, killing 12. These attacks were separated by 3623, 1080, 3501, 1, and 1420 miles, respectively. This is only a partial list of recent terrorist attacks, but I analyzed 53 al-Qaeda attacks from 1993 through 2009 to test my hypothesis that terrorists follow Lévy flights in time and space, see Figure 5.5.[5]

A simple back-of-the-envelope calculation of these Lévy flights in space produces a power law agreeing with Brockmann's 1.6! The exceedence probability of deaths as a consequence of one of these attacks also obeys a power law with exponent 1.4 (see Table 2.1 of chapter 2). Additionally, the exceedence probability of the elapsed time between attacks produces a power law with an exponent of 1.25. In other words, al-Qaeda attacks are somewhat predictable: they occur within a certain distance of one another, and exhibit bursty patterns in time, space, and consequence.

Applying the results shown in Figure 5.5, the next al-Qaeda attack will happen within 3,000 miles and 87 days of the last attack, and kill 26 people with probability 50%. This triangulation is based on the three power laws gleaned from historical al-Qaeda events. While this prediction doesn't tell us exactly when or where the next attack will take place, it does narrow down the options. But there is even better news: if terrorism is a contagion like SARS, it won't reach every corner of the world before it dies out.

Like the SARS contagion, terrorism may be limited by Yanqing Hu's conservation of energy, a property of epidemics that limits the global spread of any contagion when there are more long displacements than short ones. Until Brockmann's exponent 1.6 increases to 2.0, contagious

---

5   http://www.infoplease.com/ipa/A0884893.html

ideas, diseases, and terrorist attacks won't take over the globe. The most-likely future of terrorism is the same as for SARS—it will eventually die out. Meanwhile, societies around the world must remain vigilant and seek ways to limit terrorist's Lévy flights.

Lévy Flights and Complexity

This chapter covered so much territory and embraced so many concepts that a summary is in order. How do all the parts described here come together? How do they relate to Bak's sand pile?

Epidemics, terrorists, human and animal migrations take Lévy flights through space and time. The space-time displacements form a power law with a signature—the power law exponent. Lower exponents mean extremely long displacements occur more frequently. If the long-distance links outnumber the short-distance links, the contagion dies out.

To put the theory into practical terms, assume a disease effecting people all over the world starts from one point on the globe. The virus moves through a geospatial region looking for its victims like a shopper moving through a mall looking for bargains. It skips over immune or previously infected victims as it spreads. The distribution of jumps obeys a power law, and the power law is an indirect consequence of the social network formed by the Lévy flight.

The topology of the social network formed by foraging relates the extent of the contagion to its virulence. In the case of SARS and terrorism, the social network has a certain number of nodes (countries) and links of various lengths (jumps). The size (number of nodes and links) and shape (spectral radius) of the network, and the infectiousness of the virus determines the exponent of the power law. In turn, the exponent determines whether the contagion reaches the entire planet or dies out. If the exponent is less than 2, the contagion dies out.

Moreover, the spectral radius of the resulting social network determines persistence of the disease and how rapidly it spreads. The consequence of a contagion increases as the spectral radius increases. To reduce consequences, either thin out links, reduce connectivity of hubs, or both. Policies that reduce the spectral radius or infectiousness of the contagion also reduce the consequences. Policies that increase spectral radius and infectiousness also increase self-organized criticality. And of course, SOC relates to complexity. So SOC and complexity are consequences of the topology of the social network formed both in time and space, and this network is constructed by Lévy flights.

6

BLACKOUT U.S.A.

David Newman Ian Dobson Massoud Amin Ben Carreras

Grid Scholars: David Newman, Ian Dobson, Massoud Amin and Ben Carreras.

Living At The Edge Of Chaos

The Electric Power Grid Resiliency Workshop was a small gathering of the scholarly elite of electrical power engineering and the U.S. federal government. On one side of the room sat the grid scholars including professors David E. Newman (University of Alaska), Ian Dobson (University of Wisconsin), Ben Carreras (BACV Solutions Inc.), and Massoud Amin (University of Minnesota). On the other side sat government officials from the Department of Homeland Security, Department of Defense, and the Bonneville Power Authority. The division was both accidental and symbolic. These two groups of people rarely spoke to each other. This was their opportunity.

Carreras identified the problem with the grid, "The shifting sand pile is a paradigm for self-organized criticality, in which complex systems tend to rearrange themselves to be close to their limits, living at the edge of chaos" (Davidson 2003:1). The electrical power grid clearly supports modern civilized life, but according to Carreras, it is on the verge of collapse. There are many reasons for this and many perspectives on what to do about the problem, but not much consensus. We are here to help, said the government participants. We have a solution, said the grid scholars. Would this workshop be a rare meeting of the minds?

Carreras, Dobson, and others have been warning people for years. The U.S. power grid is perilously close to its *critical point*. Even relatively small power line failures push the system over the edge into massive outages that span large portions of the country. Natural disasters might not even be the worst-case scenarios—what if a terrorist attempted to blackout the eastern United States? It could be worse than the blackout of 2003. August 14, 2003, the date of the 2003 blackout that affected 55 million Americans and Canadians, had made the scientist's point. Now, years later, the government was starting to listen more carefully to the grid scholars gathered together in a small conference room in Monterey, California.

In a series of scholarly articles over a period spanning almost a decade, the academics modeled and simulated North American, South American, and several European power grids and found the same thing: most electrical power grids in modern industrialized nations are fragile because of decades of self-organized criticality. Moreover, the grids got that way because of how operators maintain, finance, and run utilities. In fact, upgrading the grid seems to increase its fragility instead of decreasing it! Self-organized criticality has crept into our most basic infrastructure because of the way it is managed. We should worry as much about how our power infrastructure is operated and maintained as we do about how terrorists might attack it.

Food, water and power are the basics of civilization. Without these lifeline systems, populations would quickly fall back into the dark ages. Imagine a week without electricity! Unfortunately, not many of us have truly contemplated the consequences of an extended blackout. We haven't had to live without water and power for more than a few days. With only a few unfortunate incidents (for example, Hurricane Katrina), Americans have never experienced an extended power blackout. For most of Americans, Extremistan doesn't exist.

Electric power grids are becoming more important as society moves toward a digital future powered by electrons instead of petroleum. Over the next several decades, electric cars will consume as much or more power than all the houses, factories, and offices in the country. Electric vehicles have a voracious appetite for electrons, consuming ten times the electricity of an average household. Not only do they require a lot of electricity, there are more cars in service than households! This points to an inevitable future in which we are *more* dependent on electricity than we ever were dependent on gasoline. America may be shifting its addiction to foreign oil to an electron addiction!

The grid scholar's claims of impending collapse are based on sound science. Electric power grids are complex systems that fail in accordance with the now-familiar power law. They are at their *critical point* because of steadily increasing loads (more consumption), economic optimization (maximizing profits), and routine maintenance procedures (fixing single-point-of-failure errors) (Dobson, Carreras, Lynch & Newman 2007). Not only this, but increases in transmission line reliability lead to fattening of the power law tail, which means that big failures get bigger rather than smaller (Newman, Carreras, Lynch, & Dobson 2008)! This counter-intuitive result is similar to the result I described in the chapter on forest fire simulation. The more time that elapses between failures, the bigger the failure when it does happen. Yes, power grid SOC is a form of *percolation*.

Grid operators routinely perform *N-1 testing,* which means that they are looking for single-points-of-failure, and then fixing them. For example, an N-1 test might find that a transmission line is near its limits, which means the utility company must either reduce usage or replace the line with a higher-capacity line. Replacing overtaxed lines with higher-capacity lines is standard operating procedure for typical maintenance cycles. According to the grid scholars, this makes things worse! Dobson, Carreras, and Newman showed that N-1 testing and the corresponding patching of line capacity increases the long tail of the power law. The exponent shrinks—which you now know is bad, because resilience is lowered. Bigger collapses occur more often! By doing what they think is wise and prudent, operators actually increase self-organized criticality.[1]

The challenge is vast. According to Massoud Amin, the power grid is complex due to the enormous number of combinations of things that can go wrong. Amin analyzed 20% of the North American system and identified approximately 40,000 buses, 50,000 lines, and 3,000 generators within 120 control areas. So there are 2,650,000,000 possible combinations. Operators must consider these 2.65 billion combinations in real time! Amin further pointed out that,

> The United States is experiencing an ever-increasing rate of power outages. I analyzed two comprehensive sets of data, one from the U.S. Department of Energy's Energy Information Administration (EIA) and the other from the North American Electric Reliability Corporation (NERC). The data shows each five-year period was worse than the preceding five years. In the first half of the 1990s there were 41 non disaster-related power outages that affected more than 50,000 consumers. These outages increased from 149 during 2000-2004 to 349 during 2005-2009. Adjusting for 2% annual increase in demand, the number of U.S. power outages affecting 50,000 or more consumers increased from 140 during 2000-2004 to 303 during 2005-2009, and the number of 100 MW outages increased from 156 during 2000-2004 to 264 during 2005-2009. These power outages and power quality disturbances cost the U.S. economy from upwards of $188 billion per year. (Amin to author, December 2010)

Compare this situation to Japan, which averages only four minutes of total interrupted service each year! America's power grid is more evolved toward SOC than Japan's! Ben Carreras explained, "Power grids are inherently prone to big blackouts. Trying to make them more robust can make the problem worse" (Carreras, Lynch, Dobson & Newman 2002:1). There doesn't seem to be a way out! Are we stuck on the edge of chaos? How did this happen, and what can we do about it?

---

1   David Newman objects to my use of "self-organized criticality", because it has become too common. He prefers to compare the length of power law tails before and after a change in policy.

Figure 6.1. Macro-structure of the U.S. power grid represented as a network of interconnected regions (Casazza 2003).

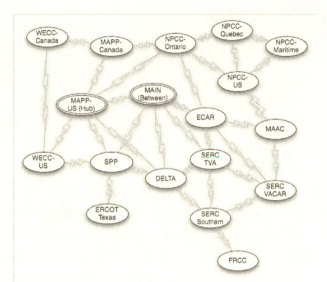

The Biggest Machine In The World

According to the largest technical/professional association in the world, the Institute of Electrical and Electronics Engineers (IEEE), the electric power grid is the biggest machine in the world. Whether power grids in any one country are bigger than the global Internet is debatable, but we do know one thing: power grids are large and complex. But they weren't always that way. In the beginning, Thomas Edison (1847-1931) envisioned electric light bulbs being lit up by direct current or *DC*. Edison's model assumed that power generation would be located close to the light bulbs, because low-voltage DC doesn't travel well. If Edison had had his way, *distributed generation* would be the norm. Distributed generation, typically in the form of small solar or windmill generators, is defined as local power, adequate to supply a shopping center or neighborhood. Transmission lines would not only be un-necessary but impractical. But Edison was wrong.

The Serbian inventor Nikola Tesla (1856 –1943), considered the greatest inventor of all time by some, had a better idea. He invented alternating current, *AC*, along with electric motors to harness the power of AC. In Tesla's model of electrical generation and distribution, large turbines generate electrical current while a transformer steps up the voltage so it can be transmitted long distances with minimum loss. At the other end, the voltage is reduced to a lower level by a step-down transformer so it can be consumed by an office, home, or factory.

Tesla's model of electric power generation, transmission, distribution, and application to electrical lighting, motors, and computers won the day. As a result, today's power grid is a network of generation plants, transformers for stepping voltages up/down, high-voltage transmission lines for long-haul transfers, and low-voltage distribution lines and substations for short-haul transfers to consumers. Edison was famous for inventing the light bulb, but Tesla invented the infrastructure needed to power those light bulbs.

Edison and Tesla were the inventors, but as described later in chapter nine—'Invention, Innovation, and Inspiration'—George Westinghouse was the innovator that made electric power a reality. Westinghouse commercialized Tesla's inventions and built the first power generators at Niagara Falls, New York, to supply markets in New York City. Transmission of electrons by high-voltage AC is much more efficient (7-8% loss) than DC, thus making the Niagara Falls to New York City circuit actually work. Coincidentally, Edison and Westinghouse nearly went broke in the process!

Tesla invented many advanced machines and devices. He held patents on radio, radio-controlled boats, torpedoes, and spark plugs for gasoline engines. He envisioned robots way ahead of his day and claimed he could extract electricity directly from the atmosphere. He received patents on a device for transmitting electricity wirelessly. On the surface, he was phenomenally successful. But Tesla was an embattled scientist more adept at inventing than turning his inventions into profits. When

Westinghouse ran into financial difficulties, Tesla gave up his patent royalties to save him. Tesla died an impoverished and lonely man.

Edison claimed Tesla's model was not only inefficient but also dangerous. He waged a campaign against AC by publicly electrocuting dogs. In fact, Edison had a point: DC current has no need of substations and transformers for stepping voltages up and down. Today many appliances such as computers, cell phones, iPods, and radios use DC instead of AC. Conversion from AC to DC requires copious use of small transformers familiar to modern consumers who must constantly recharge a variety of devices. But DC has its own drawback – it cannot turn an AC motor. In fact electric cars use an inverter to convert DC battery output into AC in order to turn the wheels. Electric motors quickly became the engine of industry, a market that DC could not address.

There are four major components in every power grid: *Generation*, *Transmission*, *Distribution*, and *Load*. Generation is done mostly by coal-burning power plants, hydroelectric dams, nuclear reactors, or natural gas-fired 'peaker' plants. Transmission is typically done by high-voltage above ground transmission towers. Distribution is typically done by intermediate and low-voltage power poles and cables. Each time voltage is stepped up or down, the electricity must be converted from one voltage to another by transformers at substations or buses. 'Load' is the name power grid operators give to consumers.

By the turn of the twentieth century, electric power operators had perfected their business model—the famous *vertical integration* model. Utilities owned all levels of the production and delivery system: generation, transmission, distribution, and everything in between. Vertical integration worked for most of the twentieth century. In exchange for efficient low-cost and accessible electricity, governments around the world granted monopolies to the utilities. The so-called *natural monopolies* operated within restricted geographical areas, serving customers from top to bottom. These monopolies ran the biggest machines in the world. It is also fair to say that they did it rather flawlessly.

For over a century, electric power infrastructures evolved into the system we currently know of as the *grid* (see Figure 6.1). Regulation had perhaps the biggest influence on shaping this huge network. Heavily regulated by FERC (the Federal Energy Regulatory Commission) and closely watched over by ISO/RTO (Independent System Operator/ Regional Transmission Organizations), the grid roughly approximates a network of loosely connected regions. Thus, we can learn a lot about its resiliency and security properties by applying the analysis techniques described earlier. In particular, cascade failures in grids are a lot like network epidemics—with a few twists that I will describe below.

Simulation of outages in the network of Figure 6.1 suggests that it is a heavy-tailed (high-risk) network, simply because of its connectivity. Recall that *spectral radius* is a number measuring some forms of self-organized criticality in networks. High values of spectral radius correspond with high link density and percolation. The continental network of Figure 6.1 has a spectral radius of 4.4, which is 1.2 times that of an equivalent random network. The hub node MAPP-US has six connections instead of the average of 3.66 links, and the maximum betweeness node MAIN is the largest middleman node with 80 paths.[2] These elevated metrics suggest that the U.S. power grid is self-organized and near its critical state. If we want to get to the heart of the problem, it is appropriate to ask why?

---

2   Recall from previous chapters that betweeness is the number of paths running through a node from/to all other nodes.

Roots of SOC

The beginning of the end of vertical monopolies in the power sector began in the 1970s, the decade of the first U.S. energy crisis. Most of the world's oil is under the control of OPEC (Organization of the Petroleum Exporting Countries), a cartel of eight Middle Eastern, two African, and two South American countries—Algeria, Iran, Iraq, Kuwait, Libya, Qatar, Saudi Arabia, the United Arab Emirates, Angola, Nigeria, Ecuador, and Venezuela. The cartel launched the first energy embargo in 1973 during the *Yom Kippur War*, initiating a global oil crisis and plunging the world into an energy frenzy that eventually produced PURPA.

PURPA 1978, the *Public Utility Regulatory Policies Act*, was designed to promote greater use of renewable energy. Utilities were forced to buy power from *qualified facilities*—non-utility power producers—at a cost equal to what the utility could generate or purchase from another source. In other words, utilities could no longer monopolize production. The government wanted to break up vertical monopolies and force them to obtain power from cleaner domestic producers. Congress also aimed to increase supply by increasing competition. When PURPA 1978 didn't produce the desired results, the government stepped up its assault on vertically integrated utilities. And this is where self-organized criticality really began to accelerate, as the electric power grid system evolved under a political framework that ignored both the physics of electricity and common business sense.

If PURPA 1978 opened a crack in the door by marking the beginning of the end of the vertical monopolies that held the largest machine together, then EPACT 1992—the *Energy Policy Act of 1992*—blew the door off of its hinges! EPACT and FERC rules 888 and 889 separated electricity producers from utilities and required the utilities to allow competitors access to all transmission and distribution lines. In effect, the law *disintermediated* the utilities—vertically integrated monopolies no longer existed. Disintermediation is the process of replacing or removing intermediary links in the value chain (for example, an online web site disintermediates a physical store when it makes it possible for a consumer to bypass the store and buy directly from the manufacturer). Instead, utilities became one of several players in an oligopoly made up of power producers, utilities, and non-profit market makers called ISOs (Independent System Operators). This separation tore the largest machine in the world into loosely coupled pieces, and discarded the centralized control so necessary for running the grid as one big machine.

After a period of litigation lasting until the U.S. Supreme Court ruling on March 4, 2000, the grid was broken into pieces: one piece for power generation, another piece for competing utilities, and a third piece consisting of ISOs designed to mediate between buyers and sellers of power. The ISO's job was akin to that of the New York Stock Exchange: to guarantee open and fair trading of electrons while maintaining the integrity and reliability of the grid. As so often occurs when dealing with complex systems, the new ISO/RTO structure immediately threw the grid out of control.

The fallout from EPACT 1992 was profound. Electricity became a commodity to be traded by companies like Enron, which in a few short years after the implementation of FERC rules 888 and 889 was found guilty of defrauding investors and gaming the wholesale electricity trading market. In less than five years, electricity was traded at a price equivalent to $450/gallon of gasoline in California. Enron had cornered the electron futures market so that when California needed electricity, it had to pay a premium to get it. In fact, predatory energy pricing toppled California's government. Arnold Schwarzenegger replaced Gray Davis as governor before Davis' term ended. Davis is only the second governor in US history to be recalled—not because people disliked his politics, but rather because he was sucker-punched by the power grid!

The second blow to the grid was more gradual. EPACT 1992 required competing utilities to share the same wires, the so-called deregulation part of EPACT. Under the new regulation, all producers of power have equal access to all transmission and distribution lines. In a crude sense, anyone could become a utility company. The unintended consequence was *more* competing utilities and *less* information flow, as competitors began hoarding what they knew about the state of the grid because it gave them a competitive advantage. Current flow became a trade secret, forcing operators to make critical decisions about the stability of the grid with little information about its state. As information dried up, the largest machine became the largest gambling casino in Extremistan.

The third blow was inevitable: due to optimization and NIMBY— 'Not In My Back Yard', the reluctance of consumers to allow utilities to build power plants, substations, and transmission lines in their communities—utilities increased the load on existing transmission lines rather than adding to their capacity. This was a true *tragedy of the commons*: individuals acting independently in their own best interest, thereby jointly depleting a common resource. And it spread like an epidemic throughout regional grids, from East to West and North to South. What is the incentive to add transmission capacity when the public opposes it and your competitors benefit from your investment? As in any such tragedy, everyone wanted more transmission capacity, but few wanted to pay for it. Lack of adequate transmission capacity is perhaps the biggest challenge facing the power grid today.

A subtle self-organized criticality began building as a consequence of EPACT 1992: the physical distance separating power generator and customer began to increase. Power plants and solar farms were pushed away from populations to satisfy NIMBY, but this required more transmission lines. It became much easier to obtain permission to put solar farms in the desert, but politicians ignored the physics of transmission. NIMBY increased the load on transmission lines because remote power generation requires longer and larger transmission lines. Thus, EPACT 1992 increased the load on an already overtaxed transmission network. Overloaded lines tend to burn out sooner, especially during the warm summer months. NIMBY and EPACT are largely responsible for increasing SOC.

A second subtle effect began to take over: *reactive power* began to go away, because power companies could no longer make money from it. Yet smooth operation of the grid depends on it. Reactive power is a form of electrical energy that sloshes back and forth between generator and load. Sloshing cancels the net-net transfer so there is no associated billing, hence there is no profit in maintaining reactive power. However, utilities must install heavier wires to handle the excess current, which is an added cost that saps profits. If power producers can't profit from it and utilities can't charge for it, then why produce it? So reactive power went away, leaving the grid less stable.

Less reactive power, less transmission capacity, and less information on the status of the grid all increase SOC. Optimizing the grid by centralizing substations and power stations increases the network's spectral radius—yet another step towards the critical point. Distributing control among a handful of ISOs makes things even worse. In 2000, loss of grid capacity and control cost consumers $20 billion, but state public utility commissions refused to increase rates. Something had to give, so in the first few years leading up to the 2003 blackout, 150,000 skilled utility workers were let go. By August 14, 2003, the over-extended operators of the Ohio portion of the Eastern Grid had inadequate situation awareness and inadequate options for handling a normal accident. As a consequence, a tripped line in Ohio toppled the Northern portion of the Eastern Grid, leaving 55 million people without electricity for more than two days. Airports, railroads, factories, hospitals, highways, Internet service providers, and emergency services were shut down across portions of northeastern Canada and the United States. At least eleven people died. And yet, we got off lucky!

Cascades as Epidemics

The slow and inevitable build up of SOC in the grid beginning with PURPA 1978 and accelerated by EPACT 1992 leads to cascade failures in the grid that obey a heavy-tailed power law according to my grid scholars—and it is our own fault. Under these conditions, even small accidents become big threats to the largest machine in the world because of a combination of high betweeness in the transmission network, high degree of concentration of control nodes, and fragmentation of control. Here is how a typical normal accident is able to snowball into a major blackout:

1. Somewhere a power line is tripped, typically by shorting out because of contact with a tree branch or because of a failed transformer in the distribution network. Since EPACT 1992 was put into full operation in 2000, the number of tripped lines has increased 6-fold.

2. Power is diverted to alternate lines to bypass the tripped line. The bypass process is so complicated and unpredictable that I chose to ignore it here! Suffice it to say the consequences are unpredictable.

3. If power demand is high, as it often is during the month of August (due to the heat and high use of air conditioners), lines overheat and eventually trip, accelerating the cascade effect. The probability of subsequent tripped lines *increases* as the number of tripped lines increases.

4. As lines are taken out of service the utility must discard power by either selling it to adjacent utilities or shutting down generators. Load shedding is a polite way of saying customers must go without power—a brownout occurs when insufficient power is delivered to customers. A blackout occurs when power drops to zero.

5. Load shedding propagates like an epidemic across the network, spreading the brownout/blackout to a greater part of the grid. The

collapse happens in a matter of minutes as operators shed power to avoid damaging components of the grid.

Cascades spread like an epidemic, but with one major difference: as lines go down and the flow of electrons shifts to remaining lines, the probability that the remaining lines will also go down *increases*. Unlike the dampening of persistent epidemics in *Lévy flights*, virulence increases as a power grid network collapses. Longer Lévy steps are *more* contagious rather than less so, although, in the case of SARS, the reverse is true. Power failures become stronger with the number of long-distance lines, rather than weaker. Thus power grid epidemics are even heavier-tailed power law catastrophes than microbial epidemics. This double-whammy adds to the speed and impact of blackouts.

Note that Edison believed in distributed generation, which requires shorter transmission lines. Today's policies push in the wrong direction as they lead to more long-haul transmission, the opposite of Edison's design. As transmission lines become longer, the grid becomes less stable. Either we need to bolster long-haul transmission or return to Edison's original design. But then again, Edison never had to deal with NIMBY.

Simulation of network collapses due to cascade failures across random, clustered, and scale-free networks shows that the most resilient grids are random and clustered networks. Simulated random failures in components such as transformers and transmission lines produces an exceedence probability curve that obeys a lop-sided power law. The question is, what policies lead to shorter power law tails and more resilient networks?

The least resilient grids are scale-free networks—networks with an exceptionally highly connected hub (recall that the hub is the most connected node). Collapses are bigger for networks with hubs, and even bigger if the hubs are the source of the initial failure. In other words, power grids become more likely to suffer major blackouts as they become scale-free and/or their hubs fail. Hubs are force-multipliers because when they fail, they also drag down the power lines attached to them. Therefore, policies that minimize hub connectivity move away from SOC while policies that increase hub connectivity move toward SOC. Current deregulation tends to grow hubs, because of socio-economic pressures. Once again, the politics of NIMBY works against physics. Ultimately, however, physics wins!

To illustrate this, consider a simulation of outages in the U.S. mid-Atlantic power grid consisting of 214 lines and 162 nodes. I simulated thousands of failures in this sub-grid and found that the mid-Atlantic grid is highly resilient against random node failure, but much less resilient if a hub fails, and even more fragile if a *betweener node* fails. Recall that the 'betweener' is the node with the most paths running through it. In this context, a betweener is the substation or transformer with the greatest load. Assuming an infectiousness rate of 10% for all nodes, the odds of 20% or more nodes collapsing because of a normal accident in a single node increases from one in 32 million for a random failure, to one in 83,000 if the hub fails, to one in 56,000 if the betweener fails. In other words, hub node failure magnifies the effect of a cascade blackout by a factor of 385 over random node failure and betweener node failure magnifies the effect by a factor of 571.

In 2005, a group of researchers constructed a network model of the U.S. high-voltage transmission grid consisting of over 14,000 generators, transmission substations, and distribution substations, and over 19,000 links representing transmission lines. They then identified the betweener nodes and, sure enough, these betweeners were the critical components of the grid. Out of the 14,000 nodes, only 140 were important enough to bring down the entire grid (Kinney, Crucitti, Albert & Latora 2005). Criticality in the power grid is highly correlated with node betweeness. Betweeness is an important property of grid structure, but few owners and operators understand this because they only test for N-1 failures.

EPACT 1992 set the stage for an emergence of criticality in the U.S. power grid. Self-organized criticality emerged in the form of a handful of betweener nodes. In order to stabilize and control the grid, it is essential to stabilize and control the flow of electricity through these betweeners. To do that, we must be able to observe the status of each component and quickly adjust flow parameters to keep the grid balanced and stable. This is where Mister SmartGrid comes in!

Mister SmartGrid

In real life, Mister SmartGrid, a Paul Bunyan-sized intellectual who was sitting in the back of my workshop room, is Massoud Amin, Professor and Director of the Technological Leadership Institute at the University of Minnesota. Amin boasts of being from the "sunny state of Minnesota," but otherwise he is as normal and personable as a schoolteacher. His pleasant and courteous demeanor hides the fact that he is the pioneering inventor of *SmartGrid*, an architecture for controlling and stabilizing the grid. He told me that,

> First off, it's helpful to define just what a smart grid is. It refers to the use of computer, communications, sensing, and control technology, operating in conjunction with an electric power grid, to enhance the reliability, resilience, security, and efficiency of the end-to-end electric power production and delivery system. A smart grid minimizes the cost of electric energy to consumers; improves security, quality, and resilience; and facilitates the connection of new generating sources-like wind and solar-to the grid. It also uses sensing and control technologies to deal with unforeseen events, minimizing their impact. (Amin in email to author, December 2010).

In January 1998, as head of mathematics and information sciences at EPRI (the Electric Power Research Institute), Amin, showed how deployment of a self-healing smart grid could alleviate the ubiquitous nature of power disturbances. The first step in building such a grid is to build a secure processor into each component of a substation. Each breaker, switch, transformer, busbar, etc, has an associated processor that can communicate with other such devices. Each high-voltage connection to the device must have a parallel information connection. These processors have permanent information on device parameters as well as device status and analogue measurements from sensors built in the component. (Amin in email to author, December 2010).

Amin's idea came from years of work on aircraft stability and other complex systems. He had been impressed by a fearless Israeli pilot who landed a jet fighter after one wing was blown off and control surfaces were damaged. The skilled pilot used thrust control to land the badly damaged airplane. This got Amin to thinking: if a pilot can control a badly damaged aircraft, then it should be possible for a computer to control the unruly electric power grid. To do so, operators need real-time information about the state of the grid at any instant in time. The challenge is to complete the loop—from power plant to transmission, distribution, load, and back—quickly enough to head off impending disaster.

Without knowing the status of transformers, power lines, and power plants across an entire grid, utilities are flying with only one wing, a blindfold, and an empty fuel tank. Chances of landing safely are near zero. Mister SmartGrid believes computers connected to embedded sensors in power lines, transformers and electricity meters can be programmed to overcome instabilities created by unpredictable faults in the network. SmartGrid equals information technology plus electric generation, transmission, distribution, and load feedback.

Amin's idea is to combine information technology with electronics and computer algorithms for analyzing feedback and making adjustments in real-time. This is a tall order. When it comes to digitized information, the power industry is starting from zero. SmartGrid information technology can measure line voltages, transformer temperatures and other parameters to gauge the state of the grid, but implementing the SmartGrid vision will require a huge investment to replace every major component of the largest machine in the world. Currently, most smart components and computer algorithms don't even exist.

SmartGrid is a vision that may take twenty to thirty years to realize because the grid is so large and expensive. Also, it is unclear whether engineers know enough about the dynamics of such large and complex systems to design smart computer programs that are actually able to control the grid. Today, SmartGrid is little more than two-way: the electric utility meters in your home that tell you and the utility company how much it costs to dry your clothes, air condition your home, and heat your shower water. But it is a start.

Energy Mash Up

Meanwhile, the United States needs an energy policy that removes SOC, revitalizes the grid, and applies what we know about hi-tech enterprises to the century-old and hide-bound power industry. Nothing short of revolutionary thinking will save it. It is one of the most important and vital of infrastructures, in the United States as well as all other modern industrial nations. We need to apply what we learned from building the Interstate Highway System and the Internet to the power grid. A successful policy mash up of Interstate and Internet systems should do the trick.

The Dwight D. Eisenhower National System of Interstate and Defense Highways, commonly called the Interstate Highway System (or simply the Interstate) is the largest highway system and largest public works project in the world. More importantly, it propelled the United States into an enviable era of prosperity. Today, virtually all goods and services are distributed via the Interstate, which at 47,000 miles is still expanding. By 2008, the public investment in the Interstate Highway System exceeded $500 billion, paid for by the Highway Trust Fund (which is stoked by gasoline taxes).

In the 1990s, the then 25-year old Internet was opened up to commercialization. This stimulated economic growth so forcefully that it produced an economic bubble that burst spectacularly in 2000. In less than 20 years, the federal government's $200 million investment in the Internet returned 100-fold—and growth is just beginning. The future of the global economy increasingly depends on the Internet. The secret to the Internet's success is simple: it is a global vending machine; a market that invites every citizen in the world to participate. For $15 per year, any commercial enterprise can gain access to the world.

The electric power grid needs a dose of innovative thinking in the form of a mash up between the continental scale transportation system and the global Internet. I'd like to propose that EPACT2020 combine the Internet business model with the network topology of the Interstate Highway System. The resulting continental energy, power, and information network would be a resilient engine of economic expansion.

It is clear that relatively modest investments in infrastructure reap exponentially large returns from economic growth, job creation, and innovation. Historically, no nation on earth (including ancient Rome) has achieved or maintained greatness, security, and prosperity, without plentiful energy, robust communications, and transportation capacity. The economy of the twenty-first century will run on electrical power and Internet packets. Why not re-think and rebuild energy and information highways that provide both?

The two major roadblocks preventing this mash up are NIMBY and the enormous cost of rebuilding a twenty-first century power infrastructure. NIMBY is currently blocking many projects because people do not want power lines in their backyards. In addition, Mister SmartGrid's convergence of electrons with information technology is an enormously expensive and perhaps unattractive investment opportunity. The existing $1 trillion electrical power grid, which is based on technology from the 1940s, will cost at least another $1 trillion and take perhaps 40 years to upgrade. More realistically, it will probably take 50-100 years and cost somewhere in the region of $10 trilllion.

NIMBY can be avoided by building underground electric power transmission lines, natural gas pipelines, and telecommunication/CATV/Internet communication lines on rights-of-way already established by the Interstate Highway System. States already own these rights-of-way, which reach nearly every part of the nation. It therefore makes sense to leverage this asset to a greater extent than it is currently. In fact, states would derive revenue from these rights because the continental power grid would be a toll road.

Existing Interstate rights-of-way can be utilized as transmission alleys crisscrossing the nation but generation still needs to be located as close as possible to high-density populations. Short transmission is better than long-haul transmission, yet it must be possible for an alternative energy entrepreneur in New Mexico to convert photons into electrons and sell them in upstate New York. This calls for a new grid architecture containing storage relays in the form of compressed air caves, flywheel substations, ultra capacitors, and storage batteries. The new architecture would have to form chains from short transmission loops connecting store-and-forward storage units located along existing Interstate Highways. I estimate it would take 1,000 storage units located approximately every 40 miles to cover the United States. On/off ramps to local utilities serving cities, factories, and farms would complete the network.

Think about this: underground storage units can be placed near the load, especially in cities. Relatively local storage would be charged up during the night when transmission lines are underutilized and discharged during peak times when consumers demand electrons. Storage would fill peak demand and because the units are placed near the load, there would be little impact on overburdened transmission lines. It would be as if the lanes of a highway were reversed in the morning and again at rush hour to accommodate peak traffic flow—a technique used every day by major metropolitan areas like Seattle, Washington.

The proposed system would be nearly devoid of SOC because of its storage surge capacity, physical and cyber security, and distributed generation and transmission architecture. It returns the grid to Edison's original idea, but with a twist—storage. Robust and redundant, able to transmit commodities such as Internet packets, electrons from solar farms, natural gas for future cars, trucks, and buses, and bountiful electrical power for future cyber businesses, the continental power grid would be a quantum leap forward for the nation and the economy. Think of it as America's twenty-first century 'moon shot.'

The Check, Please

The continental power network could be implemented much like the Interstate Highway network, which was built over a 20-30-year period at an estimated cost of $50 billion per year. I estimate that it would cost $25 million/mile to build the necessary tunnels, pipes, wires, etc. for the new power network. The Interstate is 40,000 miles long, hence a total estimated cost of $1 trillion over 20 years. While this may seem high, it represents only 3.6% of the combined revenues of the natural gas, electric power, telecommunications, gasoline, and broadcast industries combined (see Table 6.1).

The Interstate Highway System is "pay-as-you-go," with 90% of the funding coming from the federal government and the remaining 10% from the states. In its first year of construction, 1958, total costs came to $37.6 billion. By 1991, the cost was $128 billion. But these billions contributed nothing to the national debt because they were paid for by a 40-cent per gallon tax on gasoline. Title II of the Highway Revenue Act of 1956 created the Highway Trust Fund to collect and dispense funding for the Interstate Highway System. This highly successful infrastructure project looks like a bargain in hindsight.

The continental power grid can be financed in the same way—through a trust fund established by Congress. The financing plan needs to be worked out in detail, but one attractive option is to establish a GSE (Government Sponsored Enterprise) to run the continental power grid as a business. Ultimately, it must be self-sustaining, through revenues generated by its use. A toll fee could be charged for use of the pipelines, communication lines, storage facilities, and service stations. These fees could be based on existing regulated fees charged by telephone, utility, and pipeline companies—a familiar fee structure for these industries.

Ginny Mae, Sallie Mae, Fannie Mae and Freddie Mac already exist as GSEs; that is, as government backed enterprises listed on stock exchanges, and therefore, investor supported. The creation of, say, 'PowerMac' would take an act of Congress, but GSEs aren't new. It simply requires imagination. The major portion of funding could be raised from investment banks, retirement funds, and personal investors through an IPO. Like a GSE, the continental grid trust fund could be backed by the federal government, and at some point reach self-sustainability through collection of usage fees.

Glass Highways

My idea of laying down electrical power, Internet, and natural gas lines next to the Interstate Highway System is tame compared with Scott and Julie Brusaw's bold idea of glass highways stretching across the landscape.[3] But in 2010 the Brusaws were awarded a $100,000 research contract by the U.S. Department of Transportation to test the feasibility of making highways like we make television sets today. Scott and Julie have five kids and breed terriers and poodles. Scott served in the U.S. Marine Corps and volunteers as a scoutmaster, in addition to holding a Master's degree in electrical engineering—so he ought to know what he is doing! Some people are skeptical of his fantastic idea, yet big ideas like this are what built America.

Scott and Julie Brusaw want to replace current asphalt roads, parking lots, and driveways with 12' by 12' solar road panels containing embedded photovoltaic cells, transmission wires, LED displays, and storage elements, thus turning roads into giant solar farms. The glass would be tough enough for cars and trucks to drive on while the embedded electronics collect, store, and transmit solar energy to homes and businesses. These solar panels would store surplus electrons, embed displays so that roadside signs are no longer needed, and perhaps even contain sensors activated by pedestrians when stepping onto the road. The idea is so clever that one can imagine dozens of applications of the technology to safety and traffic management—as well as distributed generation and energy resiliency.

According to the Brusaw's web page, each individual panel consists of three basic layers: the glass road surface, an electronics layer containing circuitry for sensing and controlling, and a base layer containing the photovoltaic cells and transmission lines. The glass layer has to be strong enough to support the punishing pressure of trucks running over it thousands of times per day and translucent enough to allow sunlight through. The electronics layer, containing a microcomputer and sensors with associated control software, also must be tough enough to take the pounding of semi trucks and buses. This layer makes the highway smart. The base layer converts sunlight into electrons, either storing

---

3   www.solarroadways.com

it or transmitting it to consumers. The base layer might also transmit Internet and cable TV signals.

A solar roadway would be much more expensive than existing asphalt highways but also much more useful. Table 6.1 shows how to pay for a continental power grid without harvesting electrons. If the revenue from power generating solar cells is included, solar highways become attractive even though they are expensive. Scott Brusaw estimates that solar highways are capable of producing three times the national demand for electricity, assuming 15% conversion efficiency. Thus, combining photovoltaic revenue with my proposal to use the Interstate Highway rights-of-way makes the solar highway a feasible dream. Are we bold enough to do this?

Table 6.1. Sector Revenues

Sector	Revenues ($Billion)
Mobile Telephone Subscription	50
Landline Telephone Toll	190
Electric Power (Retail)	360
Natural Gas ($5/1,000 cu.ft. x 22 Tcu.ft.)	110
CATV subscriptions	125
Gasoline sales ($4/gallon x 140 bgal.)	560
TOTAL	1395

Figure 6.2. U.S. power grid mega-structure after restructuring around islands. The North-East-West-South rectangular shape of the Interstate Highway System dictates the shape of this network.

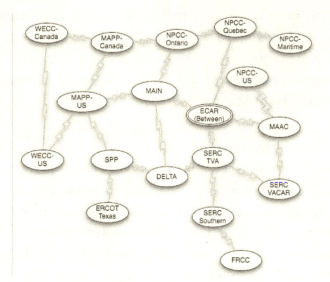

Islands in the Sun

What does $1 trillion buy? Decreases in the long tailed exceedence probability mean a more resilient and reliable power grid. The exceedence probability is improved by lowering the spectral radius of the grid. Replacing pavement with solar panels or otherwise placing transmission lines next to the existing Interstate network, reducing the length of transmission lines (using storage relays), and increasing their capacity make the grid more resilient and impervious to local normal accidents.

Mimicking the Interstate Highway System with transmission lines automatically reduces SOC because the Interstate network spectral radius is 3.10 versus 4.4 (see Figure 6.2). The immediate impact would be to shorten the power law tail and reduce blackout size by 25%. The probability of at least 20% of the grid collapsing decreases from 11% to 8.5%.

Restructuring the grid is not adequate to completely avoid catastrophic collapses. We still have to be concerned with the Black Swan event. Policy makers must face the possibility (albeit reduced) of a widespread outage that separates one part of the grid from another, thereby dragging a larger part of the grid down with a local collapse. Even if transmission lines were replaced by solar panels, the grid could be vulnerable to widespread blackouts like the 2003 normal accident!

An outage that separates a portion of the grid from all other sections is called *islanding*, because it leaves isolated islands in its wake. Network operators do their best to avoid islanding, but what if instead they did the opposite—created islands on purpose? This is the concept being pursued by the U.S. Northern Command—the division of the Department of Defense responsible for protecting the continental United States. Instead of trying to prevent the Black Swan event, suppose we mitigate its effects by re-architecting the grid?

Islanding on purpose sounds ridiculous until you think in terms of Extremistan and the effects of percolation on networks. Islanding can prevent one section of the grid from contaminating adjacent sections. An operator can create a small island by shedding load, thus relieving stress on transmission lines. But utilities have to be willing to sacrifice service to one group of consumers to keep others electrified. Additionally, islanding only works if there is sufficient storage or generation capacity within a perimeter established by the island. This is where re-design and the implementation of the ambitious plan outlined above comes in. Islanding can be maintained in an emergency if sufficient storage and generation capacity is allowed to be located close to consumers.

It is highly likely that NIMBY will prevent construction of nuclear, solar, or wind powered power plants within the city limits of major metropolitan areas where power is needed the most. Instead, innocuous storage facilities such as batteries, solar highway panels, or flywheels can be distributed throughout the city and charged overnight when the burden on transmission lines is minimal. Between midnight and 6 o'clock in the morning, electric cars and city storage facilities would be charged up for use during peak demand periods.

The energy policy for the twenty-first century is now clear: we need policies that transition the existing grid from a self-organized network into a randomized cluster network with low spectral radius and robust transmission, storage, and distribution capacity. To integrate clean energy with the grid, it is essential that the grid be able to deliver electrons generated in the New Mexico deserts to the high-density northeastern United States. When we can do that, venture capital will build solar and windmill farms without taxing consumers, and we will all enjoy islands in the sun.

7

Can you hear me now?

Samuel Morse
(1791-1872)

Alexander Graham Bell
(1847–1922)

Elisha Gray
(1835-1901)

Inventors of the modern communication system: Samuel Morse, Alexander Graham Bell, and Elisha Gray.

Hubs and Spokes

Over its 120-year history, the architecture of the U.S. communications infrastructure has evolved into a self-organized complex network because of extreme concentration of equipment in a relatively small number of *telecom hotels*—buildings containing a high concentration of switching equipment, storage, and fiber connections. These *hubs* were formed by economic, regulatory, and technical forces operating over four historical periods: the era of *unregulated beginning*, the *telecom war years*, the *regulated vertical monopoly period*, and the current *'de-regulated competitive era.'* I have put quotes around the phrase 'de-regulated competitive era,' because this latest phase of the communications evolution isn't really an age of de-regulation. In particular, recent efforts to re-regulate the industry have brought on new forms of competition on the one hand, and more regulation on the other hand. But the bottom line is that the 1996 Telecommunications Act has had the greatest impact on telecommunications since 1934—creating a self-organized network nearing its critical point.

Although the industry has not experienced a calamity on a scale equal to the 2003 Eastern power grid blackout, the two networks have evolved into a similar state of criticality because of their topology. However, there are a number of significant differences. For one thing, the communications industry has an abundance of transmission lines. There is little risk of failure due to inadequate long-haul transmission capacity. Second, the laws of physics dictating the movement of digital information is much kinder to optical transmission technology than it is to power transmission technology because there is much less friction (resistance) blocking movement of information than movement of high-voltage electrons.

Generally, the U.S. communications system is a network of hubs and spokes, as illustrated by the 30 busiest communication routes of the early 2000s (see Figure 7.1). While power grids must be concerned with transmission lines (spokes), communication networks must be concerned with switching hubs (hubs). Because economic and regulatory forces operating over the past century have distorted the hub-and-spoke system, both of these systems contain irregular wheels, at best. The 1992 EPACT is largely responsible for shaping the power grid, but the Telecommunications Act of 1996 is responsible for most of the fragility in the nation's communication infrastructure. In general, this fragility is due to self-organized criticality of hubs. This is the strong claim that I intend to back up in this chapter.

This is a story about how a combination of economic and political pressures transformed a stable and reliable telephone system into a fragile self-organized national communications system on the edge of chaos. It begins with intrigue and ends in the modern era where neglect and ignorance are most responsible for a fragile telecommunications system.

The invention of the telephone is an interesting story on its own, but international intrigue during the 1960s almost led to the extinction of modern civilization—simply for lack of a dial tone. In both cases, history would be very different if it were not for normal accidents.

Neglect and ignorance began with Congress' multiple attempts to regulate and then deregulate the industry, culminating with the 1996 Telecommunications Act. This act has severely damaged our ability to reliably communicate. This act is the single most important factor driving communications to a critical point.

Recent missteps by Congress and the FCC are particularly unfortunate because Internet traffic, cellular telephony, and e-commerce all depend on the continental wired infrastructure. Communications may be a relatively modern invention of convenience, but it is rapidly becoming an essential part of civilized living. Few of us can function for more than several days without cell phone, Internet connection, or cable TV subscription. Practically every financial transaction today—both nationally and internationally—depends on communications.

The New York Stock Exchange was shut down for a week following the terrorist attacks of 9/11 because the NYSE's backup plan lacked redundancy. And redundancy was absent because lines from two separate carriers went through the same building, which was damaged in the attacks. The building containing the primary and secondary services was a direct consequence of the 1996 Act. More on this later, but the failure of the communications infrastructure on 9/11 is a cogent reminder of how dependent civilized nations are on their communications infrastructure. It is also a dramatic demonstration of SOC and criticality.

Will neglect and ignorance further ruin this system? Perhaps not, but changes in policy are needed, which I will address later. But first, a short history of communications with emphasis on how socio-political factors shaped the industry. In the end I think you will agree that the nation's vital communications infrastructure is suffering from human-caused

SOC. My story begins with melodrama and the role of communications in the Cuban Missile Crisis of 1962.

Figure 7.1. Top 30 long-haul communications transmission hubs and links serving the U.S. circa 2005.

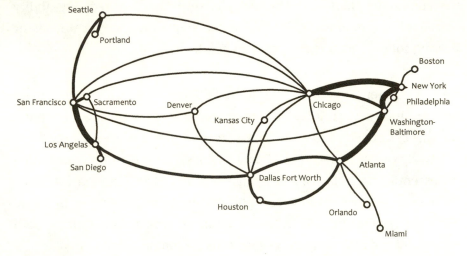

A Bad Connection

The world held its breath as it peered into the nuclear abyss. The Soviet Union had placed continental range missiles in Cuba, a mere 90 miles from the United States, prompting the young President Kennedy to draw a line in the sand: remove the missiles or be prepared to go to war. This was exactly what people had feared—nuclear annihilation due to a simple misstep in the arms race between the Soviet Union and the United States. The thirteen-day crisis precipitated runs on grocery stores, flights from major cities, declarations by the post office that it would stay open even if bombed, and robust attendance at churches around the country. Traffic on the I-5 freeway headed out of Los Angeles was unusually heavy. The situation was tense.

Negotiations between President Kennedy and Premier Khrushchev were dangerously hampered because the two leaders couldn't call one another. There was no global communication link between leaders back in October 1962. This is difficult to understand today when connecting with almost anyone in the world from a hand-held cell phone is commonplace. The first practical communication satellite, Telstar 2, didn't begin operating until 1963. Customer dialing of international telephone calls between New York and London started in 1970, and it was not until 1988 that AT&T laid the first fiber optic submarine telephone cable across the Atlantic. The word 'wired' meant something different then than it does today.

Kennedy received two critical messages from Khrushchev, one conciliatory and one bellicose. The first message agreed to a compromise. The Soviet Union would retreat from Cuba if the U.S. would promise not to attack the island. The second message demanded withdrawal of U.S. missiles from Turkey. Kennedy chose to ignore the second message and accepted the terms of the first one. Why had Khrushchev sent two different messages? Perhaps this confusion could have been avoided if an international telephone call had been possible.

The Cuban Missile Crisis had a happy ending, or else you would not be reading this! In fact, it eventually benefitted international relations and also precipitated the creation of the NCS (National Communications System) and the formation of the NSTAC—the National Security Telecommunications Advisory Committee. The NSTAC was established in 1982 by President Reagan (by Executive Order 12382) to advise the President of the United States on matters pertaining to the security and well being of the 'telephone system.' The *telecommunications* sector was renamed the *communications* sector by the Department of Homeland Security in 2009 (NIPP 2009).

The communications industry is more than just telephone or Internet systems. It embraces wired and wireless communication: landline and cellular telephony, Internet, radio and TV broadcasting, GPS navigation, global satellites, undersea cables, Wi-Fi, etc. It is bigger than the biggest machine in the world described in the previous chapter. As of 2010, there were over 3 billion cell phones, 500 million servers, and several globe-spanning optical cable networks considered part of the communications network—and the system is growing rapidly. In fact, communications is so ubiquitous we often take it for granted. Industrial controls for power, energy, banking, transportation, and business correspondence depends on robust communications. Trains, factories, and airplanes stop running when the communications network fails. It has rapidly become an essential part of the very fabric of civilization.

Figure 7.2. Mega-structure model of the U.S. communications network infrastructure.

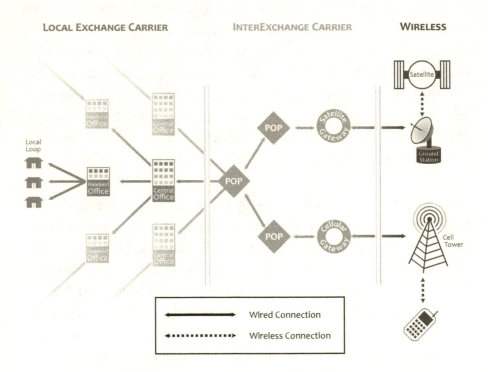

Evolution Without Darwin

Our modern communications network can be modeled at several levels. At the physical level, switches are represented as nodes and cables as links. A higher-level model equates buildings containing thousands of switches with nodes, and transmission bundles containing thousands of fiber optical cables with links. Since networks are abstract mathematical representations of what is most important to the study of a system, I use a mega-structure model here: nodes represent large telecom hotels and links represent bundles of high-speed fiber with massive transmission capacity. I am interested in the communication Black Swan events that might take out entire regions of the U.S., so a mega-structure representation is adequate (see Figure 7.2).

In some sense, the communications sector has come full circle—from digital to analog, and then back to digital. Its creators envisioned a system somewhat like today's Internet—a global broadcast network connecting everyone to everyone else. But their vision was limited by available technology going back over 200 years. Samuel Morse perfected the first commercially successful digital system called the *Telegraph*, demonstrating it in 1844 by transmitting *Morse Code*—dots and dashes equivalent to binary 1s and 0s—from Washington D.C. to Baltimore. In 1851 Western Union was formed and began, in 1861, to transmit digital messages from coast to coast, much like today's email. Thus was born the first electronic communication network for transmitting disembodied electronic messages. Technology was the limiting factor, but profitability fueled rapid advances in analog technology, obsolescing digital telephony almost immediately. Almost as soon as it was invented, an analog network replaced the first digital communication network as the standard.

Western Union enjoyed a brief monopoly of the electronic communication business until 1876, when Alexander Graham Bell successfully transmitted voice over an analog channel to Mr. Watson, his assistant. Bell filed his telephone patent only a few hours ahead of Elisha Gray of

Western Electric, a company that made the telephones and switching equipment for exchanges. Bell founded the Bell Telephone Company and quickly built the first telephone exchange network in Hartford, Connecticut, in 1877. He purchased Western Electric from Elisha Gray in 1882, and proceeded to create one of the largest of many vertically integrated monopolies of the twentieth century—the American Telephone and Telegraph Corp, AT&T. Together, Morse, Gray, and Bell created the first electronic communication system in history.

Bell Telephone linked two cities (New York and Boston) together in 1883, but it would take the company nearly another 60 years to subscribe 50% of the US population. The first mobile telephone did not appear until 1946! Compare this with the rate of adoption of the video tape recorder in the 1980s (12 years to reach 50%), and the rapid adoption of most new technologies today, such as the iPod, iPad, Internet email, and cellular handsets.

Historically and politically, it is important to note that the first cellular telephone network was built in Japan (in 1979) rather than the United States. Through most of the twentieth century, communications in the United States consisted mainly of the public switched telephone network (PSTN) owned and operated by AT&T. The slow pace of technology innovation by the AT&T monopoly eventually led to radical changes in the industry. One might be tempted to blame the break-up of AT&T on a kind of political SOC caused by stagnant leadership. Regardless of what caused the stagnation of AT&T, rapid changes in technology precipitated the Telecommunications Act of 1996, which was primarily designed to stimulate innovation and rapid adoption of new technologies. But I get ahead of myself.

Patent litigation in 1879 separated voice and data services: the U.S. Department of Justice allowed Bell Telephone to operate voice networks and Western Union to operate data networks (basically stock market quotes). The artificial separation of voice and data became a barrier to advancement of telephony until the invention of the Internet in

1969 and its commercialization in 1998. Even the *network neutrality* movement of the early twenty-first century is about content—whether voice, date, pictures, etc. should be priced separately or not. The network neutrality advocates rightly claim that all information is digital, so how can telephone and telecommunications companies charge separate rates for different encodings of ones and zeros? At the time of writing, the network neutrality advocates have won. If they eventually do not prevail, separation of content types into a multi-tier pricing strategy will have a major impact on shaping the industry.

Table 7.1. Major events in the evolution of telecommunications regulation

1837 - 1873	Telegraphy becomes the first digital communication system
1866	Western Union becomes the first telecom monopoly
1876	Bell demonstrates first operation of the telephone
1878	5,600 telephones in use
1882	109,000 telephones in use
1885	AT&T incorporates for long distance service
1894	Bell's patents expire
1898	Telecom War begins.... through 1934.
1898 - 1899	AT&T reorganizes as a patent holding company
1903	Telephone industry is dominated by independents
1907	AT&T reorganized and controlled by J. P. Morgan
1911	AT&T vertically integrated: Western Electric, Long Lines
1913	U.S. Department of Justice sues AT&T claiming violation of Sherman Antitrust Act.
1924	AT&T owns 223 of the 224 independents!
1934	Telecommunications Act of 1934
1934 – 1974	Vertical Monopoly Period
1974 - 1984	DOJ suit leads to breakup of AT&T
1996	Telecommunications Act of 1996
1996	Local exchange carriers win court battle establishing states right to set retail prices

Unregulated Beginnings

Table 7.1 lists major events in the evolution and shaping of the communications sector. As I mentioned above, the timeline contains four distinct periods: *Unregulated*, *Telecom War*, *Regulated*, and *Deregulated*. From 1877 to 1898, the industry was mainly unregulated. During this period, a large number of local companies emerged to serve local customers. This produced isolated but densely connected networks characterized by clustering around a small number of central switching offices, typically small towns and cities. Even after consolidation set in, the resulting networks were clustered and highly focused on local calls (it is worth pointing out that highly clustered networks are more resilient and less vulnerable to failures than today's national scale communication networks). Long-distance calls were virtually unheard of, and impossible except between major metropolitan areas.

The Telecom War

A 'telecom war' broke out shortly after Bell's patents expired in 1894, prompting the U.S. Department of Justice to step in and enforce the Sherman Antitrust Act of 1890 in a landmark action against AT&T in 1913. This act was designed to limit cartels and monopolies, and by 1913 AT&T had become a monopoly. AT&T dominated the industry by enforcing its equipment patents and buying out its competitors. This quickly led AT&T to monopolize the industry, eventually bringing the U.S. Department of Justice (DOJ) to file suit against the company. While the lawsuit against AT&T was very similar to the lawsuit against Microsoft in 1998-2002, the action against AT&T was much more severe. The government forced AT&T to stop buying independent telephone companies without DOJ approval, required AT&T equipment to interoperate with its competitor's equipment (the local exchange carriers, in today's language), and required AT&T to divest control of the Western Electric Manufacturing Company. The DOJ broke up the vertically integrated company, a course of action that it would take several times again in other industries.

In contrast, Microsoft was merely fined and allowed to remain intact after being found guilty of violating the 1890 act. Bill Gates, founder and CEO of Microsoft at the time of the United States v. Microsoft trial, used the 'I don't recall' defense so many times that presiding judge, Thomas P. Jackson, burst out laughing during testimony. But his verdict was not so funny. Jackson found Microsoft guilty of monopolizing the PC software industry. His remedy—breaking Microsoft into separate companies as was done to AT&T in 1984—was overturned by a higher court. Clearly, monopoly-busting isn't what it used to be!

While the action against AT&T may have seemed severe a century ago, AT&T owned 223 of the 224 independent companies within a decade of the 1913 ruling! AT&T's success illustrates one of the primary factors affecting and shaping many infrastructure systems: *increasing returns*. In economics, increasing returns is the idea that the more of a certain commodity there is, the more valuable it becomes. Increasing returns is the economic equivalent of preferential attachment described earlier. In this case, increasing returns drove AT&T toward a monopoly: the more customers connected via the AT&T network, the more valuable the network became. The more valuable it became, the more customers wanted to subscribe. This spiral ended up with AT&T in the monopoly catbird seat more than once. It also put the company in the hot seat several more times.

Increasing returns (a.k.a *preferential attachment*) accelerates the adoption of one technology and service over another largely because it standardizes the user interface, leverages the compounding network effect of being able to communicate with more people over a large network versus a small network, and motivates the owner-operator to amortize fixed costs over an ever larger customer base. It is almost a natural law that infrastructure businesses benefit from increasing returns.

In the communications business, preferential attachment works like this: as customers randomly select one of many vendors to provide telephone service, they eventually realize that more people are subscribing to one service than another. The benefits of the 'more popular' service may be intangible, but even if only a few customers decide to switch to the more popular service, this begins an avalanche of accelerated switching. Think of the vendor (competitor) as a node in a network, and think of subscriptions the links. The more heavily connected node is preferred over the less connected nodes, which accelerates linking to the heavily connected node. As more consumers subscribe to the preferred vendor node, more decide to also subscribe, which snowballs into an avalanche of connections. Thus, the popular node becomes the hub of the network.

In the end, the preferred node becomes a monopoly, as Microsoft did in the 1990s. Emergence of a monopoly has little to do with the performance of a certain company or leader, but, rather, is a fundamental property of essential infrastructure systems. When increasing returns sets in, the infrastructure company becomes the only player in the field, i.e., a monopoly. It is important to realize this because it explains why AT&T repeatedly grew into a monopoly, regardless of break-ups imposed on it by Congress and the U.S. Department of Justice.

Although the theory of preferential attachment, increasing returns, and network effects were not well understood in the 1930s, the results were the same: as a consequence of monopolies like AT&T, most customers were happy with their service, but not all. In particular, people living in rural or sparsely populated areas were without service. There, the network effect had a negative impact because it was not cost effective for the owner/operator of the telephone company to serve an isolated customer. This issue gave rise to the concept of *universal access*—the provisioning of access to all Americans regardless of where they lived.

In its wisdom, Congress bartered for universal access by granting infrastructure companies like AT&T a *natural monopoly*. The 1934 Telecommunications Act granted AT&T status as a regulated monopoly in exchange for universal access. Instead of nationalizing AT&T, Congress provided monopolistic protections for this privately owned company, on the condition that AT&T provide service to everyone, everywhere, for a flat fee. Pricing was set by amortizing connection charges over all customers. Telephone service cost the farm family located in the middle of Iowa the same amount as the city dweller located in densely populated Manhattan.

Universal access and the Telecommunications Act of 1934 put an end to the telecom war. But the bargain struck with Congress came at a price: without the incentives provided by competition, innovation slowed to a halt. On the one hand, telephone service was universally available and highly reliable. On the other, technological progress was nearly frozen. The 1950 telephone used essentially the same technology as the 1898 telephone.

Regulatory Period

The 1934 Telecommunications Act initiated the regulatory period of the communication system evolution. It provided for the regulation of telecom through the FCC (Federal Communications Commission), which answers only to Congress. It claimed the electromagnetic spectrum within the United States as public property and, as a consequence, only Congress had the right to regulate its use. A license and huge licensing fees were imposed on commercial broadcasters, telephone operators, and eventually cell phone operators. Finally, Congress required broadcasters to operate in the best interest of the public.

The 1934 Act had a huge impact on shaping the communications network of the United States. For example, the so-called 'long-lines' network established by AT&T during this period is a major component of the communications infrastructure today. The long-lines network is the backbone of the *InterExchange Carriers* (IECs, see Figure 7.2) and the protocols and standards of operation established by AT&T remain as legacy systems. This is true in the sense that the old analog protocols no longer work with the new digital protocols of the Internet, and in some cases, the protocols have to be converted in order to interoperate with newer digital protocols. Specifically, the SS (switching system) computers designed and built by AT&T/Bell Laboratories established a global standard for how telecommunications systems operate. Dial tone, touch-tone dialing, 911, and many other features introduced by the AT&T switching systems are still in use today, even if they are no longer needed!

Because AT&T was a closely regulated, vertically integrated monopoly, the system operated seamlessly from end-to-end. Equipment interoperated, networks interfaced with one another, and universal access guaranteed safe and secure operation. In many ways, the old AT&T system was more resilient and rugged than the cobbled-together networks of today. According to Richard Kuhn, "For several decades AT&T has expected its switches to experience not more than two hours of failure in 40 years, a failure rate of 5.7 x 10^{-6}."(Kuhn 1997:1) The old regulated system was extremely reliable!

Deregulated Oligopolies

The deregulated period began in 1974 and continues to this day. It took ten years for the U. S. Department of Justice to break up AT&T this time. Breakup led to the 'Baby Bells,' or LECs (*Local Exchange Carriers* in Figure 7.2)—regional telephone companies licensed to operate as monopolies within geographical areas of the United States. A total of 22 companies were granted seven operating regions, but the infrastructure remained much the same as during the regulated period. I suppose this architecture would still be used today if the Internet had not been commercialized.

Congress also sought to establish pricing, which was successfully challenged by the LECs in 1996. This ruling allowed the states to set retail prices for their citizens. Nonetheless, pricing restrictions on both the wholesaler (LEC and IEC)[1], as well as the retailer that sold telephone and Internet services to consumers, had a major impact on the performance and reliability of the network. Why build newer, faster, and more reliable networks when profitability is constrained by regulation? Once again, Congress and regulation shaped the industry, with both good and bad consequences.

The Baby Bells proved to be slow adopters of new technology and lackluster providers of better service. Telephone companies of that era operated on a 20-year maintenance and upgrade cycle, which was adequate prior to the rise of the Internet. This phase of telecom evolution may have persisted for some time if the Internet had not been commercialized in 1993-1998 by Congress and the NTIA (the National Telecommunications and Information Administration, within the Department of Commerce and created in 1978 by Executive Order 12046). Lack of motivation and imagination on the part of the Baby Bells led to another imposition by Congress.

In the late 1990's Commissioner Reed E. Hundt of the FCC worked on new legislation with Congress designed to spur innovation through competition in the lifeless communications sector. At the time they were in the midst of major upheaval, due to the rapidly evolving and growing Internet, computer, and optical communication technology. Sixty years passed before 50% of households had a telephone—Internet adoption

---

1   Local and Interexchange Carriers or 'long-haul' carriers.

reached 50% in less than a decade! But Internet speeds were too slow because twentieth century links were being used to support twenty-first century computers and communications. On February 8, 1996, President Bill Clinton signed the new Telecommunications Act into law. One of its goals was to encourage universal Internet access for everyone's home and office. Saddled with their legacy analog systems and voice-only mentality, the Baby Bells were taking too long to transition to the new digital age. This theme continues to resonate today as 'everything goes digital.' Digital convergence places even more burden on the communications infrastructure, and the Baby Bells weren't keeping pace.

The 1996 Act unbundled services—no more extra fees for services like digital data transmission (*VoIP* or voice over Internet protocol, for example). It motivated the deployment of faster networks (xDSL) and narrower ownership of Cable TV, TV, and radio stations. Most importantly, the 1996 act established *peering* as a way of life for competitors. This has led to the number one vulnerability in the communications sector: the extremely high concentration of switching equipment in one building.

Peering is the practice of sharing networks with competitors. Company A may need Company B's network to provide long distance connections for local customers. Conversely, Company B needs Company A's local connections to gain access to the 'last mile' or household/office consumer. LECs typically own and operate local exchanges, while IECs typically own and operate long lines (see Figure 7.2). In today's market, both are required; local access to get onto the long lines, and long lines to make long-distance calls.

Peering radically restructured the industry because it not only allowed, but motivated competitors to co-locate their switching equipment in close proximity to one another. The consequences were dramatic and un-anticipated: a small number—between 30 and 40 major switching facilities—emerged as preferred hubs. The law of increasing returns worked its invisible magic again, only this time the result was the creation of the number one vulnerability of the telecommunications sector: the carrier, or telecom hotel.

The telecommunications sector contains more than the wired-only network left over from the days of vertical monopolies and regulation. All communication networks depend on it. Satellite communication (with small exceptions), cellular telephony, Internet, and to a lesser degree, broadcast TV, Cable TV, and GPS navigation depend on the core capabilities of the wired network. While our wireless world appears to be free of wires, the opposite is true. Wireless networks are heavily dependent on wired networks, as shown in Figure 7.2. Wireless telephone calls, for example, are quickly routed through the wired network, using gateway switches located in telecom hotels! Therefore, a potential threat to the wired network is also a potential threat to wireless and associated networks.

Major Components of the Sector

A full discourse on the U.S. telecommunications system could easily fill an entire book, so the discussion here focuses on the top level. Figure 7.2 is a gross simplification of the communication sector as implemented in the United States. It consists of three major layers: the local exchange carriers (LECs) and their customers; the long-distance inter exchange carriers (IECs), and the various devices and services feeding into the points-of-presence (POP) gateways provided by the IECs. IECs operate long lines that connect cities and countries to one another. LECs distribute packets to local customers. The analogy with the electric power grid is obvious: long lines for transmission and shorter lines for local distribution.

Figure 7.2, reading from left-to-right, shows how a telephone call or email message makes its way from one person to another. Suppose an email sender is transmitting from one of the houses shown under the LEC column. The message travels to a *headend* switch, typically located in the neighborhood to serve up to 1,000 homes. The headend connects to a central office in the LEC, which forwards the message locally or through the long-haul IEC network. If the recipient is located within the same network, the message is routed back through tandem switches to a headend switch and then into the recipient's home. If the recipient is located far away, the message travels through a POP (Point-Of-Presence) or gateway into the IEC network.

Suppose the recipient uses a cell phone from 1,200 miles away to answer a call. The LEC must forward the message to a nearby POP switch within an IEC network, as shown in the middle column of Figure 7.2. The IEC's gateway also acts as a bridge across networks operating at different speeds and protocols (rules for exchanging messages). The sender's message may make its way across several IECs before finding a gateway that connects the sender with the receiver. Routing in this maze is an impressive technological achievement.

The nearest cellular tower transmits the 'connection signal' to a gateway within the wired IEC network when the recipient answers his or her cell phone call. A roaming cell phone registers with local towers, so the IEC and LEC switches can find the cell phone regardless of where it is. Eventually, the network makes a connection between the sender and the recipient's local tower. This all happens at nearly the speed of light, so the consumer does not notice a long delay.

The most interesting feature of Figure 7.2 is this: to work as one integrated communications system, cellular, satellite, and other means of communication depend entirely on the wired land lines. The old AT&T long-haul lines (and others) are the backbone of the national system. Cellular transmission has a range of about 3 miles, so cell phones actually connect to land lines via a nearby tower. Transcontinental cell phone calls are not possible without the long lines maintained by the wired IECs. Even satellites depend on the terrestrial wired lines. Ground stations often provide feeds to television and other broadcast media, but they need a stable and reliable wired landline network to operate. These systems are interdependent and together they form a very large and complex system.

The logical structure of Figure 7.2 shows that the telecommunications sector is a system rather than a loose collection of local components and unrelated assets. As such, this system's resiliency is dependent on the network's architecture as much as the resiliency of its individual components. For example, the highly redundant IEC layer has many POPs and gateway switches, so that the failure of one has only a minor impact on the reliability of the overall system. On the surface it appears to be a highly resilient system. But it begs the question of which components are most critical, where criticality is defined as degree of dependence of the entire system on a single component. What kind of *normal accident* can cause the entire system to collapse?

Hubs, Clusters, and Betweeners

Because of the number of redundant links in the system, communication networks are extremely impervious to single line failures. Unlike electric power grids, transmission line failures have a relatively minor impact because message packets are quickly and automatically routed to alternate lines. In fact, a protocol called the OSPF (Open Shortest Path First) algorithm constantly maintains a list of open (available) links. If one becomes overloaded or goes down, the next alternative is automatically selected. Communication networks don't fail when they become overloaded. Instead, they are removed from the list of available links in order to allow for repair or decongestion.

As far as transmission capacity is concerned, telephone and Internet traffic is relatively robust. Switching nodes are another story. If you want to do harm to the communications infrastructure, attack its hub nodes. Unfortunately, identification of the biggest hubs in the U.S.

communications network is a simple matter of googling 'telecom hotel.' Bringing down the communication network of an entire country is a matter of launching a *targeted attack.*

The simulation of attacks on random, cluster, and scale-free networks shows how vulnerable networks are to targeted attacks. I generated networks with 50 nodes and 100 links, and randomly connected node-pairs to obtain a random network. Similarly, I generated cluster networks from random networks by repeatedly rewiring links such that the *cluster coefficient* of the entire network increased. This emergent process terminated when the overall network cluster coefficient reached 50%. Finally, starting with a random network, I repeatedly rewired links chosen at random but linked by preferential attachment to a randomly chosen node, until the largest node had at least four times the average number of connections. This process produced a *scale-free network* with a relatively large hub. Recall that 'scale-free' networks are defined as *networks with a distribution of node connections that follows a power law*—that is, a network with one big hub and many nodes with only 1 or 2 connections.

In each case, an attack on a single node initiates a cascading failure that spreads to its neighbors with an infection rate of 25%—a modest rate for the spread of Internet viruses. Infected nodes are repaired in 5 time steps and, once repaired, remain immune to subsequent failure because once removed, Internet viruses typically stay removed. This simulates a susceptible-infected-recovered (SIR) epidemic, the result being that the virus spreads according to a very simple logistic growth curve. The number of nodes damaged over the life of the SIR collapse is a measure of resiliency. This number is different for random, clustered, and scale-free networks, as one would expect.

Figure 7.3 summarizes the results. Attacks on hubs are the most consequential (89% of the nodes are 'infected'), while attacks on high cluster coefficient nodes are the least consequential (a minimum of 17% for cluster attacks, and only 23% for hub attacks on cluster networks!). Clearly, attack strategy and network topology both bear on resiliency. Random and cluster networks are more resilient than scale-free networks! Self-organized criticality in this case is directly tied to hubs—and telecom hotels are clearly hubs!

A number of investigators have shown that scale-free networks are more tolerant of random attacks but are highly vulnerable to targeted attacks on the network's hub (Albert, Jeong & Barabasi 2000). But these early results did not take the spread of an epidemic into account. Clearly, attacking the hub is most consequential because hub removal also removes the maximum number of links. But a network with a large hub is also more vulnerable because an epidemic eventually reaches a hub, where it is magnified. The larger the hub, the lower the network's resilience.

It has also been shown that scale-free networks are more likely to sustain persistent epidemics, which is an important result for the communications industry because computer viruses are difficult to entirely eliminate. In fact, Wang and others confirmed this finding in an elegant and convincing network model that relates topology to persistence (Wang, Chakrabarti, Wang & Faloutsos 2003). According to the Wang et al. model, network connectivity, as measured by *spectral radius*, relates to persistence as follows: the SIR contagion is persistent if the product of infectiousness times spectral radius exceeds the rate of repair. If this condition is true, the communication network never recovers! Scale-free networks have the highest spectral radius of any network, so they are the most likely to be persistently disabled by an attack on their hub.

The opposite is true for cluster networks: they are tolerant of random and targeted attacks because they are devoid of hubs. Cluster networks are collections of nodes with relatively many links among themselves and with a few links connecting clusters. Thus, contagion is typically localized; that is, contained within a cluster. Since fewer links connect clusters to other clusters, transmission of a virus to adjacent clusters is minimized. Cluster networks are therefore more resilient against random, cluster, and hub attacks than the other two kinds of networks simulated (see Figure 7.3).

Random and cluster networks were probably the norm in the early days of the communications system, when it consisted of highly dense local distribution networks interconnected by a few long-distance transmission lines. Communication networks probably evolved from random, to clustered, and finally scale-free topologies as they matured and were shaped by the socio-political forces described above.

Additional simulations confirm that hubs are more critical than all other nodes *except* for high betweeness nodes (results not shown here). Recall that 'betweeners' are nodes with the largest number of paths passing through them from/to all other nodes. Betweeners are often also the hubs. Random and cluster networks are more resilient, but still suffer relatively high consequences when their hubs and betweener nodes are attacked. Scale-free networks suffer even more consequences because their hubs are larger. In many cases, the hub is also the betweener. This is why consequences are similar. Communication networks are more vulnerable to hub and betweener attacks than any other type of network because they contain relatively large hubs. It is easy to see the hubs in the communication network from a visual inspection of Figure 7.1. Hubs are the major source of SOC in the communications infrastructure.

Figure 7.3. Simulation results for cascading communication networks.

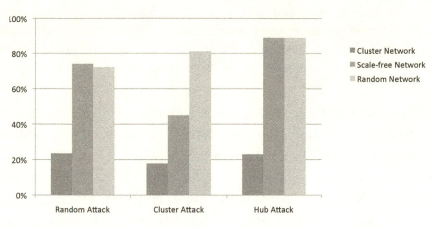

Consequences v. Attack Type v. Network Structure

■ Cluster Network
■ Scale-free Network
■ Random Network

Self-inflicted Criticality

Has the telecommunications sector reached a state of resilience, or the opposite? After 100 years of evolution, do we have a more, or less, secure and resilient communication network? I claim that the sector has become less resilient and is therefore more likely to fail than ever before. The argument for loss of resiliency is based on two main observations: firstly, after one hundred years of economic, regulatory, and technical pressure to be efficient, profitable, and politically acceptable to Congress, culminating with the 1996 Telecommunications Act, the communication system has evolved into a weakened state. Secondly, like many massively large and complex infrastructure networks with a long history of evolution, the telecom industry has reached a state of self-organized criticality (SOC) for many of the same reasons described in previous chapters. My claim is supported by the existence of critical nodes called *telecom hotels*. NSTAC identified telecom hotels as the number one vulnerability in the communications sector in 2003 and recommended their protection as the top priority of homeland security. The NSTAC report defines a telecom hotel as,

Conditioned floor space owned and operated by a commercial Landlord for the purpose of hosting multiple service providers. Tenants may include the incumbent local exchange carriers (ILEC), competitive local exchange carriers (CLEC), Internet service providers (ISP), competitive access providers (CAP), Web hosting operations, or any other non-telecommunications commercial enterprises in need of floor space to support their electronic equipment. (NSTAC 2003)

For example, One Wilshire Boulevard, a 30-story, 656,000 square foot building near downtown Los Angeles, is the single most important point of connectivity in the Western United States. It houses over 240 telecommunications companies, provides up to 75 watts of power per square foot, and connects the United States with most of Asia. Backup power of eight megawatts and 11,000 gallons of diesel provide resilience in case of power outages. If it fails, connectivity to Asia fails.

Details of telecom hotels are openly advertised over the Web—for example on www.carrierhotels.com—along with security and resiliency provisions. Thus they are not only critical, but out in the open. Vulnerability is perhaps low because of their exceptional security, nonetheless, the high concentration of LEC and IEC switching equipment placed in one location raises concern. As the first line of the NSTAC report says, "The Administration has expressed concern that the concentration of multiple entities' telecommunications assets in specific locations may have implications for the security and reliability of the telecommunications infrastructure" (NSTAC 2003).

Law of Unintended Consequences

What is happening to the communications industry fits Bak's punctuated reality model almost perfectly. Self-organized criticality is a byproduct of optimization and efficiency. After a decade of de-regulation, the national telecommunications sector has been optimized for high performance and low cost. As a result, vulnerability to massive cascade failure has increased. Damage to a small number of highly connected telecom hotels could result in major telecommunication outages.

From the beginning of modern communications history, Congress has tried to fight increasing returns, but now we know better— increasing returns (preferential attachment) is a natural byproduct of infrastructure deployment. By attempting to legislate away a natural side effect of economics, Congress has inadvertently created a bigger problem. Perhaps the reason Microsoft was not broken up in the way that AT&T was is the realization that dividing Microsoft into 'Baby Bills' would be a futile attempt to prevent increasing returns.

While the conclusion drawn here has not been verified in practice, because we have no historical precedent for such a calamity, similar SOC existed in the electric power grid prior to the 2003 blackout. Clearly, the power grid is different than the telecommunications network, but it suffers from similar regulatory forces. This suggests the possibility of a Black Swan event in the communications sector rivaling the 2003 blackout. Whether or not telecom hotels turn out to be the Achilles heel of the sector remains to be seen, but if the power law means anything, the next big one is inevitable.

On a longer time scale, the communications sector may evolve even closer to its self-organized criticality, unless policies are changed. Congressional regulation and economic forces have shaped the sector, so they can also be employed to re-shape it. If Congress were to enact legislation that dissipates telecom hotels, increases redundancy of telecom hotels, and reduces the number of betweener switches, the sector's criticality would decrease. Under this scenario, the communication network architecture would revert to a clustered or random network, with the consequence that normal accidents would be absorbed before they wipe out entire swaths of the network.

8

INTERNET STORMS

Spread of Code Red cyber exploit released into the wild July 13-19, 2001[1]. Code Red spread throughout most of the industrialized world within days.

Code Red Goes To Washington

Like a thief in the night, Code Red entered through an open door: port 80, the same door used by Microsoft Internet Explorer to access web pages from anywhere in the world. But it wasn't looking for personal information—at least not yet. Named Code Red by eEye Digital Security employees Marc Maiffret and Ryan Permeh (who were drinking Code Red Mountain Dew when they first detected it), the software *worm* sent copies of itself to thousands of randomly generated Internet addresses, blazing a Lévy Flight through the Internet. It jumped from computer to computer using the oldest cyber trick in the book—the *buffer overflow exploit*. Posing as data, buffer overflow allows malicious code into your computer so that a hacker can take control. In this case, the impostor 'data' would initiate a *distributed denial of service* attack (DDOS) on the White House of the United States. DDOS uses unsuspecting computers from all over the Internet to flood a victim computer with millions of data requests that can never be filled. Rather than a break-in, DDOS blocks anyone from accessing the victim.

---

1   http://www.caida.org

Silently and secretly Code Red spread to other computers for 20 days, lying dormant inside Microsoft's Internet Information Server until a certain time and date, when all copies simultaneously attacked www. Whitehouse.gov. The impact of this malicious program was multiplied by infecting not just one, but nearly 400,000 unsuspecting '*zombie*' computers before lashing out. Like a torrent of water released by a collapsing dam, millions of messages rushed toward the servers located in Washington DC. Only this torrent wasn't water. It was pure software— ones and zeros—that leapt from machine to machine much like the Lévy Flight of a modern Black Plague, flooding the www.Whitehouse.gov servers with meaningless data.

Code Red recruited thousands of innocent and unsuspecting computers along its swath. The unsuspecting participants, called *zombies*, became unwilling co-conspirators in a crime of national scope. Zombie computers form a kind of network called a *botnet* for the purpose of massively attacking a single target. Botnet zombies derive their power from numbers: at a pre-specified date and time the entire botnet of zombies flood the victim computer with half-completed requests for attention. But once they get the victim's attention, they ignore it!

Imagine going to a convention of 400,000 people and extending your hand to shake all 400,000 hands at once. Further imagine that the reciprocal handshake isn't reciprocated. There you stand, with your hand out, and nobody notices! Besides being socially awkward, the snubbing of your handshake confounds you and everyone around you. It would be overwhelming and confusing.

DDOS attacks are incomplete handshakes initiated by all zombies at once, hence the designation 'distributed.' The attacking computer (zombie, in this case) places a request for attention from the victim computer. The victim puts the request in a list and returns an acknowledgement to the zombie. The zombie is supposed to reply, but instead it ignores the acknowledgement. This is repeated thousands of times, once for each attacking zombie. Meanwhile, the list grows inside the target computer's memory until it eventually overflows and crashes the computer. DDOS attacks can be effective without ever cracking passwords or penetrating the victim's computer. All a DDOS attacker has to do is flood the victim's computer with thousands of incomplete handshakes.

Fortunately, the Code Red perpetrator, like many human visitors to the nation's capital, was naïve when it came to understanding Washington, DC. It was designed to use the numerical Internet protocol address (IP) corresponding to www.Whitehouse.gov instead of the symbolic www.Whitehouse.gov universal locator name itself. The government system administrators easily thwarted the attack by changing the www.Whitehouse.gov entry in the *Domain Name Server* (DNS) —the Internet telephone book—thereby directing the attack away from the actual server. Replacing the DNS entry for translating the IP address to the symbolic address foiled the DDOS. Similar techniques are used today to foil other DDOS attacks and Microsoft has patched its Internet server software so that this particular type of attack no longer works.

Internet storms—*exploits*, in the language of hackers—whip up network tsunamis. They give little advance warning and last only a few minutes, hours, or days as the wave of malicious software sweeps through millions of computers. And then, almost as quickly, they are gone. The elapsed time between subsequent DDOS attacks obeys a power law, as shown in Figure 8.1. 50% of the DDOS exploits over the past decade occurred within 120 days of one another. DDOS attacks are swift and widespread, but, so far, haven't lasted very long. Typical exploits obey Lévy Flight paths in both time and space.

Figure 8.1. Exceedence probability for elapsed time (in days) between DDOS exploits over the past decade. While the data are sparse and noisy, elapsed time obeys a power law as expected in the Casinos of Extremistan.

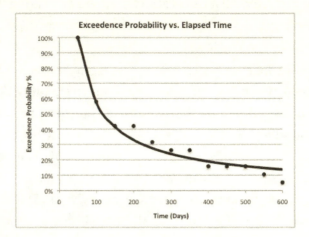

Black Hats

Black Hats are malicious hackers—people who break into networks for the purpose of doing harm. They use a variety of tools and techniques to perpetrate cyber attacks known as *exploits*. *Script Kiddies* are amateurs, but Black Hats are serious criminals. They are also very clever, often bordering on genius. Perhaps this is one reason they are drawn to cyber crime—to commit a serious cyber crime you have to be seriously clever. In some cases Black Hats establish their reputation through crime, but earn their fortunes through honest security work at reputable Internet companies. When this happens, Black Hats become White Hats, as illustrated by some of the following examples.

As I mentioned, DDOS attacks like Code Red are the oldest of all known cyber exploits. Robert Tappan Morris first demonstrated the basic technique when he was a student at Cornell University in 1988. At the time, his father, Robert Morris, was a National Security Agency scientist working on cyber security! The Morris Worm was the first computer worm set free in the *wild*, as hackers say, and the first to get out of control. Morris claims he was trying to see how large the Internet was by tracking where his worm went. Unfortunately, the Morris Worm rendered more than 6,000 machines unusable.

Pioneer Morris invented the first *worm*—a malicious program that travels on its own. Viruses have been around longer, but they require human intervention because viruses travel with humans. For example, a virus might jump from one computer to another via a shared disk drive or other storage device that is moved from one computer to another by a user. A worm, on the other hand, spreads clandestinely through the Internet, via email attachments, web pages, etc. Morris was also the first person prosecuted under the 1986 Computer Fraud and Abuse Act. He was convicted and sentenced to three years' probation, required to perform 400 hours of community service, and fined $10,000.

But his story didn't end there. Like many hackers, Morris went on to become one of the foremost computer network researchers in the country. He co-founded and sold a company named Viaweb to Yahoo for $48 million in 1995. Yahoo renamed it Yahoo Store. In 1999, he earned a PhD at Harvard and today he is a tenured professor of Computer Science at the MIT Computer Science and Artificial Intelligence Laboratory, where he researches network architectures.[2] I guess crime pays, or maybe Morris was right—there is a future in hacking. His friend and co-entrepreneur partner Paul Graham says, "Robert is never wrong."[3]

---

2   http://www.itsecurity.com

3   http://en.wikipedia.org/wiki/Robert_Tappan_Morris

Morris avoided serving time, but sixteen-year old Jonathan James achieved a small amount of fame as the first juvenile to serve prison time for hacking. He targeted high-profile organizations like NASA and the Department of Defense. According to the Department of Justice, James cracked into NASA computer systems and downloaded the International Space Station's control software worth $1.7 million. NASA was forced to shut down its computer systems at a cost of $41,000. When caught, James claimed the exploit helped him study C programming—and observed that the NASA code was "crappy" and hardly worth $1.7 million. He was banned from recreational computer use and eventually served six months in prison for violation of parole. James' ambition after getting out of jail was to start a computer security company and get rich the old-fashioned way—by earning it.

Adrian Lamo, 'the homeless hacker,' cracked computer systems at The New York Times, Yahoo, Bank of America, Citigroup, and Microsoft. He earned the 'homeless' tag because he used free computers at places like Kinko's, coffee shops, and libraries. Lamo would find flaws in his victim's information technology security, exploit them, and then tell the companies about their vulnerabilities. For example, he broke into the New York Times internal network to look at personal information, such as social security numbers. By doing so, he may have pioneered another racket because now, a decade later, cyber extortion is big business. Modern Black Hats extort World Wide Web companies by promising to *not* attack their sites in exchange for money.

Lamo was eventually caught and was ordered to pay approximately $65,000 in restitution, and was sentenced to six months of home confinement, plus two years of probation. After his probation expired on January 16, 2007, Lamo began working as an award-winning journalist and public speaker. In 2009, according to his online bio, he was working for a threat analysis company in Sacramento, California.

Perhaps the best-known Black Hat is Kevin Mitnick, the self-proclaimed 'hacker poster boy.' The Department of Justice described him as "the most wanted computer criminal in United States history."[4] Mitnick may have benefitted from overly exuberant publicity in two movies, *Freedom Downtime* and *Takedown*. Like traditional wise guy gangsters, Mitnick began his career as a small-time thief, hacking the Los Angeles bus-ticketing system for free rides. He then dabbled in *phone phreaking*, manipulating the telephone system in order to make free long-distance calls. His online bio says, "[My] hobby as an adolescent consisted of studying methods, tactics, and strategies used to circumvent computer security."[5]

Mitnick was eventually caught and convicted of breaking into the Digital Equipment Corporation's computer network and stealing software. He served five years, of which about eight months was spent in solitary confinement. He became a computer security consultant, author and speaker, appearing on 60 Minutes, The Learning Channel, Court TV, Good Morning America, CNN, and National Public Radio. He is the author of two books: *The Art of Deception* (2002) and *The Art of Intrusion* (2005).

Dark Dante, whose real name is Kevin Poulsen, worked for SRI International by day and hacked by night. His most famous hack won him a brand new Porsche. Each week the Los Angeles radio station KIIS-FM ran a 'Win a Porsche by Friday' contest. The station awarded a $50,000 Porsche 944 to the 102nd caller following a pre-announced sequence of songs. When the song sequence triggered the calling frenzy, Poulsen took over the station's phone system, blocked out all other callers, made call number 102, and drove away with the prize!

Poulson worked as a White Hat for the government but was drawn to the dark side as his skill increased and his fame spread. In another telephone exploit, Dark Dante crashed the phone lines of the TV show

---

4   http://www.itsecurity.com/features/top-10-famous-hackers-042407/

5   http://mitnicksecurity.com/media/Kevin_Mitnick_Bio_BW.pdf

Unsolved Mysteries after his photo appeared on the show. More seriously, he hacked into an FBI database containing wiretap information, perhaps to punish the FBI. Law enforcement dubbed him "the Hannibal Lecter of computer crime."[6] When he was captured, the authorities found so many hacking devices they said Poulsen put James Bond to shame. After a seventeen-month pursuit, Poulsen was captured in a supermarket and served 51 months in jail and was ordered to pay $56,000 in restitution.

Like so many other Black Hats, Poulsen got off easy, leveraged his expertise to get a lucrative job after serving time, and achieved more celebrity than notoriety. Poulsen became a senior editor for Wired News, specializing in cyber crimes and the people who do them. His most prominent article exposed 744 sex offenders who exploited MySpace profiles. It seems that our society rewards genius even when it leads to a life of crime. Who says crime doesn't pay?

Soft War

Not all cyber exploits are performed by free-lance Black and White Hats. Governments are getting into the business from the offensive side. In May 2007, President Bush authorized the National Security Agency (NSA) to launch cyber attacks on the cellular phones and computers operated by insurgents in Iraq to coordinate roadside bombings. The insurgents were recording the strikes and then posting the videos on the Internet to recruit followers (Harris 2009:1). More interesting, however, was the way the American forces used cyber exploits to deceive the insurgents. By hacking into their network and sending messages to the unwitting insurgents, the NSA operators led insurgents into a trap set by waiting U.S. soldiers. Cyber exploits in the virtual world can have serious consequences in the real world.

---

6   http://library.thinkquest.org/04oct/00460/poulsen.html

These military hacks were partly responsible for the success of the 2007 surge in Iraq. They allowed military planners to pinpoint and kill the most influential leaders with minimal collateral damage. But using this technology on the battlefield is more significant than Black Hat hacking because it introduces a new weapon into modern warfare. In fact, the war in Iraq is as much about psyops (psychological operations) and cyber countermeasures as it is about bombs and IEDs.

Strategies like President Bush's authorization of *information warfare* against Iraqi insurgents can also backfire and get out of control much as Morris's Worm did. For example, military planners rejected a proposed cyber attack on Iraq's banking system because those networks were connected to banks in France. An attack of global proportions might take down the entire banking system! A global cyber contagion may be easier to start than to stop.

General Petraeus—the commander of coalition forces in Iraq from January 26, 2007, to September 16, 2008—believes in cyber warfare. Testifying before Congress in September 2007, he said, "This war is not only being fought on the ground in Iraq but also in cyberspace"(Petraeus 2007:6). The job of the Defense Department's Cyber Command is to defend military computer networks as well as go on the offense, attacking the enemy's network infrastructure. But the United States is not the only country to go on the cyber offensive. In addition to traditional hot wars, nations are now ramping up to fight *soft wars*.

In August 2008, a dispute between the Russian Federation and neighboring Georgia over a region called South Ossetia (located on the Russian-Georgian border) initiated a vigorous and effective cyber exploit designed to augment physical conflict between the two countries' military forces. The strife began when Georgian forces launched a surprise attack against South Ossetia separatist forces on August 7. On August 8, Russia responded by sending troops into Georgian territory, which Georgian authorities viewed as an act of aggression. Cyber attacks were launched against a large number of Georgian governmental websites prior to the physical attacks. The exploits primarily defaced public websites and denied service to a number of other sites. Attacks lasted from two to six hours and damages were relatively low, but in some cases, web sites were disabled for days following the disruptive attacks.

At first, it appeared that Russian forces were behind the cyber attacks. Later, it was discovered that the attacks were carried out by Black Hats, possibly located in Russia but not necessarily supported by the Russian military. Research suggests that either way, the Russian government did nothing to stop the attacks coming from Russia (NATO 2008). It is impossible to trace the DOS attacks to their origin, because the botnet used zombies. Apparently, the aim of the attackers was to block governmental operations and discredit the Georgian government. As a result, Georgia's government was unable to get their point of view out to the rest of the world.

Another cyber conundrum of military and strategic significance is the Stuxnet attack. At the time of writing, it remains a mystery. Apparently, Stuxnet was designed to attack a specific industrial control system manufactured by the Siemens Corporation. Even more specifically, it went after the centrifuge control systems used by Iran to convert Uranium ore into yellowcake, the fuel used in nuclear power systems. Although Iran denies that any damage was done, my conjecture is that Stuxnet most likely did work, damaging the centrifuges and slowing down the production of yellowcake (Broad, Markoff & Sanger 2011). Stuxnet was so sophisticated that cyber expert Eric Byres suggested that a state supported organization rather than an individual must have constructed it. Stuxnet is believed to be the first cyber weapon to target a specific country. Stewart Baker, who once worked for the super-secret NSA said, "It's the first time we've actually seen a weapon created by a state to achieve a goal that you would otherwise have used multiple cruise missiles to achieve" (Bahari, Bergman & Barry 2010).

These examples illustrate how assaults on the information infrastructure of companies and countries are tools for both good and evil. Criminals use exploits for fame, financial gain, or mischief. Countries use exploits for political and psychological offense, and in the case of Stuxnet, for physical damage. Some experts claim that terrorist groups such as Al-Qaeda purposely do not try to destroy the Internet because they benefit from it! Like many technical innovations in history, the Internet can benefit as well as harm humanity.

In any case, offensive and defensive exploits are not unlike hurricanes—virtual storms blowing through cyberspace. Internet storms may be caused by humans instead of Mother Nature, but they also take on characteristics of natural catastrophes. They are unpredictable, extreme, and rare. But do they qualify as normal accidents in Extremistan? What is the nature of Internet storms?

Internet Storms

In previous chapters I described the principles of self-organized criticality and its relationship to cascade failures that sweep through complex systems like a virulent contagion. These principles apply also to the Internet, but with a few subtle differences. Knowing the general principles of punctuated reality gives us a tool for understanding what is happening to the Internet and how it might be improved. A short review of these principles is in order before I tell a darker story in the next section.

Worms and viruses are a lot like diseases. They spread via Lévy Flight patterns from source to destination computers. Unfortunately, they are more virulent than natural diseases because they recruit zombies along their Lévy Walk, which multiplies their impact. The hop distance along the Internet obeys a power law because worms forage as they 'worm their way' across cyberspace. Infected nodes cannot be re-infected so the worm must jump to a greener pasture, but a computer worm can take a giant stride without weakening.

Viruses, on the other hand, are transmitted by human contact. Moving a storage device from one computer to another or opening an email attachment that is actually a malicious program may facilitate contamination. Some viruses are accidentally copied from a web site into your local computer by clicking on a web page. These malicious programs can masquerade as a valid application program or utility (*Trojan Horse*), document (embedded Visual Basic in a spreadsheet), or *key logger* (a program that records your keystrokes and sends them to a hacker). Trojan horse programs can steal your information, erase your disk, and spread to other computers. An embedded Visual Basic program inside of a spreadsheet can erase data, and key loggers can capture and transmit your name, password, and credit card number to a Black Hat. This is why they are called malware and malicious!

Viruses are declining in popularity because they require the active participation of the consumer, but worms are increasing in popularity for the reverse reason—they travel and activate on their own. Fundamentally, worms hop from one computer to another by way of *ports* and communication links. Every computer has thousands of ports; electronic doors through which email, web pages, music, video, and worms pass. Port 80, for example, is the default port for every browser—Internet Explorer, Safari, FireFox, and Chrome. Port 443 is a secure browser port, and dozens of other ports exist for dozens of other media types: music, video, and database access.

For example, SQLSlammer—a single-packet-sized worm that infected Microsoft SQL Server software and crashed the Bank of America's ATM network as well as the Davis-Besse nuclear power plant safety monitoring software in 2002—spread via port 1434. *Sockets des Troie* was one of the earliest *Trojan Horse* exploits created in 1998, to attack via port 1. *Sockets des Troie* is French for 'Trojan Sockets.' Linux/Adore is a spyware exploit aimed at Linux users. It enters through port 65535 and, like all *spyware*, extracts personal information such as names, passwords, and social security numbers from unsuspecting users.

Open and unmonitored ports are obvious vulnerabilities, so every computer also ships from the factory with *firewall* software—guardians designed to protect ports. Firewalls can be configured to block ports by shutting them completely off or filtering them by selectively blocking messages from certain web sites. For example, the SQLSlammer was stopped by blocking port 1434 until Microsoft issued a patch to its database software. Everyone should set the firewall on their computer to block and filter messages. Otherwise, your computer is like a house with open doors.

Servers—computers owned and operated by an Internet Service Provider or e-commerce site such as Amazon.com—are also protected by *Intrusion Detection Systems* (IDS). These are specially programmed computers that perform more sophisticated blocking, filtering, and pattern matching. A good IDS can identify and block a DDOS attack, spam site (pushing uninvited advertisements), and other worm propagating streams. IDS vendors wage a never-ending arms race against virus, worm, and spam proliferators. Worms get through if the IDS is too lenient, but too many nuisance false positives occur if it is too strict. Worse yet, the utility of your system, web site, or email may be too restricted by an IDS. Computer security often comes down to making a trade-off between security and usability.

Unfortunately, even the best defense mechanism and most diligent systems administrators are unable to prevent all break-ins. No system is 100% secure. Damages, in terms of number of infected victims and financial losses due to scams and cyber extortion, obey a power law. So far, the power law exponent for financial loss means that the lop-sided exceedence probability steeply declines, placing cyber scams and extortion hacks in the low-risk category. In 2009, the FBI estimated the average online scam cost consumers an average of approximately

$500. While losses of $500 should not be ignored, they hardly qualify as catastrophic events.

Phishing is a popular cyber exploit, because they are easy to carry out—and people are incredibly gullible! Here is how phishing works. An email is sent to millions of consumers via a botnet, such as the hypothetical one below:

"Dear Sirs,

The Bank of Trans Atlantis has discovered $10,000,000 in an account under your name. We want to update our records and send this to you by overnight express mail, but first we need to verify your name, social security number, address, and bank account number. Please go to www.badguys.com and register immediately, so we can send your certified cashier's check for $10,000,000 by overnight express courier."

Of course the victim has to be highly gullible to fall for this unsolicited email. But if 40 million copies spam the globe, eventually a few hundred thousand end up in the inbox of an unfortunate and gullible victim. What harm can come by replying to this inviting invitation to get rich? Well, by filling out the form at www.badguys.com, the victim could loose his or her bank account or, worse yet, personal identity. This happens everyday, producing an average return of $500 per victim. Spamming costs practically nothing, so the return on investment for the criminal is significant. And in some countries, this sort of exploit is legal!

Phishing is just a means to an end; one of many tools used by cyber criminals. In 2010, the number one fraud involved impersonation of the FBI itself! The Internet Crime Report 2010, available from the National White Collar Crime Center, says FBI scams accounted for one in six complaints made by consumers; 12% of complaints were due to non-delivery of promised merchandise; 9.8% for fraudulent advanced fee solicitation; 8.2% for identity theft; 7.3% due to overpayment fraud; and 6.2% due to spam.[7] Fraudulent credit card, auction, and computer damage scams accounted for the remaining online crime.

Unlike electric power grids, infectiousness of cyber viruses and worms does not increase as an attack spreads, and unlike biological diseases that die out with length of step in the Lévy Flight, worm infectiousness does not decrease with distance. As far as we know, infectiousness remains constant at approximately 10% for Internet viruses. That is, 10% of attacked computers succumb to the worm and suffer some kind of damage. 10% is an average over all types of exploits—think of 90% as the Internet's herd immunity! Worse yet, *hubs* and *betweeners* in the routing system of the Internet act as force multipliers. Because it has extremely large hubs, the Internet likely has a high *spectral radius*, meaning that it is especially vulnerable to hub and betweener attacks. Link and node percolation makes the Internet distribution system behave like a poorly managed forest, always near its critical point.

The characteristics of the Internet—its architecture, if you will—is ideal for exploitation. Infectiousness, gullibility of consumers, low-cost access to millions of users, and poorly implemented defenses attract cyber criminals like lint on a dark suit. Hackers want a piece of the $3,600 billion per year U.S. e-commerce, and so far, getting it is relatively easy. Hacking has become big business.

Beware of the Botherders

Botnets are growing in popularity, size, and significance in the wired world of e-commerce. Control of a botnet is under a *botherder*, someone or some organization pulling the strings from behind the curtain and at a distance. Botnets automatically recruit zombies to do the botherder's

---

7   http://www.nw3c.com/

dirty work while the botherder is thousands of miles away. Attacks on the U.S. can originate from anywhere, both inside and outside the country. This poses a serious problem for law enforcement.

In 2010, the largest known botnet was *Rustock*, a gang of 1.6 – 2.4 million unsuspecting zombie computers recruited to spam the world for profit.[8] Rustock is one of many botnets run by organized crime in Russia. Wikipedia claims that the Russian Business Network (RBN), operating out of St. Petersburg, Russia, is the botherder.[9] According to Wikipedia, "It has been alleged that the RBN's leader and creator, a 24-year-old known as Flyman, is the nephew of a powerful and well-connected Russian politician."[4] It is also likely that RBN herds a number of botnets.

Botherders control botnets through a variety of communication links that essentially form a network on top of the Internet. These *overnets*, as they are called, use popular protocols like IRC—*Internet Relay Chat*— to link together massive numbers of systems. IRC melds together a coordinated army of marching zombies. Ironically (and coincidentally), overnets evolved from *peer-to-peer* (P2P) networks originally built by music and movie pirates for media sharing. P2P overnets are cheap, powerful, and resilient—just the opposite of most critical infrastructure systems!

Typical botnets control zombies (also known as *drones*) and easily spew out 250 spams per minute, night and day. Multiply this by millions of zombies and you have a problem. During the month of August 2010, one in every 300 emails contained a virus, spam, or worm, one in 500 contained a phishing exploit, and over 4,000 web sites were being blocked by a botnet every day. In 2009, Zeus was the largest known botnet in the U.S. with 3.6 million zombies in tow. The Zeus Trojan steals user names, passwords, account numbers and credit card numbers using key logger technology.

---

8   http://www.MessageLabs.com, www.Honeynet.org

9   http://en.wikipedia.org/wiki/Russian_Business_Network

Due to their immense size and capacity to spam the globe, botnets pose a serious threat to the very existence of the Internet. For example, if the 2 million zombies in the Rustock botnet were to simultaneously emit high bandwidth spams, the load on the Internet could cripple or halt traffic all over the world. The botherder could extort companies, regions, and even nations that depend on Internet traffic for everyday business, commerce, and military coordination.

Estonia's experience in 2007 illustrates the power of botnets. Estonian web sites were hammered for days after the government ordered the relocation of the Soviet-era war monument 'Bronze Soldier' from the center of Tallinn to its suburbs. Ethnic Russians rioted for two days, over 1,300 people were arrested, 100 were injured, and one person was killed in the rioting. DDOS attacks on government web sites were so severe that many public and private agencies were forced to discontinue service to and from Estonia for several days. Estonia is the most wired country in Europe, and perhaps the world (Davis 2007). Ninety percent of all bank transactions and all voting is done over the Internet. It is the home of Skype. So pulling its Internet plug is a major event.

Some of the attacks were traced back to Russia, but as we know, it is difficult to distinguish botherder from zombie. Eventually a 20-year old Estonian student named Dmitri Galushkevich was arrested and charged with launching the DDOS from his PC. Interestingly, the cyber attack on Estonia did not qualify as a military attack under the NATO definition. If it had, and if Russia or some other country had launched the attacks, other NATO countries would have been obliged to come to Estonia's rescue. Currently, NATO is not sure what to make of botherding—is it an act of war?

An even darker specter faces the virtual world. Currently we do not know what might emerge over time from botnets. After all, they are artificial societies composed of automatons much like the termites described in previous chapters. Botnet zombies tend to die if they stop communicating for a long time. They also tend to spread exponentially if given enough bandwidth and victims. So they have a life of their own—again, like the termites described earlier. Termites may seem dumb, but they are smart enough to build surprising structures. They perform Lévy Flights, consolidate wood chips into piles, and evolve their relationships from random to scale-free topologies. What if they were semi-intelligent zombies set free to exploit the entire Internet? Worse yet, what if they were capable of learning and adapting?

Figure 8.2. Ron Minnich successfully booted over 1 million Linux Kernels on 4,480 computers at Sandia National Labs to study the behavior of botnets. [http://www.socallinuxexpo.org/scale8x/blog/interview-ron-minnich-coreboot.html]

Emergent Misbehavior

According to Ron Minnich of the U.S. Department of Energy's Sandia National Laboratories, "Life on the Internet has started to really suck."[10] Minnich and colleague Don Rudish aren't complaining. Rather, they are intrigued. The Sandia scientists were the first to build a network testbed containing over one million virtual computers to study the behavior of malicious botnets as they roam around and self-organize. It takes a big testbed to simulate even a small portion of the Internet.

---

10 http://lwn.net/Articles/377391/

According to Minnich, botnets are difficult to analyze because they are spread all over the world. For example, Rustock herds over 1.6 million zombies, and other larger botnets may exist without our knowledge. Minnich and Rudish argued that a controlled laboratory experiment like theirs is the only way to study the evolution of botnets. Might the observed results teach us how to cope with cyber criminals?

Minnich has spent the past twenty years writing Linux kernel code, the deepest inner core of the Unix-like operating system that powers many supercomputers. He invented CoreBoot, basic input/output software that enables Linux to run on Intel processors. In an interview on July 28, 2009, Minnich explained his motivation,

> The achievement [of the network of a million nodes] will allow cyber security researchers to more effectively observe behavior found in malicious botnets, or networks of infected machines that can operate on the scale of a million nodes.[11]

Why simulation? The problem is, botnets are complex networks. We don't have analytical tools that can predict what will happen if botnets evolve and expand without bound. The only way to find out, according to Minnich, is to build a botnet and study it. Let it run for a few million simulated time periods and see what emerges. Nobody has studied a million zombies under the laboratory magnifying glass. Minnich started out small. He unleashed the Morris Worm on an in-house network of 50,000 nodes. The first challenge was how to observe this vast number of zombies. For example, sampling millions of nodes once per second can quickly produce more data points than the observer can analyze. And then there are the zombie behaviors. Even simple zombies become complex when millions of them cooperate.

Minnich and Rudish performed an experiment that produced results similar to the simulated results obtained from Bruce Malamud's forest

---

11 https://share.sandia.gov/news

fire simulation and Per Bak's sand pile! The states of botnet nodes were displayed on a checkerboard grid. Inactive nodes were left blank. Active nodes were colored red. Curiously, as the botnet grew from 1,000 to 10,000 nodes, its behavior became completely unpredictable. The researchers observed "avalanches" occurring with "some frequency" (Mayo, Minnich, Rudish & Armstrong 2009:15)! Occasionally the entire grid turned red. Could this be percolation and self-organized criticality all over again?

Minnich's experiment is fascinating, but it raises more questions than it answers. The truth is, we don't know what botnets are capable of doing or becoming. Emergent behavior is complex and unpredictable. Botnet societies live in a casino of Extremistan of their own making. But one thing is inevitable: the rare, unpredictable, and extreme catastrophe is waiting for us at the end of a power law. What might it look like? Is it possible that a sufficiently large botnet would be able to bring down the entire Internet?

Figure 8.2. The hierarchical DNS structure of the Internet.

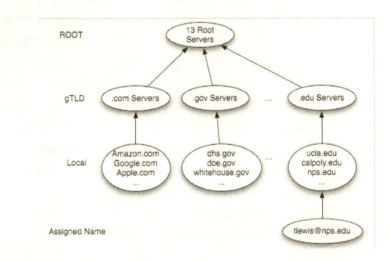

Bringing Down The House

A major invasion of the Internet by organized zombies could, potentially and theoretically, bring down the entire Internet. In fact, there have been at least two known attempts to collapse the Internet. On October 2002, a DDOS attack on the DNS *root servers* lasting twenty minutes disrupted nine of the thirteen servers. Again, on February 2007, two of the thirteen root servers were blocked by a DDOS exploit. Root servers are the grand masters of the DNS 'phone book' containing the names and numbers of everyone in the world registered to use the Internet. Communication across the Internet would be seriously hampered without a DNS server to translate names into numbers.

The World Wide Web, email, and just about everything we use the Internet for are held together by a DNS logical structure superimposed on routers, servers, and switching hardware embedded in the telecommunications infrastructure of the world. Figure 8.2 shows a simplified diagram of this logical structure. Every user has a numerical IP address that looks like 120.22.141.04, corresponding to a device such as a laptop, web server, or iPad. This IP number is difficult to remember, so it is assigned a name and server such as tlewis@nps.edu, www.Amazon.com, or www.Whitehouse.gov. Each time the name is used to send a message across the Internet it must be converted into its corresponding IP number. This is the job of a DNS server.

The thirteen root DNS servers are the ultimate authority for storing, updating, and translating names into numbers for the entire global Internet. These *critical nodes* are updated several times per day to keep the 'phone book' current. But they have helpers in the form of global top-level domain name servers (gTLDs) and local servers—DNS servers located at various levels of the hierarchy in Figure 8.2. A request for name translation works its way up this hierarchy from bottom to top, until resolved. Clearly, destruction or blocking of these DNS servers would have a major disruptive effect on the operation of the entire system.

But DDOS attacks on the root servers target only those thirteen servers and, therefore, such an exploit is unlikely to bring down the entire Internet. Of course blocking access to the root servers impacts performance, but it doesn't disconnect everyone from everyone else. Besides, the DNS hierarchy is reconstructed several times a day. Targeted DDOS attacks are like improvised explosive devices in a global war: hurtful, but not devastating. Thus far, DDOS and other small-scale attacks have been too inconsequential to be considered catastrophic.

To bring the house down, a more ambitious exploit would have to separate the *Giant Strongly Connected Component* (GSCC) core of the Internet into isolated components that cannot communicate with one another. A strongly connected component is a network containing nodes linked to each other through a labyrinth of connections so that any node can communicate with any other node through a sequence of hops from node to node. If a link is broken such that the strongly connected component separates into parts, it would mean that one group of nodes is isolated from other groups. In this case, the nodes in the isolated group become an island, unable to communicate with nodes in other components.

Broder and colleagues (Broder et al. 2000) mapped out the Internet in 1999 and discovered that most of the Internet is concentrated in a single GSCC core. At the time there were approximately 200 million servers throughout the world. They found that 56 million were in the core (27%). Additionally, all but 8% formed a 'bow tie' shaped Internet where 21% of the servers were predominantly input nodes and another 21% were predominantly output nodes. A remaining 21% were in 'tendrils,' or tributaries, loosely connected to the bow tie. The GSCC is a very big target for hackers.

Perhaps the GSCC is too big to fail. Single-target or focused attacks like the ones described thus far may be too weak to seriously damage the Internet's GSCC. But it appears that botnets can diminish the GSCC by separating it into isolated 'islands.' if enough nodes are blocked. The idea is simple but ambitious: disrupt enough servers in the GSCC to separate it into disjointed components and perhaps as many as 30% of the 600 million Internet servers (according to a 2010 estimate) would be disrupted. If cyber criminals could achieve this major feat, they could bring the house down, but a botnet such as Rustock would have to be one hundred times bigger than it is today. Is such a fantastic attack feasible?

Figure 8.3. Reduction in the size of the Internet by 'islanding.' As infectiousness goes up, reduction in the size of the largest connected component of the Internet goes up dramatically. Eventually, the Internet comes apart.

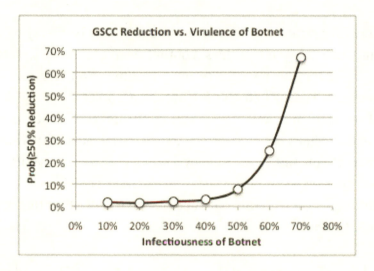

De-percolating the Net

The GSCC of the Internet was created by *percolation*, much like the percolation processes of the forest fire simulation. Percolation in a network like the Internet is the process of linking servers together. The Internet emerged by a process of link percolation combined with preferential attachment. This combination led to a scale-free GSCC. Therefore a process of de-percolation (the opposite of percolation) could dismantle the Internet. Removal or blocking of links would eventually create isolated islands. The question is, how much de-percolation does it take to destroy the GSCC?

My research (Lewis 2009) showed that scale-free networks separate into islands with probability of 25% when 40% of its links are randomly deleted. This is actually a very large number of links when applied to the global Internet. Indeed, it is highly unlikely that any botnet in existence now or in the future would be able to disrupt 40% of the communication links of the Internet. Link de-percolation is a bad strategy for botherders.

An alternative strategy is to attack enough nodes (servers) to cause islanding. How many nodes does a botnet need to remove to separate the GSCC? Figure 8.3 shows the results of a simulation I ran to address this question. I simulated the release of a botnet from the largest betweener node in a scale-free model of the Internet, containing 200 nodes and 232 links. My miniature network contained hubs because the real Internet contains hubs. Nobody knows the spectral radius of the Internet, but my network has a high spectral radius of 3.5 (versus 2.3 for a random equivalent). Recall that hubs are force multipliers that amplify the spread of the botnet.

I varied the infectiousness of the exploit from 10% to 70% and spread zombies throughout the network as far as infectiousness would allow. Infected nodes were treated as if they were removed so they could not communicate with other nodes. They blocked further spreading of botnets. Eventually these contaminated nodes separate the network into smaller, isolated parts. The consequences of the botnet attack followed a power law as expected, but instead of counting the number of infected nodes, this simulation found the largest isolated component remaining after each attack; that is, consequence is defined in terms of the reduction in size of GSCC. Furthermore, Figure 8.3 plots the probability of 50% or more reduction in size of the GSCC versus infectiousness of the botnet. As expected, the likelihood that the network is separated into islands containing 50% or more of all nodes increases with increasing infectiousness. However, the probability of separating the Internet into two large and isolated islands is relatively low for viruses that are successful less than 65% of the time (see Figure 8.3).

Figure 8.3 shows how difficult it is to dramatically diminish the GSCC by 50% or more, even by a large-scale botnet. The botnet's virulence must exceed 65% before it is likely to greatly diminish the GSCC. Catastrophic islanding is not only rare, it is difficult to achieve without an extremely infectious botnet. However, it is still possible for a *highly* infectious botnet to separate the Internet into non-communicating islands! Furthermore, the separation likelihood rises *exponentially* with infectiousness beyond 65%. Such a rare and extreme event places the Internet in the Casinos of Extremistan.

Taming Cyberspace

Eventually the Internet will have to be tamed, but Internet culture was originally defined, designed, implemented, and run by anarchists and remains perhaps the largest experiment in anarchy in human history! It has no hierarchical authority controlling it and virtually no laws regulating it. Rather, it is 'run' by volunteers who enforce a strict *open source* code of behavior. For example, every aspect of the Internet—how it operates and how standards are set—is documented online in a series of RFCs (Request For Comments) and BCPs (Best Common Practices). It is bigger than any government, has no army or navy, and has very few rules governing its behavior. It is the largest unregulated infrastructure ever devised.

On the one hand, the lack of centralized command and control is perhaps one reason botnets exist and botherders thrive. On the other hand, the Internet is perhaps the most successful enterprise ever conceived, which raises interesting questions about self-organization in other segments of modern society. But that is the subject of another book!

The Internet appears to have evolved in much the same way as other, more highly regulated and controlled systems have evolved. In contrast to the electric power grid, the Internet is more efficient as a distribution network, but much less secure. Compared to the Interstate highway system, the Internet is chaotic and unruly, but reaches deeper and farther than any road network in history. While the Internet depends on the communications sector, it is quickly reshaping and dominating it, while operating as an unregulated overnet. Politicians don't quite know what to think of it!

Punctuated reality is the most likely future of the Internet. At some point, the online world will reach a critical point because of social, political, and economic self-organized criticality. Whether this is due to an unexpected botnet storm, a national security catastrophe, or some unimaginable calamity, the inevitable build up of self-organized criticality will eventually motivate politicians to tame the Internet. And, that means regulation—the worst thing that can happen to Internet culture in the opinion of Internet anarchists. What lies beyond this tipping point?

I can only speculate on how regulation might shape the Internet, but eventually regulation will come. Here are some possible scenarios to consider. The first restriction most likely will come in the form of consumer protection. The exponential rise in theft of personal information, hacked credit card names and numbers, and stolen online financial information is already causing concern in government. Several remedies—ranging from severe penalties imposed on e-commerce companies that loose personal identity information, to consumer protection mechanisms such as key lock card systems to control access—are likely topics of regulatory reform over then next decade or so. The Environmental Protection Agency already imposes severe fines on energy companies responsible for accidental oil leaks and other environmental accidents. The EPA and local public health organizations exercise control over drinking water purity, pollution emissions, and so forth. It is therefore an easy step from environmental and consumer protection regulation, to regulation of e-commerce. For example, large e-commerce sites may be subject to penalties if say 10,000 or more personal identity files are hacked. This would motivate e-commerce sites to spend more on security.

Beyond insider attacks, password hacks are the most prevalent form of security breach. People don't change passwords often enough and when they do, they use simple names and dates. Pet name lists are the first to be checked by *war dialers* (a war dialer is software that dials every phone number in the book, or every possible Internet Protocol number, looking for unprotected computers). Hackers are fully capable of testing all 600,000 words in the English language, using war-dialing techniques, until they stumble onto valid passwords. The best protection against key loggers, war-dialers, and clever code breakers is to change passwords frequently.

One solution is to require *temporal passwords*. Temporal passwords change every 60 seconds, foiling the war-dialer and code breaker. For example, some organizations distribute credit-card-sized random number generators to employees. To login, authorized employees augmented their individual passwords with a random number produced by their individual random number generator card. The augmented password is decoded by the server, which also runs a synchronized random number generator. Because the number changes every 60 seconds, it becomes very difficult for the hacker to steal the temporal number and use it later. By the time the hacker tries, the password has changed! This technology can easily be miniaturized and incorporated into a credit card.

A third line of defense would require deployment of standardized cyber security countermeasures. It is clear that deploying even the most rudimentary security measures greatly diminishes successful exploits. Encrypting password files, properly setting up firewalls and intrusion detection systems, and performing regular security audits have been shown to be very effective deterrents. Updating operating system patches, performing background checks on key information technology employees, and auditing network traffic are other obvious precautions that may eventually be required by law.

Nobody likes regulation, but all other critical infrastructure systems in modern societies are regulated to some extent. Some, like the energy and power sector, are thoroughly regulated. So far, only the Internet has escaped this inevitability. Unfortunately the day is rapidly approaching when regulation may be the only remedy. Unless of course, the industry voluntarily establishes stronger practices than those that exist today.

9

INVENTION, INNOVATION, AND INSPIRATION

| Vladimir Zworykin | Philo Farnsworth | David Sarnoff |

The Inventors and innovators of modern television: Russian-American Vladimir Kozmich Zworykin (1888 –1982), Philo Taylor Farnsworth (1906 – 1971), and Russian-American David Sarnoff (1891 – 1971)

The Inventor

Philo T. Farnsworth was just a teenaged Idaho farm boy in the 1920s when the Delco electric power generator on his father's farm stopped and the lights went out. The family had just moved to Rigby, Idaho, from Beaver, Utah, to set up farming, and Philo's father knew nothing about electricity—an exotic subject in the early 1900s. To everyone's surprise, the young farm boy effortlessly repaired the device and turned the lights back on. You see, Philo's hobby and passion was building electric motors in his parent's attic. He once repaired a discarded electric motor and used it to power his mother's washing machine. Fixing the Delco generator was easy.

By the 1920s, Thomas Edison had already perfected the electric light bulb and motion pictures, and Guglielmo Marconi's (1874–1937) radio was transmitting information over long distances without wires. Henry Ford was selling more cars than imaginable only a decade earlier, and fortunes were being made in railroads, steel, banking, and retail. It was the Roaring Twenties and anything was possible.

But nobody had been able to transmit motion pictures over long distances by radio waves. This was the young farm boy's life-long goal. Philo's unusual intellect and curiosity drove him to do what others could not: invent television. Like a tsunami that comes out of nowhere, television was a normal accident—rare, but not impossible. And like the flood that wiped out New Orleans, television caused waves of *chaotic adaptation*, an expected consequence of Black Swan events, as described by Bak's theory of punctuated reality (see chapter 1).

Farnsworth was not alone in his pursuit. Electronics fascinated and attracted many inventors and entrepreneurs of that period, much in the same way that the Internet fascinated and attracted software inventors and entrepreneurs of the 1990s. Edison's motion picture invention captured images and played them back through a motion picture projector, and Marconi's radio transmitted sound into people's homes. It was only natural to take the next step by combining these two technologies into one, and voila! You have television.

Farnsworth reasoned that it should be possible to capture and send motion pictures through the air just like sound waves are captured and transmitted by radio waves. How might this be done? This question stumped Philo for months until he was inspired by a rather convoluted idea that sounds fantastic even today. Here is how it works: capture reflected light from an image, break it into horizontal strips, encode each strip as a radio wave, transmit the wave to a receiver where the signal is converted back into an image strip, and then reconstruct the entire image by stacking the strips on top of one another—and do it fast enough to trick the human eye into seeing the original image! Simple in concept, but not easy to do in practice.

Eventually Farnsworth devised a way to capture reflected light from an image in a jar, convert it into a radio wave, and then magnetically deflect each line one at a time at the other end so that the scanned lines together formed a moving picture. Today we know this as *progressive scanning*. For example, a high-definition television screen capable of 1080p draws

1080 lines from top to bottom of the screen quickly, so the human eye sees only a solid image. It is called 'progressive scanning'; because the image is composed of successive lines stacked one adjacent to the other until 1080 lines have been drawn.

Philo was inspired by the fantastic technological feats of Edison, Ford, and Tesla. But he had a problem: when his father died, Philo, then sixteen years old, became the sole provider for his two brothers, two sisters, and mother. His life seemed to be over before it began. Nonetheless, he overcame many hardships along the way, making slow and bursty progress. He was accepted into the U.S. Naval Academy, but turned down a free education when he learned that the U.S. government would own his intellectual property! Instead, Philo attended Brigham Young University and taught himself how vacuum tubes and cathode ray tubes worked, while supporting his family and pursuing his goal of combining motion pictures with radio.

Philo shortened his name to Phil and continued pursuing his passion, sharing his ideas with family friend Cliff Gardner, who wisely advised him to patent his devices. This would become critical in later years when Phil's inventions were challenged by Radio Corporation of America (RCA) and David Sarnoff. Cliff brought other assets to the party. His sister Elma 'Pem' Gardner Farnsworth (1908–2006) and Phil fell in love. They married when Phil was nineteen and Pem was seventeen. The teenagers got married and moved to Hollywood, California, to continue working on his invention.

The living room of their Hollywood home became Phil's lab. His brother-in-law Cliff became the chief glass blower, a skill needed to make tubes called *image dissectors*. Image dissectors were devices that used the photoelectric properties of cesium to dissect an image line-by-line prior to being converted into radio waves and transmitted. Cliff's ability with glass was also needed to build the first TV tube—it was an inverted chemistry flask!

Soon the first primitive TV was ready. The first demonstration was underwhelming, as Farnsworth's invention produced a horizontal line on a glowing background! But the demonstration was adequate to establish his claim on TV. Phil filed his first fully electronic TV patent on January 7, 1927—considered the official date of the invention of television. On September 3, 1928, The San Francisco Chronicle described Farnsworth's television as "smudges and blurs" that needed more work, but perfecting the device was merely a "matter of engineering."[1] The teenager from Idaho had achieved his goal. Invention, however, was the easy part.

By 1927, Farnsworth's partners had invested $60,000 more than planned. They wanted to cash in, but Farnsworth wanted to keep going. Unfortunately, he didn't have enough money, and without money to further develop his inventions, Farnsworth's television would remain an idea rather than a product. Phil learned the hard way that invention is distinctly different from innovation. Innovation takes an idea to the next level; it perfects, promotes, and spreads ideas, products, and services to a wide audience of consumers. What Farnsworth needed more than a good idea was an innovator.

The Innovator

A poor fifteen-year old Jewish immigrant from Minsk, Russia, named David Sarnoff moved to New York City with his family in 1900, where he supported his father, mother, three brothers and a sister by selling newspapers. With little education, money, or future prospects—but a lot of motivation—Sarnoff started moving up the ladder of success. He worked as an office boy for Commercial Cable Company and eventually Marconi Telegraph Company of America. Marconi sold wireless communication devices to shipping companies who used them to track their cargo at sea.

---

1   http://www.vigyanprasar.gov.in/scientists/PTFarnsworth.htm

In thirteen years, Sarnoff moved up the corporate ladder to become commercial manager of the company, having learned the wireless business from the ground up. But hard work wasn't what distinguished Sarnoff from all the other workers at Marconi. Sarnoff was inspired. Like so many innovators before and after him, Sarnoff was a genius when it came to reality distortion. He knew that, for many people, perception is reality, especially when it comes to innovation. During the Titanic sinking of 1912, Sarnoff claimed to be the lone wireless operator tirelessly tending his radio in support of the rescue operation. According to Wikipedia, "Sarnoff falsely advanced himself as the sole hero who stayed by his telegraph key for three days to receive information on the Titanic's survivors ... some modern media historians question whether Sarnoff was at the telegraph key at all."[2]

Apple Computer's visionary CEO Steve Jobs would be accused of similar promotional antics seventy years later. And like Sarnoff, Jobs was no technical genius. Neither innovator was an inventor, but both men understood the potential of their respective products and ideas. Sarnoff understood the potential of radio and television before most others. Earlier he had advised Marconi to build and sell a *radio music box* to amateur radio enthusiasts. Jobs had advised his supervisors at Hewlett-Packard to build personal computers. Alas, both men had their ideas firmly rejected by their employers.

Eventually, Marconi Telegraph Company of America was purchased and rolled into RCA, Radio Corporation of America. RCA bought its first radio station in New York and launched NBC (National Broadcasting Corporation) and ABC (American Broadcasting Corporation). Sarnoff was put in charge of RCA and NBC, and the rest is history.

Very early on, Sarnoff recognized radio as a stepping-stone to television—the big prize. But, he needed devices that worked. So, in 1928 he hired Westinghouse engineer Vladimir Zworykin to build, buy, or otherwise

2   http://en.wikipedia.org/wiki/David_Sarnoff

obtain the technology necessary to combine motion pictures with radio waves. Zworykin was also a Russian-American with big ideas of his own. He patented devices similar to Farnsworth's but also did pioneering work leading to the electron microscope and infrared imaging.

As RCA's vice president and general manager, Sarnoff soon became interested in Phil Farnsworth's pioneering work. It may be more accurate to say that Sarnoff became interested in Phil Farnsworth's patents, because RCA used radio patents, including Marconi's patents, as a weapon of business war. Every company that manufactured radios paid royalties to RCA, but these patents were due to expire. Without fresh patents, RCA would go the way of Studebaker and Hudson automobiles. Sarnoff had no choice but to build a patent portfolio in the 'next big thing.'

Sarnoff sent Zworykin to see Farnsworth in San Francisco under the pretext of licensing Farnsworth's patents. Zworykin was so impressed he told Sarnoff to look for himself. When Sarnoff later saw Farnsworth's television camera and receiver, he offered to buy Farnsworth's entire company, Television Labs, for $100,000. Farnsworth declined, even though the Great Depression was in full swing and $100,000 was easily a fortune. Farnsworth's refusal set off a competition that would not end well for television's inventor. Decades later Farnsworth would be forced to accept $3 million for his company and its patents—a disappointing outcome for the Farnsworth family.

Invention was one thing, innovation another. In fact it is rare to find both inventive genius and innovative genius in the same person.[3] Invention creates an idea, product, or service, while innovation introduces it to the world. Farnsworth created a product, but he was unable to introduce it to the world. Unfortunately, Farnsworth never seemed to realize this.

---

3   http://www.merriam-webster.com/dictionary defines 'invention' as "a product of the imagi-nation", and 'innovation' as "the introduction of something new."

Over time, Sarnoff and RCA would win the innovation race. According to Hal Landen's account on VideoUniversity.com:

> The RCA legal guns were quite experienced in these kinds of battles. They attacked the Farnsworth patents in the U.S. Patent Office. Phil's attorney was also an engineer and asserted that Farnsworth had developed his original idea at the age of 14. And to prove it, they located Phil's old science teacher who came to Washington and sketched the idea Phil had drawn on the blackboard back in his school days.

The U.S. Patent Office decided in favor of Farnsworth, but RCA adopted a common 'David-and-Goliath' tactic. They pressed on with appeals that taxed Farnsworth's bank account, hoping to win the war by attrition. Goliath RCA continued its legal attack for years, but without success. After Sarnoff had spent $10 million and Farnsworth's company had spent $1 million, the RCA lawyers decided to offer a cross-licensing deal to Farnsworth in 1938. Farnsworth accepted and purchased an 80-acre farm in Maine with the $3 million he received as part of the deal. The most profound invention in media history was sold to the broadcast innovator for a paltry sum.

Hal Landen recounts the early impact TV had on the world:

> In April of 1939, Franklin D. Roosevelt became the first president of the United States to appear on television. Even though the demand for television sets was skyrocketing, the [Farnsworth] company was unable to get back on its feet. In 1949 it was sold to International Telephone & Telegraph. Phil stayed with ITT in Fort Wayne until 1967. Then he retired and moved back to Salt Lake City. As he saw what television had become he wondered if all his work had been worth it. Then in 1969 he and Pem watched a man walk on the moon and he knew his work had been worthwhile. Philo Farnsworth was named one of TIME Magazine's 100 Greatest Scientists and Thinkers of the 20th Century. Philo T. Farnsworth died in 1971.[4]

---

4   http://www.videouniversity.com/articles/the-birth-of-television

The Stigmergy of Invention-Innovation

Zworykin is sometimes called the father of modern television because he applied for a patent on the electron scanning tube—a primitive TV camera called an *iconoscope*—in 1923. Farnsworth was the first to successfully demonstrate the transmission of television signals on September 7, 1927. Another inventor of the time was John Logie Baird, a Scottish engineer and entrepreneur who demonstrated a mechanical television on March 25, 1925. These inventors stood on the shoulders of others too numerous to include here. Sooner or later, someone would have invented television. But in this case it would take the innovator David Sarnoff to make it happen sooner.

Farnsworth, Zworykin, and Baird were creative inventors, but Sarnoff was the innovator. Without Sarnoff, Farnsworth may have never received credit for inventing television. Whether or not you agree with his tactics, it is clear that Sarnoff brought the inventions of others to market; that is, he played a critical role in spreading TV to the world. This is the key difference between invention and innovation. One cannot succeed without the other. They are different sides of the creative process.

Farnsworth's invention and Sarnoff's innovative ability to commercialize television illustrate the important roles of each. Invention often languishes without innovation, and the reverse. This raises several important questions regarding the inventive and innovative processes. In the remainder of this chapter, I explore the concept of invention as a *normal accident*. Do inventions occur rarely and dramatically like avalanches in Bak's Sand Pile? If so, does invention obey a power law?

Similarly, is innovation a normal accident? I claim that innovation is simply a chaotic adaptation spreading through society as it reacts and adapts to the shock created by an invention. One can argue that atomic bomb, television, and Internet are normal accidents, each of which caused chaotic adaptations in its wake. Invention is the rare event, while innovation is a series of adaptations that may spread throughout society for decades. Atomic power, television, and Internet have all produced waves of innovation, but they are all based on a single invention. If my theory is true, invention and innovation illustrate punctuated reality once again.

An important facet of the invent-innovate cycle relates to *stigmergy*—a term coined by French zoologist Pierre-Paul Grasse in 1959 (Theraulaz & Bonabeau 1999). It is derived from two Greek words: *stigma* (mark) plus *ergon* (work), meaning 'mark+work,' or 'stimulated work.' Work is stimulated by some environmental feature, which leads to a modification in the environment, which leads to more stimulus, etc. Grasse illustrated this feedback mechanism using termites![5]

I use the term stigmergy to describe the product of individuals who work independently but are stimulated by the work they and others do. That is, I hypothesize that the invent-innovate cycle works much like the stigmergy stimulus-response flocking behavior observed in herd animals. Invention stimulates innovation, which leads to more invention, and so forth, in a never-ending cycle.

This is an intriguing and unorthodox idea—invention as stimulus and innovation as response. After each cycle, the stimulus-response pattern repeats. And as the pattern repeats, society progresses forward like termite nests emerging from chunks of pheromone soaked dirt. If my theory is right, power laws should describe invention and innovation. Does invention and innovation fly through time like a Lévy flight and produce unexpected outliers like we find in the Casinos of Extremistan?

---

5   OK, so I stole the idea.

Table 9.1. Breakthrough inventions and innovations related to the Internet seem to follow a Lévy flight. DeltaT is the elapsed time between events, in years.

Date	ΔT	Event
1958	0	Eisenhower administration creates ARPA: Advanced Research Projects Agency of the US Department of Defense.
1969	11	ARPA creates first 'Internet': Arpanet goes online in December.
1971	2	Ray Tomlinson invents e-mail.
1973	2	Vint Cerf and Robert Kahn invent Transmission Control Protocol/Internet Protocol (TCP/IP).
1983	10	Jon Postel and Paul Mockapetris invent the Internet's Domain Name System (DNS).
1988	5	Robert Morris invents first worm that shuts down about 10% of the world's Internet servers.
1989	1	Tim Berners-Lee of CERN (European Laboratory for Particle Physics) invents HTML and the World Wide Web.
1993	4	Marc Andreeson and Eric Bina invent the first graphical browser, Mosaic.
1998	5	Internet is commercialized by U.S. Department of Commerce.
1999	1	Shawn Fanning invents Napster for music sharing; Social networking site MySpace is launched.
2001	2	Jimmy Donal 'Jimbo' Wales invents Wikipedia.
2005	4	Chad Hurley, Steve Chen, and Jawed Karim create YouTube, signaling the beginning of 'Internet TV.'
2007	2	Activision Blizzard's online virtual reality *World of Warcraft*, surpasses 9 million subscribers.
2010	3	First commercially successful tablet computer, the Apple iPad, launched in April 2010, selling 3 million units in 80 days.

Figure 9.1. Frequency plot of elapsed time between major inventions and innovations leading up to the Internet shows that they obey a power law. Data obtained from Table 9.1.

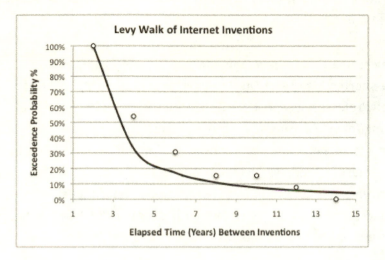

Patterns of Inventiveness

The problem of measuring the impact of invention and innovation on society is epistemologically insurmountable. How can we determine the impact of electric power, television, computers, and the Internet on society? For example, the U.S. Government spent $200 million inventing and developing the Internet, but what has been its impact? Two hundred billion dollars? Two hundred trillion? It is impossible to calculate. Instead, I analyzed the pattern of invention and innovation in time and asked—do inventions and innovations walk a Lévy walk through time? Do inventions qualify as normal accidents? Using a timeline of inventions and innovations in the field of electrical power over a period of 185 years from 1800 to 1984, I obtained a good fit to a power law with exponent of 1.6, the 'magic number' obtained earlier for Lévy Flights.[6] That is, the distribution of elapsed time between major events leading up to modern electrical power systems obeys a power

---

6   http://inventors.about.com/od/timelines/a/electricity_timeline_2.htm

law akin to the power law characteristic of Lévy Flights. Invention and innovation is bursty, therefore they behave like normal accidents—at least in time.

But electrical power development is only one example. Consider the much shorter history of the Internet. Starting with a glimmer in the eye of Professor Joseph Carl Robnett Licklider (1915–1990) of MIT working for ARPA (the Advanced Research Projects Agency), right up to the recent launch of the innovative Apple Computer iPad in April 2010, Internet progress has been punctuated by bursts of innovation and invention followed by relatively long uneventful periods. The data in Table 9.1 also fits a power law with exponent of 1.6—an exponent that matches the Lévy flights described in chapter five!

Table 9.1 contains a list of major inventions and innovations leading up to today's Internet. I chose the entries in Table 9.1 because they qualify as Black Swans in my theory of 'invention as normal accident.' While many inventions and innovations contributed to the ubiquity of today's Internet, these were my picks because of their profound effect on the Internet. The plot of Figure 9.1 shows a rough match between the raw data and a power law, but the fit is good considering the small sample size. Whether inventions are recorded over a period of two hundred years or a few decades, they appear to obey a Lévy flight power law!

Normal accident theory and punctuated reality theory apply to other creative endeavors, too. For example, the consequences of hit movies (measured in gross revenues) obey a power law with exponent of 1.6 (see Table 9.2). The long tail of movie hits is even more pronounced for elapsed time between hits; its exponent is 3.3, suggesting an extremely short time lapses between hits. Apparently, hit movies 'accidentally' happen in spurts, separated by as much as six years. The average separation in time between box office hits is only nine months! It is of course possible to hypothesize that the annual Academy Awards have something to do with the short elapsed time between hits.

Table 9.2. The top ten highest grossing movies in the US, in adjusted dollars.[7]

Rank	Title	Adjusted Gross	Year
1	Gone with the Wind	$1,606,254,800	1939
2	Star Wars	$1,416,050,800	1977
3	The Sound of Music	$1,132,202,200	1965
4	E.T.: The Extra-Terrestrial	$1,127,742,000	1982
5	The Ten Commandments	$1,041,450,000	1956
6	Titanic	$1,020,349,800	1997
7	Jaws	$1,018,226,600	1975
8	Doctor Zhivago	$986,876,900	1965
9	The Exorcist	$879,020,900	1973
10	Snow White and the Seven Dwarfs	$866,550,000	1937

Invention, innovation, and its underlying inspiration qualify as normal accidents in the Casinos of Extremistan. They are simple and yet complex systems supporting events that appear to be random, but are actually rather predictable. Indeed, the exponent 1.6 commonly appears in these power laws, which means there is a 50% chance of a major invention or innovation occurring every $2^{1/1.6} = 18$ months. This estimate conforms to Moore's Law, which says that the number of transistors inscribed on a computer chip doubles about every eighteen months. Does complexity theory explain Moore's Law? No, but this result begs the big question of this chapter, 'what causes one bright idea, invention, or innovation to rise above all others to become a significant advancement for society?' Why do most innovations fail, and a few succeed?

---

7   http://boxofficemojo.com/alltime/adjusted.htm

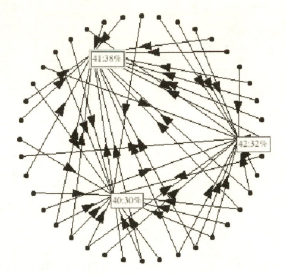

Foraging and Flocking in Social Networks

Humans have an uncanny ability to create new ideas, products, and services, so ideation is not such a big deal. It is perhaps naïve to assume everyone can create something new, but there are so many humans trying that it is safe to assume that new ideas, products, and services are constantly and randomly being generated throughout the world. Like foraging and flocking animals, ideas are taking Lévy flights every day. So, why do some ideas catch on while others die off? Why did Farnsworth invent television instead of Zworykin or Baird? Why do some inventors succeed while others of equal creativity and ability fail?

The answer isn't blowing in the wind. It is quite simple: humans prefer winners. Humans flock around winners at the expense of lesser ideas, products, and services. In more formal terms, new ideas, products, and services rise to the top through a kind of *preferential attachment*, which crowds out second-place. Recall that preferential attachment is the network equivalent of increasing returns whereby highly attractive ideas, products, and services gain more market share simply because they have more market share! This vicious cycle propels obscure, but slightly more attractive products, to dominance. The more market share Microsoft Windows has, the more it gains; the more popular Apple Computer's iPhone is, the more popular it becomes. The more money a hit movie makes, the bigger its audiences, which translates into even more ticket sales. How is this mechanism at work in the spread of novel ideas?

Consider a social network as a vector for spreading products, ideas, or services through a society. Nodes of the social network are divided into two classes, *competitors* and *consumers*. Competitors make and sell products, ideas, or services to consumers. In my network model of an economy (shown in Figure 9.2), consumption is represented by a link from a consumer to a competitor. The more links a competitor has, the more market share it has, which is a measure of success. In fact, market share can easily be calculated as the percentage of links pointing to a competitor node.

Products, ideas, and services—let's refer to them simply as *products* for brevity—are generally divided into *innovations* and *imitations*. An *innovation* is the first in its category, while an *imitation* is a variation on the innovation. For example, the first TV, VCR, telephone, and personal computer to achieve widespread adoption were innovations, while enhanced and improved TV, digital video recorder, and personal computer were imitations. Business people often debate the merits of being an innovator versus an imitator. This question is explored here using complexity theory and simple social network analysis.

Whether an idea spreads by innovation or imitation, we refer to the process whereby it is adopted as *diffusion*. Adoption is a consumer's decision to make use of a new product, idea, or service, based on information provided to the consumer through various marketing mechanisms. For example, word-of-mouth diffusion occurs when people talk to one another about a product, and media diffusion occurs through advertising on a web site or television screen. Diffusion is modeled as an insertion of a link between a consumer node and a competitor node. Further, *rapid adoption* occurs when links are added quickly, relative to the number of competitors.

Product adoption by various methods of diffusion is essentially an *emergent process*. Recall that various forms of emergence reshape networks by rewiring them. Emergence can transform a random network into a scale-free network with a hub, such as a congested electric power grid with betweener nodes, or a social network with a dominant leader. In this case, diffusion based on simple measures of product acceptance, such as *popularity*, transforms a random network into a scale-free social network with a dominant competitor as the hub. Consumers may use other measures of product acceptance to select a competitor, too. But in general, consumers evaluate products on the basis of a *value proposition* such as price, quality, availability, or peer pressure. Value proposition is a general measure used by consumers to discriminate among products, so I will use it here also.

Innovation is essentially a diffusion process. Sarnoff and Jobs were extremely successful innovators because the ideas and products they advocated rapidly diffused throughout society. Large-scale adoption of television was Sarnoff's achievement. Large-scale adoption of the graphical user interface, personal music player, and tablet computer are Jobs' major achievements. In both cases, their innovations were responsible for widespread diffusion of ideas (graphical user interface) and products (iPods, iPads, TVs).

How this mechanism works is of keen interest to businesses because it can mean the difference between success and failure. I will examine three broad cases. First, I model a single-product market and show that it is easy for a monopoly to form. Then I model a multi-product market and show that oligopolies tend to form, rather than a monopoly. This surprising result is perhaps due to choice and high demand for goods and services in a 'rich society.' Finally, I explore the impact of market speed on market dominance. Markets are considered 'fast' if demand outstrips supply. As it turns out, different strategies apply to fast and slow markets.

Innovation and Diffusion

Successful diffusion often leads to a monopoly. A competitor achieves a *monopoly* when it has an overwhelmingly large market share. In the social network model of a market, the more consumer links that point to a competitor, the more market share that competitor has and, therefore, the more dominant is the competitor. If the network contains one large competitor hub, it is a scale-free social network. Therefore, in this context, a *scale-free* social network is essentially a monopoly network because the number of links equates with market share. A *duopoly* network has two highly connected competitor nodes and an *oligopoly* network has three or more competitor nodes whose market share total is dominant. What emergent properties of such a social network lead to monopoly, duopoly, or oligopoly? Is it inevitable that small competitors always die out?

Of course, it is not necessary to use network science to model product diffusion. In fact, the earliest models of diffusion were based on mathematical *epidemiology*. Even today, the terms 'viral marketing' and 'going viral' are used to describe the use of epidemic modeling to describe the diffusion of an innovation. The early equations describing diffusion of an innovation or imitation were identical to the equations describing the spread of an infectious disease. The more infectious the product is, the faster its diffusion. In terms of product marketing, the number of infected consumers is a measure of *market penetration* or *market share*, instead of infection density. *Adoption rate* is used instead of infection rate to describe the speed with which an innovation spreads.

Frank Bass was the first to apply an epidemic model to explain product diffusion (Bass 1969). His equation produced adoption/diffusion curves identical to the S-shaped logistic curves of contagions. Figure 9.3 shows some well-known adoption curves for common products, and sure enough, they are S-shaped just like curves describing the spread of SARS or H1N1! Ideas, products, services, and diseases are alike in this respect. This is the prevailing 'traditional' model of diffusion.

One interesting inference from Figure 9.3 is the observation that the length of time to reach 50% of consumers has declined by a factor of ten or more over the past 100 years. Diffusion rates increase with an increase in communication and transportation technology. Television and the Internet have greatly sped up the diffusion process. In a way, the Internet is a disease vector! Thus, modern Internet technology has introduced another factor in market diffusion: speed. Social networks are becoming major force multipliers that greatly accelerate the spread of new products. Speed is another factor that cannot be overlooked when modeling markets.

Bass's traditional diffusion model assumes homogeneous mixing of the market population and ignores the topology and modern speed of social networks. It therefore does not explain all forms of social network diffusion. Specifically, it does not explain the emergence of one or more market leaders in markets involving multiple products, nor does it explain strategies that work in fast markets. The resurgence of Apple Computer in hi-tech markets is an example of competition in multi-product markets, and the dethroning of the Sony Walkman with the introduction of Apple's iPod, iPhone, and iPad illustrates the importance of speed.

Figure 9.3. Diffusion of new innovations through society: market penetration as fraction of the total population that adopted the product since its invention. Smooth S-shaped logistics curves are fit to data points shown as special symbols.

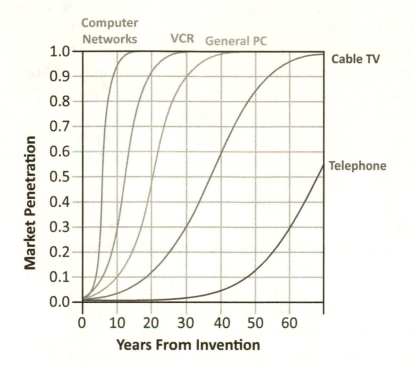

Monopoly Networks

How does a monopoly form? Consider the following social network simulation as it undergoes transformation from a leaderless random network to a structured monopoly network. Start with a randomly wired directed network containing a large number of consumer nodes, and a small number of competing nodes. I assume that the network is random initially, and connect each link to a randomly chosen competitor node. Starting in this way means there is no apparent structure and no clearly dominant competitor. But this random structure soon goes away as the network is rewired according to preferential attachment. The rule is very simple: select a link at random and rewire it to another randomly selected node if the number of connections to the second node is greater than the number of connections to the initial node. Repeat this forever.

Figure 9.2 illustrates such a network with three competitors and 40 consumers. Links are directed from consumer to competitor nodes, indicating that the consumer subscribes to a product offered by the competitor. Market share is defined by the percentage of links pointing to a competitor. Competitors move toward the center of the circle as their market share increases. Consumer nodes are arranged in a circle and the three competitors are drawn as rectangles. Multiple (but not duplicate) links attached to a consumer node are interpreted as split loyalty, or represent different products from different competitors. If there are more links than consumers, I assume the social network represents a multi-product marketplace.

Rewiring randomly selected links by connecting them to the node with the higher market share simulates monopolistic *flocking behavior*—people flock to the dominant competitor because they want to own what other people own. This form of flocking leads to a monopoly network because, over time, consumers eventually connect to the competitor with the highest market share. The market share of all other competitors drops to zero. So the rate of adoption of the monopoly node obeys a logistics growth curve as predicted by Bass's equation and shown in Figures 9.3 and 9.4.

Figure 9.4 shows the results of a simulation based on this sort of flocking behavior. One competitor grows its market share faster than all of the others. The others' market share initially rises, but then drops off after peaking. One lucky competitor out-performs all the others, so its market share continues to rise, leveling off as it nears 90%. In fact, left unchecked, the monopoly competitor may reach 100%! But as I will show later, monopolies are rarely left unchecked!

This form of flocking cannot predict which competitor will win, only that one (randomly) chosen competitor will rise to the monopoly level. Flocking produces a winner, but which competitor wins is pure chance. In general, if this simulation is repeated dozens of times, a different competitor node rises to the top each time. Preferential attachment is a form of stigmergy that selects an unpredictable winner. Becoming a monopoly is a normal accident!

Figure 9.4. Plot of market share versus time for random network with 100 consumers, 5 competitors, initially, and 100 links. Only one of the five competitors reaches a dominant share approaching 90%.

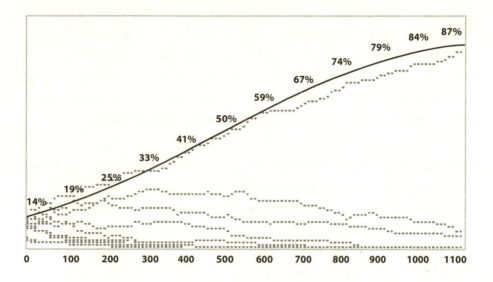

Oligopoly Networks

A more interesting and realistic social network model contains multiple competitors offering multiple products. Each consumer has multi-product *preferences*, which may be spread across multiple competitors. In fact, consumers are likely to have allegiances to more than one competitor, represented here as a social network with more links than consumer nodes. Because of the abundance of links, the multi-product network will evolve into an *oligopoly* network. Oligopolies support multiple products at the same time, represented here by multiple surviving competitors.

I modeled this social network the same way as before, starting with a random network, followed by repeated application of flocking. Once again, a dominant competitor emerges, but in addition, a number of other players and laggards emerge. Players are competitors that vie for dominance and laggards are competitors that have little chance of dominating. Typically, laggards hold onto less than 26% of a market. Surprisingly, in a multiple-product market, these players and laggards are able to co-exist with a dominant, even monopolistic, competitor. In a single-product market, such as operating systems for personal computers, only one Microsoft is needed. But in a multi-product market, such as music players and cell phones, many competitors—for example, Apple Computer, Microsoft, and Google—can co-exist. In fact, diversification of a competitor's product line is one way to compete in a social network where consumers flock toward market leaders.

I concluded that monopolies emerge and thrive in poor social networks and oligopolies emerge in rich social networks, where 'poor' and 'rich' refer to the density of links in the network. This means that sparse social networks evolve into monopoly networks, while rich social networks evolve into oligopoly networks. This suggests that affluent societies are able to support many competitors, so a variety of products are more likely to be found in rich societies. Or, perhaps I am stretching the analogy too far!

Nascent Market Speed

A *nascent market* is a market in development, meaning that the number of customer links starts at zero and steadily increases over time corresponding to increasing demand. As the number of links increases, new competitor nodes appear to address the growing demand. Typically, a single innovator introduces a new idea and enjoys a monopoly for a period of time. This innovator is also known as the *first-mover*. Soon other competitors join in, especially if the first-mover is making a profit. These imitators are known as *fast-followers* for obvious reasons. The rise of personal computers in the 1980s, the rise of the Internet and e-commerce companies in the 1990s, and the rise of international terrorism in the 1970s are examples of nascent markets.

A contemporary example of first-mover versus fast-follower is Research In Motion, RIM, maker of the Blackberry cell phone, versus Apple Computer, maker of the iPhone. RIM was the first-mover, bringing out the first smart phone to support email. RIM had a commanding lead for years, until Apple Computer introduced the iPhone—an even smarter smart phone. For the next several years, fast-follower Apple Computer eroded RIM's market share. The smart phone market is still nascent as I write this chapter, so the evolution of this nascent social network continues. Will Apple's iPhone eventually be replaced by another fast-follower?

As demand increases due to stimulation of the market by the first-mover and fast-follower competitors, more competitors jump in, and so forth, until the market is fully populated by competitors. But at some point demand peaks and the number of links remains constant. The nascent market becomes a *mature market* and the number of competitors begins to decline because of competition. This is known as the *shakeout phase*, because less successful competitors lose market share and go out of business. Eventually, only a handful of competitors remain.

What are the dynamics of nascent markets? Do they obey the traditional S-shaped logistic adoption model of Figure 9.3? Do they always result in a monopoly, duopoly, or oligopoly? What is the best strategy for a competitor that wants to become the dominant player? What happens to novel products during the nascent market stage? Does speed matter?

Consider a simulated nascent market initially monopolized by a single competitor—the first-mover. Demand, in the form of additional links, is assumed to steadily increase at a constant rate. The speed of a market is defined as the ratio of the growth rate of links to the growth rate of new nodes. For example, let a new customer link be added once every fifth time period. Suppose fast-followers are added once every twentieth time period. The *speed* of the nascent market is 20/5 = 4, because links are being added 4 times as fast as competitors. In other words, demand is increasing 4 times faster than competitors are being created to fill the demand.

As it turns out, fast markets produce different networks than slow markets—a new and unexpected result. Once again, simulation shows that it is more likely for a first-mover to be replaced by a fast-follower in a slow market because a slow market gives the fast-follower plenty of time to gain on the first-mover. Why? In the very early stages of a nascent market, a change in one or two links can alter the leadership position 'by accident,' simply because there are few links. In a slow market, there is time to rewire existing links in between the introduction of new links. This means there can be many changes of leadership position in the early stages of emergence. But in a fast market, the number of rewiring steps in between the introduction of new links is limited. This limits the ability of a fast-follower to overtake the leader.

Another unexpected result from simulation of nascent market diffusion is how many competitors survive preferential attachment. Regardless of initial number of competitors, the nascent market network evolves into a 3-way oligopoly with the leader achieving a near-monopoly. In general:

1. With two initial competitors, a leader will emerge with approximately 72% of the market and the other competitor will emerge with only 27%.

2. With more than two competitors, only three dominant competitors initially emerge, and the top two will achieve at least 63% and 26% of the market, respectively.

3. As the speed of the market decreases, the first-mover advantage decreases; slow markets may be monopolized by fast-followers. The slower the market, the better chance a fast-follower has to disrupt the market leader. Recall that market speed is proportional to the rate of new links being created as compared with new competitors being created.

Competing in Internet Time

In today's communication-rich culture, inventions and innovations exist in a multi-product world. Fast innovation is essential because today's social networks form fast markets. Furthermore, simulation suggests that it is unlikely that today's multi-product networks are able to support more than two or three competing products at once. We live in an oligopoly. Once an oligopoly is established, it is difficult to remove, unless a competitor self-destructs. As it turns out, self-destruction is a fundamental property of capitalism! And self-destruction is more significant today than ever before, as markets change in Internet time.

Creative Destruction Networks

Up to this point, I have assumed that all products have the same perceived value. In reality, consumers make selections by comparing many properties of a product, service, or idea, which I lump together and simply designate as *product value*. Product value can be tied to price, quality, fashion, or psychological value, and may have little to do with the intrinsic value of the product. Regardless of how consumers rank competitive products, their decision to buy one product over another inevitably comes down to a *value proposition* based on the perceived value of the product.

Competitors gain or lose market share based on changes over time in product value. A certain company may gain market share by lowering the price of its television, increasing its performance, or increasing advertising to make its television more appealing. In an unregulated capitalistic system, failure to keep pace with constant improvement leads to loss of market share and eventually to the competitor's demise.

The ability to improve on a product's value proposition sometimes declines as a competitor becomes a market leader. One can argue that success leads to a market leader's increase in size and corresponding decrease in agility. As an organization grows, it takes more time to make decisions, and as it becomes more successful, it becomes risk-averse and opts for more conservative improvements. This burden can lead to reduction in the value proposition of the leader's products. For whatever reason, it is an observable fact that a competitor's rate of innovation tends to slow down as market share increases.

Clayton Christensen, for example, attributes this slowdown to the *innovator's dilemma*, which explains why large, established market leaders ride a *sustaining technology* path of incremental improvement instead of continuing to innovate (Christensen 2003). In Christensen's view, it is much safer to incrementally improve one's products by gradual improvement in its sustaining technology—the highly evolved and proven technology that made the company successful in the first place. On the other hand, a radically new technology—a *disruptive technology*—often comes by that is initially inferior and of lower-quality, but also cheaper. The disruptive technology improves faster until it meets or exceeds an ever-expanding market. In many cases, the disruptive technology replaces the sustaining technology, and can lead to the demise of the dominant competitor. Therefore, the innovator's dilemma is this: follow the sustaining technology to its penultimate level, or risk everything by switching to the next big thing—the disruptive technology? Play it safe or risk everything to remain the leader? Failure to recognize if and when to switch technology platforms makes market leaders vulnerable to technological surprise by an upstart innovator.

In contrast to a safe and secure sustaining technology path, an innovator rides the *disruptive technology* path characterized by products with lower performance, lower price, and marketing with an intense focus on an underserved segment of the market. If the innovator is able to move fast and make rapid improvements in its technology's performance, the innovator's product may soon exceed the value proposition of the incumbent's offering. Before the market leader knows it, its market is gone and the innovator starts the cycle over again.

What value proposition drives consumers to a new product, service, or idea, and away from other, older ones? We know that a certain loyalty in the form of *stickiness* (defined as consumer resistance to switching from one product to another) exists in most markets. Stickiness is often due to high *switching costs* that make consumers resistant to change. For example, a consumer may not want to use a new computer or software application because of its steep learning curve, or buy a new car because he or she prefers the styling of the old car. It may be easier for a consumer to continue to use an existing product, simply to avoid paying tangible or intangible switching costs. Thus, the incumbent may hold on to a portion of the market even while being disrupted by a disruptive technology.

History has shown, however, that switching costs are eventually overcome and entire industries capitulate to a disruptive technology. The switch from chemical photography to digital photography, mainframes to personal computers, proprietary network protocols to TCP/IP (Internet) protocols, and vinyl records to digital downloads and MP-3 music players are well-known examples of disruptions of entire industries. In each case, the challenger started out as a lower-quality, lower-performance niche product and then quickly improved it until it exceeded the minimum value proposition required by the consumer.

For whatever reason, market leaders and monopolies are destined to decline and be replaced by new innovators. The rise and fall of market leaders is a natural consequence of capitalism, not the exception. Joseph

Schumpeter referred to this as *creative destruction*, famously advancing the case that 'economic progress means turmoil' (Schumpeter 1942). His theory explains how capitalism perpetuates itself through competition, constant invention, and subsequent waves of innovation. You might say Schumpeter was the economic equivalent of Per Bak, because he believed in destruction!

Creative Destruction Emergence

Schumpeter was perhaps the first to observe the cycle of innovation-leadership-decline in a capitalist system. His *creative destruction* theory describes a cyclical process of early stage innovation, followed by a rise to the top, then by eventual decline and downfall as the market leader encounters a challenger with a new or better product. In Schumpeter's worldview, creative destruction "incessantly revolutionizes the economic structure from within, incessantly destroying the old one, incessantly creating a new one" (Schumpeter 1942:82). Creative destruction is an essential fact of life in a capitalistic system. Does this sound like punctuated reality?

In the following I describe a social network model of creative destruction based on a value proposition that attracts customers to high-valued products at the expense of lower-valued products. Switching is still influenced by preferential attachment, but, in addition, customers weigh the value proposition of each competitor's products as well. If both value proposition and market share falls below that of a challenger, the consumer switches to the better product. For example, customers select a product on the basis of cost and popularity.

On the other side of the equation, competitors are constantly aware of shifting consumer values, so they adjust their value proposition upward to attract customers. This is done in a number of ways, such as cutting prices, increasing quality, and so on. But competitors are also greedy, so they try to maximize profits, compelling them to adjust their value proposition downward when they can. As long as a monopoly is able to maintain a commanding lead in market share, why sacrifice profits? Such a monopoly is tempted to reduce the value of its product and risk loss of share to an upstart to maximize its profit. If market share begins to slip, however, the leader must resort to increasing value by improving its product's quality, price, or advertising budget—all at the expense of profits. Thus, competitors constantly shift between profit-taking when they enjoy a commanding lead and value-increasing when they suffer market share loss.

Challengers attack the leader with a compelling value proposition designed to destroy the market leader. Having less to lose and possibly some market share to gain, the innovative challenger sacrifices profits in the short term for market share in the long term. It does this by giving the consumer a better deal—higher quality, lower price, or more advertising. In the extreme, a challenger may 'buy market share' by selling at a loss; a short-term strategy that can reverse the leadership position.

As an approximation of value, I propose the following: let switching be proportional to the square root of the ratio of two competitor's value propositions. This *square root law* leads to constantly shifting consumer demand as the ratio of value propositions fluctuate. For example, I currently own a Ford, but my next car is going to be either a Toyota or a Ford. If a new Toyota costs $36,000 while the equivalent new Ford costs $32,000, will I switch? After comparative shopping, I estimate both cars are worth about the same, say $40,000. I base my estimates on the style, ride, comfort, gasoline mileage, and electronics in each car. So here is the value proposition: I can get $40,000 worth of transportation for either $36,000 or $32,000. Switching costs me $36,000, while staying with Ford costs me $32,000, so the square root of the ratio of value propositions is square root of ($32,000/$36,000), which is 0.94. The exact number is not important, only the fact that I perceive the Ford to be of greater value than the Toyota. So I decide not to switch. I am still driving my Ford.

Switching takes place only when a challenger has a more attractive value proposition than the incumbent. But in the simulation, value propositions constantly change as competitors try to attract customers on the one hand and maximize profit on the other. Customers are attracted to high value, and profit is greater when market share is maximized. To make the competition more interesting, I limited market share to a maximum value of 72% and a minimum value of 26%, because the previous simulations showed that market share varies between a low of 26% and 72%. A competitor decreases value (takes more profit) when its market share exceeds 72% and increases value (takes less profit) when its market share falls below 26%.

Intuitively, market share leadership should oscillate between competitors. First, the challenger increases value proposition until it achieves a leadership role, while the leader is focusing on taking a larger profit. When positions are reversed, the leader must do the same. Thus, we expect the exchange of leadership position to oscillate between 26% and 72% forever. But this is not the case. What happens instead should surprise everyone.

Once again, start with a random network. What happens when we simulate competition using the square root rule? The field of competitors quickly narrows to two competitors, because of preferential attachment. This is creative destruction in action! As soon as a competitor surpasses the minimum threshold of 26%, it begins to increase its value proposition to gain more market share. When the competitor reaches the monopoly threshold of 72%, it does the opposite—decreases its product's value to increase profit. When this happens, the new leader is challenged by a fast-follower, and the process repeats.

So far, no surprises. Leadership oscillates back and forth. But the amplitude of subsequent value propositions is slightly lower than the previous one and takes longer to reach. Sooner or later, the value of all competitors reaches one. When this happens, products are reduced to a commodity (that is, reduced to a product that, in the eyes of consumers, is indistinguishable from its competitors), and the network reaches its stable *attractor* or *critical point* (see Figure 9.5). Creative destruction eventually destroys all differentiation between competitors! The top two remaining competitors form a stable duopoly network!

All but two competitors drop out of the value-proposition market. The result is not radically different than the previous simulation, suggesting that creative destruction merely accelerates the inevitable rather than altering it. New products must still compete on the basis of preferential attachment. And as the reader well knows by now, the winner of a preferential attachment competition is unpredictable. Microsoft could just as well have been Digital Research, the first-mover company formed by Gary Kildall (1942 – 1994, the creator of the CP/M operating system) to supply operating systems to personal computer manufacturers, and Cisco Systems could well have been some other startup company selling Internet switches. Preferential attachment guarantees dominance, but it doesn't determine which competitor will become dominant.

Figure 9.5. Value of top two competitors in the second phase of creative destruction, shakeout. Initially, random network has 100 customers, ten competitors, 100 links, and value proposition is 1.0 for all competitors.

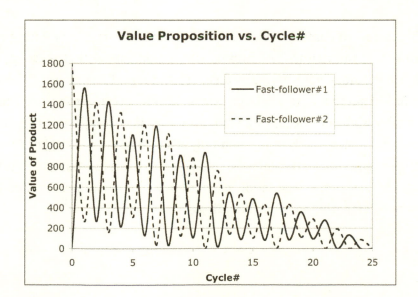

Mergers and Acquisitions

Surprisingly, creative destruction using the square-root algorithm leads to a duopoly. The thresholds used in these simulations determine how much market share each survivor ends up with, but typically one competitor achieves 60-72% while the other achieves 26-40%. These numbers are consistent with previous simulations. The more interesting conclusion is that only two competitors survive, regardless of the number of competitors initially in the social network.

According to Schumpeter, creative destruction is an inevitable result of competition; human ingenuity and network effects make it so. Mergers and acquisitions, on the other hand, provide a more direct means of controlling market share among competitors. When two competitors merge into one, it is hoped that the value proposition of the combined entity increases and makes the new business more competitive. While this may or may not be true in all cases, a merger does increase market share for a time simply because the merged entity's share equals the sum of the two competitor's market shares. Thus, acquisition of a competitor is one way to increase one's standing in the market.

Is it possible to come from behind by employing a strategy of merging with other competitors? Additional simulations show that merging is helpful, but does *not* guarantee a rise to the top of the capitalist food chain. Merging has the effect of increasing the speed with which the inevitable shakeout occurs by eliminating weaker competitors sooner rather than later. Merging is commonly used to bump up market share and gain economies of scale in the real world of business, but simulation suggests that mergers generally do not alter the inevitable. Eventually, only two competitors are left standing.

A Market of Ideas

Farnsworth the inventor and Sarnoff the innovator lived in a world of physical labor, relative isolation, and limited opportunity. Much of their success or failure depended on their ability to monopolize patents and keep trade secrets. Patents locked in an idea long enough for a company to gain a monopoly market share and block competitors from entry. Once Farnsworth got his patents, he had little competition from other inventors. And once Sarnoff monopolized the right patents, he had little competition from other innovators. Their world was largely hegemonic. No wonder the Gilded Age (1877 – 1917) was characterized by so many monopolists!

The Gilded Age no longer exists. Instead, we live in a highly connected, opportunity rich environment dominated by an incredibly fecund market of ideas. If Farnsworth were working on a new technology today, he would face competition from perhaps thousands of people with ideas much like his own. Inventions are rampant, and innovators are abundant. Patents assure inventors of nothing because fast-followers are clever and capable. Typical research labs at large corporations file patents to block others rather than to innovate. Rarely do big corporations invent anything truly new, and innovation is still an individual sport. For example, in 2009, IBM, Samsung, and Microsoft received 11,380 patents, while Apple Computer received 289. IBM, Samsung, and Microsoft have huge research labs, while Apple has none. Which company do you consider an innovator? In the same year, individuals filed over 18,000 patents.[8]

Even if a new idea or product catches on for a time, consumers are fickle and rapidly change their tastes. Cell phones, computers, televisions, and automobiles become unfashionable or obsolete before breaking or wearing out. Diffusion of ideas is nearly real-time, which means that new products appear and disappear with alarming speed. Big products

8   http://www.uspto.gov

like smart phones, movies, and apparel are good for about eighteen months at most, and are soon replaced by the next big product.

At least technological products appear to work this way—disruptive inventions appear to create shock waves of chaotic adaptation through entire industries. A sort of self-organized criticality builds up until reaching a critical point, which is then released in a catastrophic event that changes everything. The television largely replaced radio, the personal computer largely replaced the mainframe, the automobile largely replaced the horse and carriage, etc. This all adds up to one thing: invention and innovation remain outliers—bursty normal accidents that may occur more frequently than 100 years ago, but obey a power law nonetheless.

I claim that this form of normal accident is good. Society benefits from most inventions and innovations because they generally raise socio-economic well-being. Normal accidents do not always have to damage society. They can produce positive waves of chaotic adaptation.

Per Bak would say this is how the world works.

10

BOIDS,
POLITICIANS,
AND TERRORISTS

Winston Churchill, Franklin D. Roosevelt and Joseph Stalin at the Yalta Conference, February 4-11, 1945

Punctuated Cold War

Russian forces were marching westward towards Berlin while Allied forces pressed eastward toward the German capital. It was 1945 and 'the Big Three'—Winston Churchill, Franklin Roosevelt, and Joseph Stalin—met at the Crimean Black Sea resort town of Yalta to divide the spoils of war and decide the future of the world. World War II was winding down and the *Yalta Conference* was the second of three meetings among the victorious leaders. At that point in time, the Big Three were the most powerful men on earth. They held the fate of humanity in their hands, and yet there was little consensus among them. The decisions made at Yalta set into motion a long series of reverberations that rippled across the globe for the remainder of the twentieth century, and what took place over the next 50 years once again illustrated Bak's concept of punctuated equilibrium.

The two closest of the allies, Churchill and Roosevelt, barely agreed on how to deal with Germany after the war. In fact, a 'Committee on Dismemberment' was set up to divide Germany into as many as six pieces! The fates of Poland and other Eastern Eureopan nations were handled like poker chips in the deadly game that became known as the Cold War. The poker players were placing bets on behalf of most of humanity.

Negotiations were discordant and not very binding. The Yalta meeting took place six months before the atomic bomb was used to end the Pacific War, and America still played second fiddle to Great Britain. In fact, Roosevelt was the weakest of the Big Three because his strategy was to give Stalin "everything I possibly can" for "a world of democracy and peace," believing appeasement to be the best policy when dealing with Stalin (Miscamble 2007:52). In his eagerness for peace, Roosevelt focused on ending the war as quickly as possible and underestimated Stalin's ruthlessness. He wanted Russia's help to defeat Japan—a goal that would prove to be costly.

Roosevelt was in poor health and conceded much to Stalin. For example, he agreed to Stalin's demands to take over Latvia, Lithuania and Estonia (to this day, many Latvians, Lithuanians and Estonians consider Roosevelt a traitor). He also conceded to the Soviets veto power in the United Nations Security Council, in exchange for Russia joining the emergent United Nations in October 1945. History would not be very kind to Roosevelt's poker-playing skill. Churchill faired better because he was the more astute of the two Western leaders. He had a better understanding of history and the importance of preventing the Eastern European countries from becoming Soviet satellites, and he simply didn't trust Stalin. He sought free elections for Poland and warned Roosevelt that Stalin was a "devil"-like tyrant (Miscamble 2007:51). The Brit was leery of Stalin's land grab in Eastern Europe. As it turned out, Churchill was right, but he had no leverage with either of the other two.

Stalin eventually agreed to free elections, but they never happened. He wanted more real estate, and he got what he wanted. In the end, Stalin and the Soviet Union dominated the negotiations, a prelude to the Communist state's influence over world events for the next 46 years. Stalin was the most powerful of the Big Three, and the Soviet Union the most influential country surviving the war because his swing vote counted more than the other two.

The Yalta Conference negotiations illustrate an important property of complex systems and social networks: power and leadership can be derived from the clever manipulation of social network structure. Stalin played Churchill against Roosevelt through his 'swing vote.' In the terminology of complex systems theory, Stalin's swing vote equated to network *betweeness value*. Recall that 'betweeness' is the number of paths passing through a node from and to all other nodes in a social network. Stalin's superior betweeness at Yalta allowed the Soviet Union to win vast territories and exert great influence over world events for the remainder of the twentieth century. How manipulation of social network structure and network betweeness leads to influence over others is the major subject that I will address next. But first, I want to convince you that the struggle between Communism and Capitalism as practiced during the post-World War II era is in fact yet another example of the Casinos of Extremistan.

Figure 10.1. U.S. war casualties and Cold War Lévy flights in time obey the Power Laws of Extremistan.

a. Exceedence probability of U.S. war fatalities (1775-1991). Exponent is 1.1.[1]

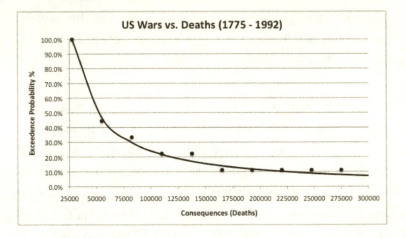

b. Exceedence probability of time between Cold War incidents (1945-1991). Exponent is 1.6. Data shown in Table 10.1.

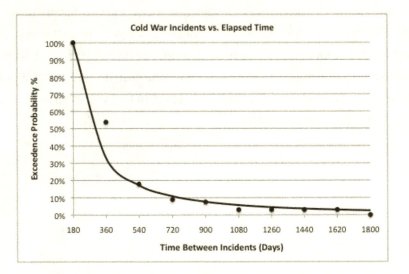

---

1   http://www.fas.org/

Table 10.1. Cold War incidents (1945-1991)[2]

1945	February 4-11	Yalta Conference Cold War Begins
	August 6	United States used atomic bomb in war
	August 8	Russia enters war against Japan
	August 14	Japanese surrender End of World War II
1946	March	Winston Churchill delivers 'Iron Curtain' Speech
1947	March	Truman declares active role in Greek Civil War
	June	Marshall Plan is announced
1948	February	Communist takeover in Czechoslovakia
	June 24	Berlin Blockade begins
1949	May 12	Berlin Blockade ends
	July	NATO ratified
	September	Mao Zedong, a Communist, takes control of China
	September	Soviets explode first atomic bomb
1950	February	Joe McCarthy begins Communist witch-hunt
	June	Korean War begins
1951	January 12	Federal Civil Defense Administration established
1953	June 19	Rosenberg executions
	July	Korean War ends
1954	March	KGB established
		CIA helps overthrow regimes in Iran and Guatemala
	July	Vietnam split at 17th parallel
1955	May	Warsaw Pact formed
1956	October - November	Rebellion put down in Communist Hungary. Egypt took control of Suez Canal; U.S. refused to help take it back

2   http://library.thinkquest.org/10826/timeline.htm

1957	October 4	Sputnik launched into orbit
1958	November	Khrushchev demands withdrawal of troops from Berlin
1959	January	Cuba taken over by Fidel Castro
	September	Khrushchev visits United States; denied access to Disneyland
1960	May	Soviet Union reveals that U.S. spy plane was shot down over Soviet territory
	November	John F. Kennedy elected President
1961	April	Bay of Pigs invasion
	July	Kennedy requests 25% spending increase for military
	August 13	Berlin border closed
	August 17	Construction of Berlin Wall begins
1962	October	Cuban Missile Crisis
1963	July	Nuclear Test Ban Treaty ratified
	November	President Kennedy assassinated in Dallas, Texas
1964	August	Gulf of Tonkin incident
1965	April	U.S. Marines sent to Dominican Republic to fight Communism
	July	Announcement of dispatching of 150,000 U.S. troops to Vietnam
1968	January	North Korea captured U.S.S. Pueblo
	August	Soviet troops crush Czechoslovakian revolt
1969	July 20	Apollo 11 lands on the moon
1970	April	President Nixon extends Vietnam War to Cambodia
1972	July	Strategic Arms Limitation Talks (SALT) I signed
1973	January	Cease fire in Vietnam between North Vietnam and United States
	September	United States helps overthrow Chile government

	October	Egypt and Syria attack Israel; Egypt requests Soviet aid
1974	August	President Nixon resigns
1975	April 17	North Vietnam defeats South Vietnam
1979	July	Strategic Arms Limitation Talks (SALT) II signed
	November	Shah of Iran overthrown; Iranian Hostage Crisis
1983	October	U.S. troops overthrow regime in Grenada
1985		Iran-Contra Affair (arms sold to Iran, profits used to support contras in Nicaragua)
		Mikhail Gorbachev ascends to power in Soviet Union
1986		Gorbachev ends economic aid to Soviet satellites
	October	Reagan and Gorbachev remove all intermediate nuclear missiles from Europe
	November	Iran-Contra Affair revealed to public
1987	October	Reagan and Gorbachev agree to remove all medium and short-range nuclear missiles by signing treaty
1989	January	Soviet troops withdraw from Afghanistan
	June	China puts down protests for democracy; Poland becomes independent
	September	Hungary becomes independent
	November	Berlin Wall falls
	December	Communist governments fall in Czechoslovakia, Bulgaria, and Rumania; Soviet empire ends
1990	March	Lithuania becomes independent
	May 29	Boris Yeltsin elected to presidency of Russia
	October 3	Germany reunited
1991	April	Warsaw Pact ends
	August	Collapse of the Soviet Union; Cold War Ends.

Thus began the Cold War, 46 years of *chaotic adaptation* lasting from February 1945 to the fall of the Soviet Union in August 1991. Chaotic adaptations occurred in small, medium, and large waves following the punctuated reality of World War II. From 1945 through most of 1991, the world was frequently rocked by political tectonics and, in rare cases, shocked by catastrophic events (see Table 10.1). As the reader now knows, these adaptations obey the lop-sided power law you have come to know and appreciate as the universal signature of the Casinos of Extremistan.

Table 10.1 is not my list. Rather it is compiled from ThinkQuest at Oracle Corporation's educational site (see library.thinkquest.org/10826/timeline.htm). I don't make this stuff up! To further confirm the generality of normal accidents and power laws, consider a longer period of history. Consequences (deaths) of major wars fought by the U.S. since its inception in 1775 obey a power law with exponent in excess of one (low-risk), as shown in Figure 10.1a.

So it is no surprise that the elapsed time between major incidents during the Cold War obeys a Lévy flight path through time, as shown in Figure 10.1b. This figure shows that Cold War events as defined by ThinkQuest were bursty. Most events occurred close together in time, while a few rare events occurred after long lapses of time. In a very broad sense, the Cold War was punctuated by rare but dramatic political events followed by numerous smaller events near the big event in time. The numerous smaller events were chaotic adaptations, subsequent collapses and crises, or both. For example, the explosion of the first atomic bomb over Japan precipitated a flurry of political moves ranging from Japan's surrender, Churchill's criticism of the Iron Curtain, creation of the Marshall Plan, to the Blockade of Berlin. This pattern of moves and counter-moves repeated over the 46-year period of the Cold War.

Consequences were mostly incremental, but occasionally catastrophic.[3] For example, invasions of countries (Czechoslovakia), the construction of the Berlin Wall, and an ensuing Space Race were rare, but they did happen. Like termites foraging through time and space, incidents of the Cold War obey a lop-sided power law with such fidelity that they are almost textbook perfect! This all fits Bak's model of punctuated reality.

Bursty patterns repeat throughout history because leaders understand one of the universal laws of politics—'Waste No Crisis!' Hardly anything difficult or demanding is possible during good times, but almost everything is possible during 'bad times.' People are more willing to accept change immediately after a catastrophic event than during stable periods. Taking advantage of catastrophe is an art among successful politicians. Whether despotic or democratic, nearly all leaders practice this universal law. 'Waste No Crisis!' is how things get done.

A dramatic example of this occurred on October 4, 1957, when the Soviet Union won the first round of the Space Race. *Sputnik* was the first artificial satellite to orbit the earth—produced by the Soviet Union, not the US! The 180-pound beach ball wasn't much of a satellite, but its launch ushered in profound political, military, technological, and scientific developments that reverberate through today. The success of Sputnik sent political shockwaves around the globe. How could Soviet Communists recover from the ravages of World War II and beat Western victors into space? It tarnished *U.S. exceptionalism*, the belief that the United States holds a special place in the world because of its long history and tradition of hope for humanity, and personal and economic freedom. It damaged American's national pride. According to the *Sputnik* entry in Wikipedia, "The launch provided both pride for the Soviet people and embarrassment for the Americans."[4]

---

3   Catastrophic means the consequence appears in the tail of the power law.

4   http://en.wikipedia.org/wiki/Sputnik_1

But here is my point: this Russian achievement rallied politicians in the West and sent waves of chaotic adaptation, not only throughout the United States, but also around the world. A series of U.S. Presidents exploited these chaotic waves to the benefit of the country, but to the chagrin of their political rivals. American-made cars with fins were made possible because of Sputnik! More seriously, American exceptionalism accelerated beyond imagination because of Sputnik, setting the stage for putting a man on the moon and creating the Internet, among other advances.

Sputnik is a direct cause of the development of modern personal computers, cell phones, the Internet, and American war-fighting supremacy today. The *Space Race*, as it became known, challenged American willpower, ingenuity, and determination. President Eisenhower and Congress established DARPA (Defense Advanced Research Projects Agency) and NASA (National Aeronautics and Space Administration) in 1958 to prevent more technological surprises like Sputnik. These two agencies were key players in the development of the micro-miniaturization needed to build personal computers and cell phones. DARPA created the forerunner of today's Internet, Arpanet— an experiment that evolved into DARPANET and eventually became the Internet in the 1990s. The chaotic adaptations of Sputnik are felt today every time a cell phone is used to navigate by global positioning system (GPS) satellites or send email.

In many ways, Eisenhower and his successor John F. Kennedy leveraged the Cold War crisis to get what they wanted. What they were really doing was setting up a series of complex system forces that led to unimaginable progress. 'Waste No Crisis' is a kind of organizing force that can shape entire societies when used by skilled leaders. The political will of the American people was shaped by threats of Soviet domination, a global Communist contagion, and a nuclear holocaust. These presidents seized the day and built interstate highway networks, intercontinental ballistic missiles, GPS-guided bombs, powerful computers, and lunar-landing vehicles. In a sense, the Cold War, Space Race, and Atomic Bomb set the stage for a kind of Cold War herd mentality. Americans fell prey to being led like a flock of sheep.

Socially and politically, the Cold War proves the point of this book: that Pascal's triangle and the Normal Distribution are inadequate to describe world events. Instead, history obeys power laws. But the social and political movements precipitated by the Cold War era caused something else to happen—a new political organizing force emerged. What exactly is this organizing force and how does it work? If we want to understand history, we can learn a lot from *boids* and terrorists.

Herd Instinct

Even before the BTW experiment exposed the deep nature of complex systems, Craig Reynolds had a brilliant idea related to complexity of simple systems. Reynolds does research for Sony Computer Entertainment in Foster City, outside San Francisco, California.[5] His unconventional thinking becomes clear when one takes a glance at his life. He boasts that his two children selected him and his wife as parents, rather than the other way around. When friends told him to 'get a life,' he thought they meant he should study *a-life*—artificial life forms generated by computer. So he did. Craig's life is more surreal than real. Instead of just having fun, however, Craig invented an entirely new way to simulate living things.

When he went to work for Sony in 1998, Reynolds was already a big name in the film industry, specializing in computer-generated animation. He discovered and perfected a *flocking algorithm* in 1986 (Reynolds 1987), and won an Academy Award for the application of his flocking algorithm to three dimensional computer animations in 1998. Reynold's flocking algorithm, for example, animated penguins for the 1992 Tim Burton

---

5   http://www.red3d.com/cwr/reallife.html

film *Batman Returns*. Since then there have been many spin offs of his technology, which are described in greater detail on his web site, http://www.red3d.com/cwr/.

Reynolds called his first simulation/animation *boids*, a play on words since his simulated flock of flying birds are self-organized droids. Boid behavior explains why and how birds flock, fish school, and buffalos organize into herds. As it turns out, animals don't have to be very smart to flock and form herds. And this is the connection between world events driven by the Cold War, the behavior of politicians, and the self-organized social behavior of terrorists. What do they have in common? They all exhibit flocking behaviors.

The key to understanding boid animation is to realize that group behavior is mostly determined by the actions of individuals and much less determined by leaders! Individual boids are influenced only by nearest neighbors, but neighborhoods spread their influence to adjacent neighborhoods, which eventually influences the entire flock. Politicians may appear to lead from the front of the pack, but in reality they are steered by the masses or other influential individuals in society. The key to understanding how to influence a group is to appreciate the complex interplay between individuals and their neighbors. What is the nature of this interplay?

Boids obey three simple rules: 1. Steer away from neighboring actors to avoid crowding, 2. Aim in the direction of the average heading of neighboring actors, and 3. Move toward the center of mass of the local neighbors. When Reynolds applied these simple rules to artificial animals on the big screen, the computer-generated animals behaved just like the real thing. They clung together, swarmed fluidly and beautifully, and once in awhile, darted in unpredictable directions. The similarity between boids and groups of humans is unmistakable. Boid behavior conjures up controlled chaos, just like Bak's Sand Pile.

There is no central control or published flight plan for the alpha boid to follow. The alpha boid is steered by his or her nearest neighbors. Change in flight direction is a collaboration among nearest neighbors, but because neighborhoods overlap, local perturbations propagate to adjacent neighborhoods. Most of the time, deviation from straight flight is minor, but on rare occasion the deviation is so extreme it might be considered an outlier. This should sound familiar because complex systems do the same—behave normally most of the time, but deviate dramatically some of the time. Flocking is the ultimate *normal accident* because small perturbations are magnified and propagated to the entire flock through overlapping neighborhoods (coupling). The ultimate direction of the flock emerges from the complex interactions, instead of a central plan.

Numerous scientists and technologists have extended boid algorithms to serve as the brains of robots and explain the emergence of human behaviors. For example, boid algorithms have been used to understand panic and crowd control (Helbing, Farkas & Vicsek 2000). Reynolds lists a few of these behaviors on his web site:

- Seek and Flee
- Pursue and Evade
- Wander
- Obstacle Avoidance
- Path Following
- Crowd Path Following
- Leader Following
- Collision Avoidance
- Queuing at a doorway
- Flocking

Stigmergy to the Max

Reynolds showed that the flowing behaviors of animal flocks, herds, schools, and gaggles are nothing more than simple actions performed by extremely simple-minded automatons acting as individuals. Surprisingly, uncoordinated simple-minded 'artificial creatures' create elegant flowing motions that appear to be 'intelligent.' In more technical terms, you might say that meaningful patterns emerge from self-organization. Flocking, foraging, fleeing, stalking, power grabbing, and negotiating are emergent properties of self-organizing systems. Reynold's flocking rules help us understand human nature.

In complex systems such as the electric power grid, transportation systems, or communication networks, emergent patterns can be harmful because they amplify inevitable collapse. In complex social systems, as illustrated many times during the Cold War period, emergent patterns can either benefit or harm society. Politicians such as presidents Eisenhower and Kennedy were steered toward a positive result. Politicians such as Stalin were steered in opposite directions. Emergence in social systems is analogous to emergence of boid behavior in physical and biological systems.

Craig Reynolds reduced the simple self-organizing behavior of flocking animals to a simple algorithm. Behaviors are mechanical, but surprising—and even elegant. His animals are not as smart as presidents and dictators, but like all animals they nevertheless share a common trait: emergent behaviors shaped by social interactions within overlapping neighborhoods. While some are more complicated than others, both are the consequence of self-organization. It is this build-up of SOC that seems to underlie many unrelated phenomena.

In both cases—human social systems and herds of boids—*stigmergy* is at work. Recall from the previous chapter that stigmergy is derived from two Greek words: *stigma* (mark) plus *ergon* (work), meaning 'mark+work,' or 'stimulated work.' Work is stimulated by some environmental feature, which leads to a modification in the environment, which leads to more stimulus, etc.

Biological termites (as opposed to my artificial ones) build elaborate nests without a blueprint or supervisor. How do they do it? Termites randomly walk around picking up small pellets of soil and dropping them at random. But they also impregnate the bits of soil with a pheromone that attracts other soil carriers. Thus, bits of soil accumulate in a random pile of smelly particles! The shape of the pile is recognized as a building block for a nest, which triggers a different response in the termites. At some point the pheromone wears off, which stops more termites from coming.

Some ants are uncanny in their ability to find the shortest path between their nest and food. How do they do this? Ants are not capable of calculating optimal routes like some erudite mathematician. Instead, the ant herd spreads out randomly from the nest in a random walk that obeys the lop-sided rules of a Lévy flight. Eventually an ant stumbles onto the food and hustles back to the nest, leaving a trail of pheromones behind. Other ants follow the pheromone trail to the food. Each returning ant excretes a trail of pheromones as it returns. Thus, the initial trail is enhanced, which attracts even more ants. This form of *preferential attachment* continues until the food is depleted and the pheromone trail evaporates.

Now here is the secret: ants don't know which trail is shortest, but they do know enough to follow the tail left behind by the first one to return to the nest with food. Ants all travel at about the same speed, so the first one to return must have found the shortest path. In fact, the path isn't always the shortest one possible in all cases, but it is close, because a longer path would take an ant more time to travel. Hence, ants optimize foraging by self-organization. Ant stigmergy appears to be brilliant, but in fact it emerges from randomness.

The algorithm for stigmergy is simple: stimulus, response, stimulus, and response, etc., until a halting stimulus is reached. In the simple termite example, the first stimulus occurs by accident when a random termite impregnates a piece of soil and drops it near another termite. The neighboring termite follows the scent to the soil and drops more impregnated soil on top of the first one. This increases the stimulus (more pheromones), which increases the feedback attracting more termites and more soil. At some point the pheromone evaporates, which reverses the triggering stimulus, and the termites seek out greener pastures. At this point the small pyramid is completed.

Like Lévy flights and preferential attachment, stigmergy is a form of self-organization that creates patterns. These patterns emerge because of local individual behaviors. Termites do not know that they are building nests and ants are ignorant of mathematical optimization algorithms, but their local behaviors produce social structures nonetheless. A larger social structure emerges from combining local smaller structures, and so on. This is a common property of every self-organizing system, whether it is a political, economic, or physical system.

Flocking and stigmergy are possible explanations of human interactions and behaviors. Although humans are vastly more complex, is it possible that stigmergy operates at an unconscious level among groups of humans? What I am suggesting lacks a certain aesthetic value because who wants to be compared with boids, termites, and ants? Besides, if the socio-economic and political course of history is simply a Lévy flight or emergent behavior of herds, then what hope do we have of saving humanity?

On the other hand, if leadership is a form of stigmergy where the most powerful steering tool is 'Waste No Crisis,' then formation of leadership, the power of influence over the herd, and persuasion are easily explained as *attractors* in simple but complex systems. Recall from the first chapter that 'simple but complex' means that these systems *appear* to be simple, but their behavior or structures in fact turn out to be complex. That is, herd behavior is another game of chance in the Casinos of Extremistan. To become masters of the game, perhaps the players should study ants and termites more carefully.

Figure 10.2. The follow-the-leader self-organizing flock algorithm: random links are switched to nodes with greater value.

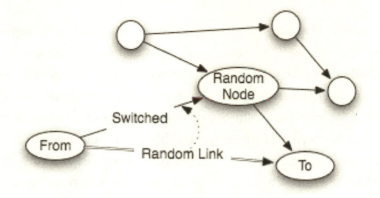

Steering the Flock

Is it possible that social interactions among humans also create patterns? Can humans be steered by social flocking? To answer these questions, I performed one of my simple experiments. Suppose a few very simple rules of stigmergy are applied to a group of people represented as a social network (see Figure 10.2). Each person or *actor* is represented by a node, and links represent the influence one person has on another. This social network is directional because a link points to a node that it influences. In Figure 10.2, the node labeled 'from' influences the 'to' node because the link extends from the 'from' node to the 'to' node.

Now suppose a very simple stigmergy rule is introduced into the social network: links are randomly switched to nodes of higher value than the node to which they currently point. So, in Figure 10.2, a random link is switched to point to a random node if the value of the random node is greater than the value of the 'to' node. Obviously, the random node and link are selected randomly, and this process of evolution repeated forever (remember stimulus-response?). Eventually, a new social structure emerges; that is, the network self-organizes into a topology that increases each nodes' influence over other nodes. Like Stalin at Yalta, the actor with the greatest influence gets what he or she wants.

I call this the *follow-the-leader* self-organizing flocking algorithm because it mimics real life. Power-seeking humans are attracted to other individuals with more power. This form of flocking is repeated forever so that this social network will evolve into a stable network with a radically different topology than it started with. Eventually random switching of links stops because it becomes impossible for a 'from-node -> to-node' link to improve its position. When this state of self-organized criticality is reached, the social network is at its *attractor* or *critical point*. This attractor state is in equilibrium because the social network remains unchanged unless some catastrophic event destroys the linkages that bind the social network together. What measure of power should I use? What is the shape of the evolved network?

Power in social networks isn't really some arbitrary value assigned by the follow-the-leader flocking algorithm. Rather, power in a social network is proportional to how much information an actor node controls. In other words, power is proportional to *betweeness*. The node with the highest number of paths passing through it is the most powerful node, because it exerts the most influence over its neighbors (adjacent nodes). If the betweener node cancels or enhances messages passing through it, it also blunts or sharpens the possible behaviors of the group. Another way to look at this is in terms of boid behavior: boids are influenced by nearest neighbors. This influence is transmitted (or blocked) by invisible links between neighboring boids. If the neighbors dart in one direction, the connected boid also darts. Once again, global group behavior is influenced by local individual behavior. Neighbors steer the flock.

My follow-the-leader flocking algorithm uses both directed and bi-directional betweeness to determine power. Directed betweeness counts the number of directed links from nodes to all other nodes along directed paths. Assuming that links point in the direction of nodes with higher betweeness, directed betweeness is a measure of how high up in the social hierarchy a node is. Bi-directional betweeness ignores the direction of links and so counts all paths. This betweeness is a measure of how influential a node is to all nodes in the network.

So here is how my follow-the-leader flocking algorithm works: I alternate between applying bi-directional betweeness maximization for a few hundred iterations with directed betweeness because nodes try to increase both their influence over the entire network and consolidate their power over the nodes beneath them (in the hierarchical sense). How do I know my strange definition of betweeness defines power in a social network? I don't know for sure, so I tried several termite experiments.

Suppose I repeat the artificial termite experiments described in chapter 5, but with the following variations. Instead of linking together wood chips that are dropped with chips that are picked-up, suppose the termites apply one of the following rules: link to the picked-up chip only if, 1) it has more links than the dropped chip; 2) it reduces the distance between itself and all other chips in the network; or 3) it increases its betweeness. After running thousands of termite simulations, the betweeness metric produces the most self-organized wood chip network of all—it has the highest spectral radius, therefore it is the most organized.

Still not convinced? I next created a random network containing 62 nodes and 150 links and applied the follow-the-leader flocking algorithm repeatedly for several thousand iterations. The reason for modeling a network with 62 nodes and 150 links will become apparent later. A handful of leaders emerge as the simulation unfolds. Then I rank the leaders by their normalized bi-directional betweeness value.[6] The most influential node is assigned a value of 100%, while other nodes are assigned a value less than 100%. Nodes are ranked accordingly, establishing a pecking order among actor nodes. Leaders are assumed to be the highest-ranking nodes. Table 10.2 shows the result of applying the follow-the-leader flocking algorithm on initially random networks.

Table 10.2. Ranking by betweeness by evolved follow-the-leader flocking networks containing 62 nodes and 150 links. These numbers were obtained by averaging over five samples each.

Rank	Betweeness
1	100%
2	56%
3	48%
4	46%
5	44%
6	43%

The number of paths running through the highest-ranking node increases as flocking increases. This is not surprising because the flocking algorithm aims to increase betweeness. The highest-ranking nodes that produced Table 10.2 increased their betweeness from an average of 514 bi-directional paths to 827 paths. The leading node consolidates power throughout the network. This also has the effect of restricting the flow of information to other nodes because their betweeness goes down. In terms of social network influence, I claim that leaders like to hoard information, and the simulation bears this out.

The drop-off of betweeness shown in Table 10.2 is precipitous—it obeys a power law. Once again, this is an indication of consolidated power, as the highest-ranking nodes are the ones with the highest betweeness. In general, follow-the-leader flocking is another example of preferential attachment, but the preference is for betweeness.

---

6 Normalization means that each betweeness value is divided by the largest betweeness value, so all betweeness values lie in the interval [0, 100%].

This simple experiment into social stigmergy suggests that one way to gain influence in a group is simply to follow the most influential members of the group. By aligning with the influential actors, one can gain influence over the entire group. If neighbors can steer the leader, they also steer the group. Does this work in real life?

You may still be unconvinced that betweeness in abstract networks has any meaning whatever in the real world. The result of termite simulations and emerging networks may simply be a coincidence, and, indeed, my experiments have never been performed on actual people. So I undertook one more analysis to see if boids, termites, and terrorists have anything in common. In the next section I apply this follow-the-leader logic to the 9/11 terrorist network to determine who the masterminds of 9/11 were.

The Masterminds

Mohammed Mohammed el-Amir Awad al-Sayed Atta was born in Egypt on September 1, 1968. His strict father demanded his children be educated, so Atta attended Cairo University to study architecture. In 1992, Atta entered the Carl Duisberg Gesellschaft international student exchange program and moved to Germany. There, he lived in a house provided by a Hamburg couple while attending the Technical University of Hamburg-Harburg and majoring in urban planning. Upon graduating, he worked for Carl Duisberg as a tutor and seminar participant throughout Germany during the period 1995-97.

While studying and working in Germany, Atta became more religious and more critical of the Gulf War and U.S. policy in the Middle East. The 9/11 Commission Report says Atta expressed anti-Semitic and anti-American sentiment and condemned the "global Jewish movement centered in New York City" (9/11 Commission Report 2004:161) that supposedly controlled the financial world and the media. Atta considered New York City the heart of America. If you want to kill America, strike its heart.

Mohammed Haydar Zammar claims that he recruited Atta into al-Qaeda. According to the FBI, Atta established the Hamburg cell of the al-Qaeda terrorist network when he moved into an apartment with alleged terrorists Said Bahaji and Ramzi Binalshibh in November 1998. Many other al-Qaeda members lived in the same apartment, including Marwan al-Shehhi, Zakariya Essabar, Waleed al-Shehri, and others. Twenty-nine men claimed the apartment as home while Atta's name was on the lease, including the 9/11 mastermind Khalid Sheikh Mohammed who occasionally occupied the apartment.

In late 1999 through early 2000, Atta, al-Shehhi, Jarrah, Bahaji, and Binalshibh studied terrorist tactics with Osama bin Laden at Tarnak Farms, near Kandahar, Afghanistan. The CIA observed Atta buying large quantities of chemicals after returning to Germany in 2000, but did not act on this intelligence. During this time, Atta contacted 31 flight schools in the United States regarding flight training. Then he traveled to Prague, stayed overnight, and departed for the United States, arriving in Newark, New Jersey. The CIA stopped watching Atta after he entered the United States on June 3, 2000. After all, the CIA doesn't spy inside the United States!

Atta and other hijackers in the United States began flight school training in July 2000. He and Marwan al-Shehhi enrolled at Huffman Aviation in Venice, Florida, where both men earned their instrument certificates from the FAA in November. They continued flight training by watching flight deck videos purchased from Sporty's Pilot Shop in Batavia, Ohio. They even practiced flying commercial jets using the Boeing 727 simulator at the Opa-locka Airport near Miami. Atta and al-Shehhi were awarded pilot's licenses on December 21, 2000.

Throughout the summer of 2001, Atta visited Boston, San Francisco, Las Vegas, Spain, and Switzerland, apparently meeting fellow terrorists to plan the 9/11 attacks. In July, according to U.S. officials and the Spanish police, he drove halfway across Spain to meet with hijackers Wail and Waleed al-Shehri, and Bin al-Shibh. Pere Gomez, manager of Hotel Monica in Cambrils, Spain, said the receptionist on duty refused to rent them a room because she didn't like the look of Bin al-Shibh. They later returned after the receptionist left and stayed the night. The growing network of hijackers reportedly met al-Qaeda's Spanish point man Imad Yarkas during this trip and coordinated the details of the 9/11 attacks. They ruled out an attack on a nuclear plant, and instead decided to hit the World Trade Center.

The day before September 11, 2001, Atta joined al-Omari at the Milner Hotel in Boston, and drove to a Comfort Inn in Portland, Maine, where they spent the night in room 232 only to return by airplane back to Boston the following morning. Authorities speculate that this maneuver was designed to avoid stricter security checks at Logan Airport in Boston. At 6:45 am on September 11, al-Shehhi called Atta to confirm that the attacks were ready to begin.

The plane departed Boston with 81 passengers at 7:59 am. At 8:24 am air traffic controllers heard a voice believed to be Atta's saying, "We have some planes. Just stay quiet and you will be OK. We are returning to the airport. Nobody move, everything will be OK. If you try to make any moves you'll endanger yourself and the airplane. Just stay quiet..." (9/11 Commission Report 2004: 11). Atta is believed to have been the pilot of the plane when it crashed into the north tower of the World Trade Center 23 minutes later, at 8:46:40 a.m.

Figure 10.3 shows the social network of the nineteen attackers and their supporting co-conspirators. The organizational structure of the 9/11 terrorists was formed by the links between them as shown in Figure 10.3. The links were obtained from Krebs (2002). I calculated betweeness as shown in each node. The layout is around betweeness, so the largest betweeness nodes move toward the center, with the lowest betweeness nodes at the periphery of the layout.

Were there self-organizing social factors that held this network together, and what were the simple but complex behaviors that made it work? Does the follow-the-leader self-organizing property of termites and abstract networks described earlier apply to this real network? Is it possible to identify the leaders of the 9/11 terrorist social network using betweeness?

Figure 10.3. The 9/11 terrorist social network containing 62 actors (nodes) and 150 links (relationships), is shown here with the directed betweeness value of the top six terrorists and their names [Krebs 2002].

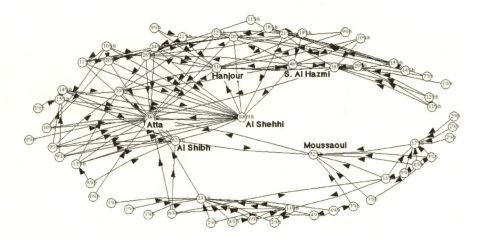

Terrorist Flocks

From Figure 10.3 it is clear that the so-called ringleaders of the 9/11 terrorist network were al-Shehhi, al-Shibh, Atta, Hanjour, Moussaoui, and S. Al-Hazmi, in that order. How did I conclude this from Figure 10.3? Network analysis of the social network formed by the 62 co-conspirators of 9/11 reveals that these six actors were the most influential members of the social network. They controlled the most paths according to the follow-the-leader flocking algorithm.

The nineteen terrorists who actually died on 9/11 were #3 Mohammed **Atta**, Satam al-Suqami, Waleed al-Shehri, Wail al-Shehri, Abdulaziz al-Omari, #1 Marwan **al-Shehhi**, Fayez Banihammad, Mohand al-Shehri, Hamza al-Ghamdi, Ahmed al-Ghamdi, #4 Hani **Hanjour**, Khalid al-Mihdhar, Majed Moqed, Nawaf al-Hazmi, #6 Salem **al-Hazmi**, Ziad Jarrah, Ahmed al-Nami, Saeed al-Ghamdi, and Ahmed al-Haznawi. These formed the core of the social network shown in Figure 10.3.

Does betweeness predict leadership in a social network? There is no theory to support this conjecture, but when I applied the two follow-the-leader flocking behaviors to a random network of equal size, I obtained the results shown in Figure 10.4. The rank order of nodes (as defined by normalized betweeness) of my evolved and averaged random networks roughly match the 9/11 terrorist network. The coefficient of correlation between evolved random network and the terrorist network is high (99.2%). The power law exponents are 0.40 and 0.47, respectively with R-squared[7] values of .93 and .89, respectively (I report the R-squared values here because this result is hard to believe!). In other words, follow-the-leader betweeness self-organization produces social networks very similar to the real 9/11 terrorist's social network. In this case, the follow-the-leader flocking algorithm tells us who the leaders are simply by measuring betweeness.

I also simulated the formation of self-organized networks using one other algorithm as a sanity check. Preferential attachment flocking rewires the random network to link a node to another node with more links. Of course this creates a hub and other highly connected nodes. In this case, Atta is a hub, but the resulting preferential attachment network does not fit the real network as well as betweeness emergence. This is shown in Figure 10.4 as a dotted line that crosses the two follow-the-leader lines.

---

7   R-squared is the 'root-mean-square-error'. A perfect fit would have an R-squared value of 1.0.

What can be learned from stigmergy, flocking, and self-organization of social networks? First, human behavior is intriguingly similar to the stigmergy behaviors of ants, wasps, and termites. This alone should be humbling, if not mind-boggling! Second, follow-the-leader emergence is a rather surprising predictor of social network organization. At least it did a good job of explaining the 9/11 terrorist social network. Third, betweeness increases as follow-the-leader emergence increases, suggesting that leaders consolidate power through control of messaging. Apparently, knowledge is power!

Figure 10.4. Comparison of three different follow-the-leader flocking algorithms with the 9/11 terrorist network betweeness structure shows betweeness emergence is a better fit to the actual 9/11 terrorist network. Correlation coefficient is 99.2%.

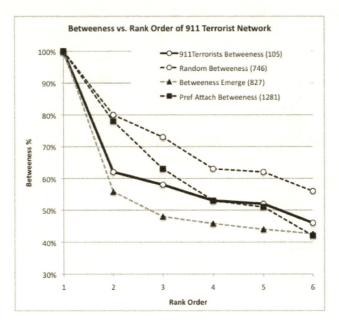

Ontogeny Recapitulates Phylogeny

Ontogeny is the growth and development of an individual organism. A chicken starts as an egg, evolves into a chick, and eventually grows up to be a full-sized hen or rooster. Phylogeny is the evolutionary history of a species. Chickens started out as single-celled animals that evolved into small dinosaurs, continued mutating, and eventually evolved into the junglefowl (Gallus gallus) that is a close relative of the domestic chicken (Gallus gallus domesticus). *Ontogeny recapitulates phylogeny* is a discredited theory going all the way back to the 1790s, which suggests that individual maturation rapidly repeats evolutionary development. Thus, individual chickens grow up by repeating their evolutionary past—progressing from a single cell, to a chick that looks like its dinosaur ancestors, to the modern version, all in rapid succession.

Like I said, it is a discredited theory. Yet it has been applied to many simple but complex systems in biology, anthropology, and education theory. I decided to apply it to social network theory as follows: when social networks fall apart they reform by repeating the (social) evolutionary processes of humankind. That is, groups repeat the stages of civilization following a catastrophic event that shatters the group. After a horrendous earthquake, flood, or fire, the social network rebuilds through stages that mimic the social development of the species. At least, this is my theory. What are these stages?

Anthropologists, sociologists, and amateurs (like me) divide social phylogeny into four stages: scavenger/looter, hunter-gatherer, agro-stationary, and urbanite. Homo habilis survived by scavenging/looting about 2.5 million years ago. Homo erectus was a hunter-gatherer approximately 1.8 million years ago. Homo sapiens invented a non-nomadic agricultural civilization about 10,000 years ago, and settled down in farms and villages. Urbanites specialized so that it became advantageous to build cities about 5,000 years ago. During the twentieth century, people created complex social and physical networks we now know of as *mega-cities*. We are in the latter stages of urbanization.

Scavenging/looting is typically done by individuals or in small groups—packs. These nomadic packs migrate from place to place in search of food and shelter. As far as anthropologists know, Homo habilis had minimal social structure—a very disconnected social network, if any at all. Think of this stage of social evolution as individual nodes in a network with very few, if any, links. Did they trace out Lévy flights while foraging? Most likely homo habilis foraged like most other animals.

Because humans were smaller and less powerful than the animals they hunted during the hunter-gatherer stage, Homo erectus formed larger groups to bring down a more powerful prey. Group hunting required creation of a social network called a tribe, but the tribe was still nomadic. Tribal social networks are more connected and robust than scavenging/looting packs. Think of this stage of social evolution as disconnected clusters of small networks tightly connected within their own social networks.

The emergence of agricultural societies supported even larger groups—so large, in fact, that they required the development of governments, leaders, and specialization of skills. These were the urban or city-dwellers of modern Homo sapiens. So-called *urban* life has emerged from very large social networks in excess of a million individuals. This model has been very successful. In fact, the number of people on the planet living in cities exceeded 50% during the twentieth century. Most modern humans embedded within very large urban social networks enjoy the benefits of extreme specialization, sophisticated infrastructure, and a high standard of living. Think of this stage as a vast social network with millions, perhaps billions, of links connecting nearly everyone to everyone else.

The four stages of social development, from scavenging to urban socializing demonstrate a kind of *social phylogeny*—social evolution of the species. Social phylogeny is equivalent to network percolation—the formation of ever-larger societies by a process of adding links. In fact, Malamud's forest fire simulator described earlier provides a metaphor for social phylogeny and the evolution of ever-larger social networks. The distribution of sizes of local social networks (clusters in the forest fire simulation) obeys a series of power laws, with longer and longer tails as population density increases; that is, mega-cities become both larger and more common as human population increases.

First, it is interesting that the size of tribal and urban clusters—tribes, villages, and cities—is distributed according to a power law. Second, it appears that restoration of society immediately after a catastrophe is akin to social phylogeny, as a shattered society rebuilds from scavenging to tribal, agro, and eventually urban social networks. For example, rampant looting took place immediately after Hurricane Katrina devastated New Orleans in August 2005. "Hurricane Katrina washed away the New Orleans criminal justice system," according to Garrett and Tetlow (2006). New Orleans society had to be rebuilt from that of scavenger/looter, hunter-gatherer stages, and eventually back to its urbanite stage, over a period of time.

The Big Three—Roosevelt, Churchill, and Stalin—led shattered societies in 1945. They had to rebuild their societies or risk a reversal of social phylogeny, sinking from weakened post-war urban societies back to the scavenger/looter stage. Follow-the-leader influences such as the Marshall Plan were used to mend their social networks. The quick actions of the victors of World War II prevented reverse social phylogeny, but their decisions were not perfect. History tells us that there is no guarantee that every damaged social network will rebuild itself into a healthy urbanite social network. An interesting question to ask is, what lies beyond the urbanite stage? Recall the botnet discussion in chapter eight. Might self-organization of urbanite cultures destroy themselves by inadvertently creating social viruses? This is the final topic of this chapter.

Flocking and the City

Luís Bettencourt and his colleagues at Los Alamos National Laboratory in New Mexico studied scaling laws in urban societies and found flocking behaviors similar to the results I have shown here (Bettencourt, Lobo, Helbing, Kühnert & West 2007). Their research explains why social networks evolve into urban structures, and possibly suggests what might lie beyond the urbanite stage. Basically, cities and their correspondingly large social networks are a product of scaling along a number of dimensions—economic, infrastructure, intellectual, and political. There is no surprise in how cities and their infrastructures behave, but the fact that cities generally obey power laws may be unexpected.

The Los Alamos researchers observed power laws across different nations and different human activities. Activities with short tails (exponent greater than one) benefitted from *increasing returns*—they were super efficient—while activities with long tails (exponent less than one) benefited from *economies of scale*, where efficiencies modestly reduce the per unit cost or other property. These power laws were obtained by plotting the number of activities on the vertical axis and the population of cities along the horizontal axis. Specifically, Bettencourt and his colleagues list economic, intellectual, and creative activities as benefitting from increasing returns, as measured by wages, gross domestic product, consumption of electrical power, number of inventors, patent applications, and research and development jobs. They also list dysfunctional behavior, such as serious crime, as an increasing returns activity of urbanites. It scales with scaling of large urbanite networks.

Activities benefitting from economies of scale (exponent less than one, so the power law has a long tail) were more likely to be related to physical infrastructure. For example, the number of gasoline stations, length of roads, and length of electrical cabling in U.S. and German cities had exponents less than 0.87. Without economies of scale, these activities—actually, the infrastructure—would not be efficient at all. Without efficiencies, doubling the population means infrastructure also has to double. Instead, doubling the population increases infrastructure by $2^{0.87}$ or a factor of 1.83. For example, doubling the population of a city requires 83% more roads – not the expected 100%.

Like flocking ants and termites, humans tend to organize infrastructure assets in efficient ways. Flocking has advantages—social, economic, and intellectual activities scale according to increasing returns (power laws created by preferential attachment) and infrastructure facilities that benefit from economies of scale (increasing efficiency) as population increases. City efficiency is not always positive. Serious crimes also rise due to increasing returns. For example, doubling population causes serious crime to increase by a factor of $2^{1.16}$ or 2.23. A city with 100,000 inhabitants and 10 murders per year will have 22 murders per year when its population reaches 200,000.

If in fact 'social viruses' such as serious crime increase faster than the population, at what point does an urbanite society reach its critical point and collapse? In addition, if urbanite societies apply economic, creative, and intellectual increasing returns towards nefarious activities such as the construction of botnets with the power to crash vast infrastructures, at what point does urbanite society destroy itself? After all, Bak's punctuated reality includes the (slight) possibility of extinction. As modern urbanite societies become more efficient and mega-cities optimize utilization of resources, do cities eventually reach their critical points? This is left as an exercise for the reader!

11

IF I
WERE KING

Queen Victoria (1819-1901), sovereign ruler of the United Kingdom of Great Britain and Ireland from 1837 to her death in 1901. She was the longest serving monarch in the history of the British Empire

The Queen

Alexandrina Victoria—daughter of Prince Edward, Duke of Kent and Strathearn, and his German-born wife, Princess Victoria of Saxe-Coburg-Saalfeld—became Queen of England at the age of eighteen and went on to rule one-fourth of the entire world's population for 63 years. One can argue that during her rule, England became a world power and enjoyed perhaps its most prosperous and peaceful period in history. Victoria was an extremely successful leader. But was she a Black Swan?

Victoria's rise to power and longevity was no accident, normal or otherwise. If you plot the length of reign of all kings and queens since the beginning of the British monarchy, going back to Egbert, Ethelwulf, and Aethelbald circa 800AD, their Lévy flight in time does *not* obey a power law! In fact, the current queen, Elizabeth II, has already logged more than 58 years of rule at the time of writing this. I dare not accuse her of being a Black Swan, nor does the data support it. Rather, the longevity of British monarchs defies the power law and refutes Bak's theory of punctuated reality. British monarchs tend to reign for periods of time more in line with Mediocristan than Extremistan.

I am not going to explain why British monarchs last so long or why they are such successful leaders. Instead, I am going to place myself in their robes and ask, *what would I do about Extremistan, if I were king?* Parliaments and presidents don't have the power that monarchs do, nor should they. But does it take more than a parliament or president to deal with the enormous problems and opportunities posed by Extremistan? In this final chapter, I analyze the challenges of Extremistan from an idealized perspective, one without the limitations of most modern leaders. So if I were king, what would I do?

Beyond Monarchs

Bak's Sand Pile is a metaphor for complex, non-linear, critical, outlier events that happen almost every day! By now you should be convinced that modern life is not like it used to be—Black Swans, normal accidents, and random catastrophes follow Lévy paths through space and time (of course, it is not clear that non-modern life was any different, but perhaps the modern time-scale is compressed). These events aren't governed by General Brownian Motion or the bell curve; if they were, we could expect the average incident to happen most of the time. And since they are not, we should be concerned for the long tail event—the big event that changes everything. After all, our very survival may be at stake. Asteroid Apophis, headed our way in 2036 could end it all. Current estimates of the likelihood of impact by this 885 ft diameter rock are one in 250,000. This is equivalent to a power law catastrophe with exponent equal to 2.7, assuming Apophis is the worst asteroid disaster of all time. The Tunguska explosion, thought to have been an exploding asteroid, obliterated 2,000 square kilometers of Siberia in 1908. If such an event happened over the New York metropolitan area it would lead to 3.9 million deaths, 4.7 million injuries, and $1.5 trillion in property loss (Mignan, Grossi & Muir-Wood 2010).

If annihilation by asteroids is too remote to worry about, perhaps we should worry about self-inflicted extinction through climate change! A study by Sandia National Laboratory in 2010 estimates that global climate change is likely to cost the U.S. economy $1.2 trillion by 2050. The exceedence probability versus GDP curve for losses due to climate change obeys a power law with exponent of 1.54. While this power law has a longer tail than that of asteroids, both are still considered low-risk hazards.

We can do something about both asteroid strikes and loss of GDP due to climate change. For example, we could launch a space program capable of diverting future meteors and eliminate pollution of the atmosphere to head off global warming. But since both of these unthinkable consequences are extremely unlikely and distant, should we worry more about other potential catastrophes? In a complex world, almost anything can happen—especially the unanticipated, unthinkable, and rare Black Swan.

Big Systems, Big Consequences

Even if end-of-times catastrophes are too remote and unlikely to be concerned about, the randomness of the Casinos of Extremistan leave plenty of room for game-changing disasters to occur. Hurricane Katrina, California wildfires, and mega-sized tsunamis are disastrous and frequent enough that we should do something about them. Add to these natural events human-made disasters, such as the 2010 Gulf oil spill, the 2003 blackout, and 9/11 terrorist attacks, and power laws should be on everyone's minds. In chapter two, '*Normal Accidents*,' I showed how to classify natural and human-made disasters into low- and high-risk categories. We should be prepared to respond to low-risk hazards because they are relatively frequent, while working to prevent the consequences of high-risk hazards as much as possible.

Human-engineered hazards are often self-organized networks or network-like systems containing hubs and betweeners, with invisible or obscure interconnections that often end up in critical states. They are subject to risk and reward, normal accidents, NIMBY, Lévy flights and walks, preferential attachment, flocking and foraging, chaotic adaptation, and punctuated reality. If we want to avoid big collapses of systems that we can do something about, we have to change the policies that govern them. In the simplest possible terms, this means reducing SOC by increasing redundancy and surge capacity, and operating them below maximum levels. For example, power systems, hospitals, and highways are more resilient when they run far below their maximum capacity.

In the following, I'll summarize what I think are some potential showstoppers lurking ahead and suggest appropriate policies to mitigate the key challenges confronting us. For the most part, it won't be pretty, but I believe that if we have bold leadership and determination, we can avoid another 2008-sized financial meltdown, global socio-economic meltdown, or near-extinction at our own hands. Call me Pollyanna, but I think we are on the verge of a historical improvement of the systems we depend on daily.

Without its critical infrastructure, no nation can be great for very long. In particular, great nations depend on fundamentals, such as clean water, ample supply of energy, and world-class transportation and communication technology. It is doubtful that modern mega-cities would remain civilized if deprived of water for more than a week, or energy for more than a few days. Cities of the size of New York have never gone for more than a day or so without electricity. It remains to be seen how long a civilized nation can exist without telephone service, or systems such as commuter rail, automobile, and truck transportation. Few urbanites have ever contemplated a protracted breakdown in fundamental services for very long. Most of us cannot go for more than a week without visiting a grocery store!

Perhaps the biggest challenge facing all great nations is *climate change* and the lack of an operational energy policy able to realistically deal with the increasing hazards of burning carbon-based fuels. On the one hand, these fuels are energy-dense and relatively inexpensive sources of energy. A pound of gasoline, for example, contains 100 times the energy of a pound of the most sophisticated battery today. In the United States, it takes the energy equivalent of one-half pound of gasoline to sustain one person for a day. The same person would require the energy of 11,000 AA batteries to keep on going for a day.

On the other hand, burning carbon-based fuels pollutes the atmosphere and has unacceptable long-term consequences. Every pound of gasoline burned in an automobile, airplane, truck, or train produces three pounds of pollution, because during combustion, carbon combines with oxygen to form CO_2! In the United States, the per capita consumption of gasoline ranges from 100 pounds (630 gallons) per year in Wyoming to 6.5 pounds (41 gallons) per year in California. The average American manufactures 200 pounds of CO_2 every year as a byproduct of gasoline consumption. And these statistics ignore pollution created by burning petroleum, natural gas, and coal to produce electricity.

Energy Policy

The 'energy problem' will only worsen as modern society transitions to an increasingly electronic infrastructure. Trains are already hybrid electric transporters. As entire nations transition to electric cars and trucks, demand for electrons and the means to produce them will continue to increase. Consumption of electricity will continue to rise as long as nations prosper, even as gasoline consumption declines. To remain a great nation, modern civilizations must eliminate CO_2 as a byproduct of the production of electricity.

In '*Blackout USA*,' I recommended that the United States begin rebuilding the fundamental infrastructures it will need for the twenty-first century: electrical power, natural gas, and ultra-high bandwidth communications. I suggested this infrastructure be buried in tunnels alongside of the nation's 40,000 miles of Interstate Highway. The Interstate Highway System is intrinsically stable because its spectral radius is low, the rights-of-way are already owned by state governments, and the Interstate reaches every corner of the country. As an energy and communication highway, it would pay for itself from a user toll of approximately 3.5% on revenues generated from the sale of energy and information. In addition, it can be green—open only to the transportation of energy and information produced by clean fuels.

This is an enormous undertaking, but it is perhaps the cheapest and easiest way to transition to a safe, secure, and carbon-free energy infrastructure by the end of the twenty-first century. How do we get there? The first step is to change the Energy Policy Act (EPACT) currently in effect.

If I were King, here is what I would do:

1. Eliminate NIMBY as a barrier by using existing Interstate Highway rights-of-way for the transportation of energy and information. These rights are owned by the states and adequate to support underground utility lines.

2. Set national interoperability, safety, and security standards for the energy and information highway utilities: electricity, liquid natural gas, digital transmission.

3. Allow only clean energy and information produced by clean energy to rent the utility—a national asset that allows vendors to reach all parts of the country.

4. Regulate maintenance, safety, and security practices in order to assure the system's physical and political longevity.

5. Establish wholesale and retail rents that sustain the infrastructure indefinitely, and yet stimulate innovation such as using superconducting transmission lines, advanced storage technology, robotic maintenance, and ultra-secure communication protocols.

I believe this infrastructure could be a 'field of dreams'—build it and the venture capitalists will come. The opportunity to produce an electron anywhere in the country and sell it anywhere else would be irresistible. Electrons produced by solar farms in New Mexico could be transmitted and sold to consumers in Connecticut. I believe that there is a market for electrons produced by windmills in Kansas and Texas that is as big as the market for beef produced on Kansas and Texas ranches. The transformation would be profound.

Cyber Security Policy

One of the major benefits of the Interstate Highway energy and information network is the potential to provide broadband on a national scale—a literal information highway that reaches the entire population. Everything in communications is converting to IP (Internet Protocol). This means that in the not-to-distant future, in addition to the Internet and World Wide Web, radio, television, movies, SmartGrid control, commuter trains, airplanes, and telephone signals will be 'broadcast' in the Internet language. This convergence makes interoperability across all media possible, but it also makes the communications infrastructure vulnerable to cyber attacks. If we want to be a great nation, we will have to fix this.

The physical communications infrastructure network is self-organized and near its critical point because of telecom hotels, as I explained in chapter seven, '*Can You Hear Me Now?*' There are thirteen root servers and another thirteen global top-level domain servers in the world, each of which, technically, represents hundreds of thousands of actual computers. In addition, there are another 25-50 Tier-1 Internet Service Providers and Metropolitan Area Exchanges supporting the global communications network. I estimate that fewer than 200 servers make up the core of the global communications infrastructure. These 200 servers are the most critical assets in the sector.

The 1996 Telecommunications Act requires peering, which encourages formation of telecom hotels. Telecom hotels are large network hubs, and as I explained in chapter four, '*California On Fire,*' hubs increase a network's spectral radius, thereby increasing its fragility. This act must be changed to make the communications infrastructure more resilient. The first step is to remove telecom hotel hubs from the network.

But concentrating assets into fewer than 200 locations in geo-space and cyberspace is not the number one problem. Current deployment of a national broadband network is limited by inadequate access and inadequate security. Every office, factory, and home will need gigabit access (1,000 times greater than today's cable TV 'Internet') if we are to take the next step towards 3D Internet, fully immersive entertainment, digital factories, globe-spanning offices and distributed knowledge workers. To make this possible, consumers will have to be protected from exploitation by botnets, spams, phishing, and plain old fraud. In chapter eight 'Internet Storms,' I claim that it is very difficult to dismantle the Internet by de-percolation. It is very easy, however, to saturate the Internet with botnets like Rustock.

The Internet is an unregulated 'wild west,' ripe for exploitation by outlaws and unfriendly governments. It is perhaps the largest infrastructure in the world to operate as a purely self-organizing system. As a result, it has grown like a sprawling metropolis without law enforcement or public safety. It is *carpe diem* for outlaws and *caveat emptor* for consumers. After 40 years of unruly development, the Internet needs to be tamed.

If I were king, here is what I would do:

1. Governments should establish safety, security, and licensing standards for all IP-based communications. Call this the Cyber Safety and Security Act.

2. Licensed Tier-1 ISPs, Metropolitan Area Exchanges, and telecom hotel operators should be subject to the most stringent standards specified in the Cyber Safety and Security Act. For example, they should be required to provide strong physical and cyber security, employ strong encryption of both storage and transmission, verify authenticity of all users, properly operate strong intrusion detection systems, and maintain current software updates and patches.

3. Licensed E-commerce and web sites serving 10,000 or more consumers should be subject to penalties for loss of consumer

information such as names, addresses, social security numbers, health records, etc. They should also be required to implement the highest standards for secure storage, transmission, and physical/cyber access to consumer information. For example, they should be required to operate VPN protocols (Virtual Private Network protocols, which, among other things, hide the source and destination addresses in every packet of information). Moreover, they should be required to encrypt all consumer data and follow best common practices for fending off denial of service attacks, preventing the spread of malware, operating firewalls properly, and screening transactions for worms and viruses.

4. Consumers should be required to use 'credit cards' containing electronically embedded temporal passcode generators. A temporal passcode generator is a pseudo-random number generator that generates a new random number every 60 seconds or so. This passcode is appended to the user's password each time the user logs into his or her online account. The passcode enables non-repudiation—the inability of a user to deny that he or she was the person logging into a system. In this way, the identity of everyone using the Internet can be verified. For personal privacy reasons some of these regulations may be subject to warrants or other legal protections. Spoofing would no longer be possible.

5. Software publishers should be required to implement simple authentication in their operating systems software and application software. For example, a check-sum might be required. A check-sum is simply a number obtained by summing the contents of computer memory. If the computer memory contains an application program, the check-sum is matched against the publisher's check-sum before the software is allowed to enter the computer system. This simple mechanism would

avoid most unauthorized spreading and activation of malware, such as key loggers and Trojan Horses.

Pandemic Policy

Deflecting asteroids may be easier than deflecting a mutated germ. In chapter five, '*Lévy Flights*,' I traced the spread of SARS from China to far points of the globe. Preliminary evidence suggests that SARS quickly fizzled after a rampant start because it ran out of 'energy.' Modern air travel amplifies the spread of contagions, but it also saps the strength of the virus. I also showed that other kinds of Lévy flights and walks do the opposite—they get stronger as Lévy jumps increase. For example, electric power grid cascades gain strength as the fault propagates from one place to another. A power grid normal accident can be more virulent than an Internet virus!

Pandemics prey on dense social networks. High spectral density can even lead to persistent diseases that never go away unless the host is eliminated! Hubs and betweeners act as super-spreaders that magnify the consequences of an outbreak. If we want to reduce the likelihood of extinction due to a persistent incurable disease, we have to lower the spectral radius of social networks. But the human population is going in the opposite direction.

700k → 3B

In 1950, 30% of the 2.5 billion people in the world lived in cities and New York was the only metropolitan area with ten million inhabitants. Today, 50% of the world's six billion people live in cities and there are over twenty cities with ten million or more inhabitants. In 2008, metropolitan Tokyo had 34 million inhabitants; Guangzhou and Seoul were home to 24 million, and Mexico City, Delhi, Bombay, New York, and Sao Paolo were close behind with at least 20 million, each.[1]

---

1   http://www.citypopulation.de/world/Agglomerations.html

Add to the spectacular growth of cities the fact that airlines transport over a billion passengers every year. Packing 100-300 people into the close quarters of an international flight increases the chances of communicable diseases spreading around the globe. All of this packing together means that the spectral radius of today's social networks are soaring! And as spectral radius increases, so does SOC.

Sooner or later the pandemic Black Swan will appear again. Perhaps it will materialize as a new strain of SARS that does not weaken as it travels, or a resistant H1N1 virus immune to vaccines. If the Spanish Flu of 1918-1919 were to hit today's population of 6.5 billion, approximately 225 million people (3.5%) would die in the first six months (50 to 100 million of 1.8 billion died in 1918)! How many casualties might a *mutated*, and therefore more virulent, Spanish Flu cause? Whatever lies in wait, the huge rise in social network density and the expansion of global transportation around the world are early warning signals not to be ignored.

Part of the solution is to increase research leading to the development of vaccines, promote healthy practices, and improve sanitation around the world. Another is to reduce link percolation in global social networks. Of course, quarantine is an undesirable method of reducing link percolation because it limits personal freedom, negatively impacts the economy, and is difficult to enforce. Unfortunately, nearly every effective approach requires a political will that does not exist today.

If I were King, here is what I would do:

1. Increase research to speed delivery of vaccines with an emphasis on mutations of known highly infectious diseases, in order to reduce the spread of contagions around the globe.

2. Implement bio-shield detection and checkpoint systems throughout the travel network: at train stations, airports,

seaports, points of entry at national borders, and shipping ports-of-entry. Technology currently exists for detecting the presence of some chem-bio contaminants by 'sniffing' the air in airports, and train stations, for example. And when prevention fails, quick response to an outbreak of highly contagious contaminants like anthrax and Ebola can go a long way toward minimizing the damage. In fact, in 2004 the United States initiated the ten-year, $6 billion Project BioShield to provide exactly this capability (although Congress cut $2 billion from the program in 2010 and it is in danger of being terminated as I write this).

3. Implement a global information system for disease surveillance. This real-time reporting system would provide early warning and tracking of outbreaks around the globe. Infectious diseases are better stopped earlier rather than later. Currently, 80 global and 60 U.S. laboratories participate in surveillance for influenza outbreaks. If this network were extended to the entire world and expanded to record all kinds of infectious disease incidents, diseases like SARS and H1N1 could be quickly suppressed.

Unfortunately, there is little motivation to implement these precautions until a 'near-miss' happens. So leaders must wait for the crisis and then 'Waste No Crisis,' as I described in chapter ten, '*Boids, Termites, and Politicians*.' 'Waste No Crisis'—perfected by politicians in the self-organizing liberal democracies of the twentieth century—turns out to be an extremely effective leadership tool. But recall how leaders are herded by the masses in a form of flocking and follow-the-leader emergence.

Engine of Prosperity

The Black Swan of total extinction of the human species is less likely to happen than a catastrophic collapse into a less technologically advanced society. Civilizations don't last forever, after all. Is it possible for modern society to disintegrate and return to the European Dark Ages? Might terrorism, political turmoil, climate change, cataclysmic natural events, or a nuclear holocaust send the world into darkness?

It is more exciting to contemplate the ruination of society than its longevity and prosperity. Hollywood movies cash in on stories about end-of-time disasters at the hands of evil businessmen, alien invaders, and nuclear warmongers. There is big money to be made in negative press, and the computer graphics are much more spectacular.

It is much more challenging to be optimistic. I like a challenge, so here I go. In my Casino, invention and prosperity go hand-in-hand, according to power laws described in chapter nine, '*Invention, Innovation, and Inspiration*,' and the positive consequence of punctuated reality described in chapter ten, '*Boids, Termites, and Politicians*.' Recall that scientific and technical advancement is a Lévy walk in time. Societies advance in spurts along social, political, and technical dimensions. But the path to innovation is bursty and unpredictable, just like a sand pile. Societies that successfully exploit invention and innovation make quantum leaps forward; societies that repress them lag behind. Therefore, invention and innovation need to be nurtured like a perpetual newborn infant.

If I were King, I would emphasize education:

1. Invention and innovation start with inspiration and education. Education is the big leveler with benefits: it secures the state and increases the standard of living. America is facing an education crisis. "Based on the latest data, around 7,200 students drop out of high school each day, or about 1.3 million a year. Nationally,

about 68.8 percent of students who start high school graduate four years later, but there are huge local differences. While 83 percent of the students in New Jersey graduate each year, only 41.8 percent of Nevada's students do." (Wingert 2010)

Globalization opens the world of producers to vast markets, but it also opens the world of producers to competitors. As advanced nations create new industries such as the electronics and software industries, the number of customers for computers, Internet e-commerce, and cell phones skyrocket. But competitors capable of manufacturing refrigerators, cars, cell phones, and computers also emerge. Western nations invented globalization for the benefits, but overlooked the drawbacks: along with new consumers, globalization conveniently creates competition for producers.

There is only one way to win the globalization game. Invention and innovation are the engines of prosperity in a world awash in cheap materials, cheap labor, and abundant investment capital. To stay competitive, Western nations must invest heavily in education, research and development, and reduce restraints on creativity. Materials, labor, and money may be a commodity, but creativity remains precious. As a society becomes a leading producer of commodity goods, the societies they displace must move on to more advanced and creative endeavors. Germany may have invented the automobile and, together with Japan, it may dominate automobile manufacturing. But the future of both is in nanotechnology, information technology, biotechnology, and other technologies, as Korea, China, and India commoditize automotive manufacturing.

Principles of Bak's Sand Pile

It is impossible to avoid the Casinos of Extremistan with their power laws and punctuated reality. But according to Bak, if we want to reduce risk, we have to back away from the modern idea of optimality with its penchant for optimal, just-in-time efficiency. Modern science and advanced technology have brought the highest standard of living to the greatest number of people in history. But perhaps we have gone too far! At some (critical) point, modernity reaches a tipping point. As during the excesses of the 2001-2008 economic period, the very systems we depend on may be stretched too far.

Ultimately, Bak's Sand Pile is about how things work, and as it turns out, they don't work as we previously thought. Extremistan is the rule, Mediocristan the exception. Extremely rare, punctuated Black Swans matter much more than White Swans; outliers matter more than inliers; and catastrophes matter more than smooth sailing. In the modern real world, normal accidents and Black Swans advance civilization while the ordinary has virtually no impact at all. I am not being negative; I am simply interpreting real-world data.

The rules of punctuated reality are the rules of complex systems. The fundamentals of Bak's Sand Pile and complex systems in general are: complexity equals connectivity, emergence, self-organization, simple-but-complex non-linear behavior, Lévy walks in both space and time, and chaotic adaptation.

Complexity Equals Connectivity

Complex systems are connected, emergent, self-organized networks. The network model is rather flexible—nodes represent anything of interest and links represent any form of coupling or connectivity. A financial system is a network of banks (nodes) connected through their transactions (links); a nuclear power plant is a network of components (nodes) and their interactions (links); and an earthquake is a network of tectonic plates (nodes) and their interfaces (links). Network models of complex systems embrace the three fundamental properties of all complex systems studied in this book: coupling, emergence, and self-organization.

Complex systems evolve—they change over time. In most cases, one or more properties of a complex system emerge out of randomness or disorder as the system responds to transformative forces. Efficiency and optimal restructuring is perhaps the most common form of transformative force. Whatever the motivation, emergence is the byproduct of a thermodynamic process whereby energy goes in, and structure comes out. It takes effort to change a system even though it might appear that the system has reorganized itself.

As a system consumes energy to reshape itself, a new form of organization emerges from the less organized configuration of nodes and links through dynamic processes that are often hidden or occur so slowly that they go un-noticed. It has taken the U.S. energy sector over 100 years to arrive at its current form of self-organization. The same observation applies to other large and complex systems such as transportation, telecommunications, and various forms of government.

In many cases, self-organization increases system risk by reducing resiliency as SOC transforms a system from a non-critical to critical state. For economic and NIMBY reasons, network systems form hubs, betweeners, and critical nodes and links. The telecom hotels of the national communications infrastructure evolved out of the 1996 Telecommunications Act. The critical nodes and links in the electric power grid evolved out of NIMBY. The increase in vulnerability to terrorism in the modern industrial world as a consequence of high population densities in cities is yet another example of self-organized criticality.

Why? Random systems lack organizational structure—the parts of the system are linked together haphazardly. Organized systems exhibit less disorder, meaning there is a distinct pattern in the way the parts are linked together. For example, a scale-free network containing a highly linked hub and many sparsely linked nodes is more organized than a random network. The U.S. telecommunications system has structure because of its telecom hotel hubs. The electric power grid has a few nodes with high betweeness, hence more structure than a random grid. When a highly organized system reaches its critical point, insignificant incidents become significant because they can collapse the entire system.

We call a system self-organized when it evolves from a random network into a structured network 'on its own' (of course, it doesn't do this entirely on its own, but as a reaction to a hidden or subtle force). As self-organization increases, typically in the form of larger hubs or nodes with high betweeness properties, the complex system also becomes more vulnerable to targeted attacks and normal accidents. The extreme case of self-organization is SOC—a state in which small changes are likely to create large effects.

Abrupt Change is Catastrophic

This is where non-linearity becomes important: small changes can create large effects. As a system nears its critical point, consequences grow exponentially in size. As SOC grows, so does the multiplier effect on the overall system. SOC is a force-multiplier. In terms of the power law used here to measure criticality, we say that SOC stretches the long tail. It makes the Black Swan outlier bigger and more likely to happen. Non-linearity comes into play because consequences are not gradual with SOC. Instead, effects grow out of proportion to the cause. Sudden collapse without warning, the sporadic dripping of water from a leaking faucet, the non-linear jumps in the spread of SARS, and the Lévy bursts of world events are all examples of non-linearity.

Complex systems evolve discontinuously through space and time and violate General Brownian Motion. Instead of obeying the bell curve, events move through space and time according to Lévy flights and the power law. Such systems appear to have no memory; that is, the past is *not* a prelude to the future. Instead, the future of a complex system is highly irregular and unpredictable. If any generalization can be made about the future of a complex system, it must be related to the build up of SOC. If we want to influence the future state of a complex system, we must control its self-organization. Otherwise, the more a system is dominated by self-organizing dynamics, the less the past predicts the future.

Simple But Complex

Simple rules lead to complex and unexpected patterns. I have repeatedly called a number of systems in this book 'simple but complex.' What I mean by this contradictory phrase is that complex systems are typically governed by simple rules, but behave in unpredictable ways. We see this effect repeatedly in government, business, and daily life. It is the basis of normal accident theory. In principle, automobile transportation is a simple mechanical system that works as expected 99.999% of the time. And yet, 40,000 people die in accidents every year. Driving a car is simple, but complex.

Punctuation

System collapse does not resolve complexity, but merely starts a new cycle of self-organization. The dot-com bubble, financial meltdown of 2008, Gulf oil spill, 9/11 terrorist attacks, and Hurricane Katrina did not resolve the complexity of any of these systems. Rather, they simply started a subsequent build up of SOC following a period of chaotic adaptation, as described in chapter one, *'Bak's Paradox.'* There will be future financial bubbles, environmental catastrophes, terrorist attacks, and natural disasters, but they will be different—surprising and unpredictable—as a new round of self-organization takes over.

Bak's paradox is this: systems become more complex as they are improved; as they are made more efficient, less expensive, and more capable. They also become more self-organized. Therefore, the more we improve these systems, the more likely they are to collapse unexpectedly. And yet, it would be foolish to make these systems less efficient and more expensive.

Bak's admonition must be taken to heart: "Equilibrium equals death. Change is catastrophic. We must adapt because we can't predict."[2] Stasis means the end of civilization, but catastrophe means renewal and brings on a new round of change. We lose unless we learn to adapt.

The question is—adapt to what?

---

2   http://www.paulagordon.com/shows/bak/

BIBLIOGRAPHY

9/11 Commission Report. (2004). *The 9/11 Commission Report: Final Report of the National Commission on Terrorist Attacks Upon the United States (Authorized Edition)*. Washington, DC, National Commission on Terrorist Attacks Upon the United States.

Albert, R., Jeong, H. & Barabasi, A. (2000). 'The Internet's Achilles' heel: Error and attack tolerance of complex networks.' *Nature, 406*, 378-382.

Amaral, L. A. N. & Meyer, M. (1999). 'Environmental changes, coextinction, and patterns in the fossil record.' *Physical Review Letters, 82*(3), 652-655.

Appleyard, B. (2008, June 1). 'Nassim Nicholas Taleb: The prophet of boom and doom.' *The Times* (London). Retrieved February 12, 2011, from http://business.timesonline.co.uk/tol/business/economics/article4022091.ece

Backus, G., Lowry, T., Warren, D., Ehlen, M., Klise, G., Loose, V., et al. (2010, May). 'Assessing the near-term risk of climate uncertainty: Interdependencies among the U.S. States.' *SANDIA Report: SAND2010-2052*. Albuquerque, NM, Sandia National Laboratories. Retrieved February 12, 2011 from https://cfwebprod.sandia.gov/cfdocs/CCIM/.../Climate_Risk_Assessment.pdf

Bahari, M., Bergman, R. & Barry, J. (2010, December 20). 'The shadow war.' *Newsweek*. Retrieved February 12, 2011, from http://www.newsweek.com/2010/12/13/the-covert-war-against-iran-s-nuclear-program.html

Bak, P., Tang, C. & Wiesenfeld, K. (1987). 'Self-organized criticality: An explanation of 1/f noise.' *Physical Review Letters, 59*, 381-384.

Bak, P. (1996). *How Nature Works: The Science of Self-Organized Criticality*. New York, Copernicus Press.

Barabasi, A-L. (2003). 'Scale-free networks.' *Scientific American, 288*(5), 60-69.

Barabasi, A-L. (2005). 'The origin of bursts and heavy tails in human dynamics.' *Nature 435*, 207-211.

Bass, F. M. (1969). 'A new product growth model for consumer durables.' *Management Science 15*, 215-227.

Bernstein, P. L. (1998). *Against the Gods: The Remarkable Story of Risk.* Hoboken, NJ, John Wiley & Sons.

Bettencourt, L. M. A., Lobo, J., Helbing, D., Kühnert, C. & West, G. B. (2007). 'Growth, innovation, and the pace of life in cities.' *Proceedings of the National Academy of Sciences, 104*, 7301–7306.

Bhatt, U. S., Newman, D. E., Carreras, B. A. & Dobson, I. (2005, January). 'Understanding the effect of risk aversion on risk.' *Proceedings of the 38th Annual Hawaii International Conference on System Sciences (HICSS '05),* 64b.

Boyer, C. B. (1991). *The History of Mathematics.* Hoboken, NJ, John Wiley & Sons.

Broad, W. J., Markoff, J. & Sanger, D. E. (2011, January 15). 'Israeli test on worm called crucial in Iran nuclear delay.' *New York Times*. Retrieved February 12, 2011, from http://www.nytimes.com/2011/01/16/world/middleeast/16stuxnet.html

Brockmann, D., Hufnagel, L. & Geisel, T. (2006). 'The scaling laws of human travel.' *Nature, 439*, 462-465.

Brockmann, D. (2010). 'Follow the money.' *Physics World (February)*, 31-34. Retrieved February 12, 2011, from http://rocs.northwestern.edu/publications/index_assets/brockmann2010pw.pdf

Broder, A., Kumar, S. R., Maghoul, F., Raghavan, P., Rajagopalan, S., Stata, R. et al. (2000). 'Graph structure in the web.' *Computer Networks, 33,* 309-320.

Buchanan, M. (2000). *Ubiquity: Why Catastrophes Happen.* New York, Three Rivers Press.

'California wildfires largest 'fire event' in state history.' (2008, July 14). MSNBC.com. Retrieved February 12, 2011, from http://www.msnbc.msn.com/id/25681607/ns/us_news-life/

Cann, R. L., Stoneking, M. & Wilson, A. C. (1987). 'Mitochondrial DNA and human evolution.' *Nature, 325,* 31-36.

Carreras, B. A., Lynch, V. E., Dobson, I. & Newman, D. E. (2002). 'Critical points and transitions in an electric power transmission model for cascading failure blackouts.' *Chaos, 12,* 985-994.

Casazza, J. A. (2003). 'What's wrong with the electric grid?' *The Industrial Physicist, 9*(5), 8-13.

Cheesebrough, T., Stenzler, J., Langbehn, W. & Hanson, M. (2009). 'RAPID: Supporting risk-informed strategic policy and resource allocation decisions at DHS.' Washington, DC, U.S. Department of Homeland Security, Office of Risk Management and Analysis.

Christensen, C. M. (2003). *The Innovator's Dilemma: The Revolutionary Book that Will Change the Way You Do Business.* New York, Harper Collins.

Clauset, A., Young, M. & Gleditsch, K. S. (2007). 'On the frequency of severe terrorist events.' *Journal of Conflict Resolution, 51*(1), 58–87.

Davidson, K. (2003, August 15). 'How a butterfly's wing can bring down Goliath/Chaos theories calculate the vulnerability of megasystems.' SFGate.com. Retrieved February 12, 2011, from http://articles.sfgate.com/2003-08-15/news/17502761_1_complexity-theory-power-systems-system-collapse

Davis, J. (2007, August 21). 'Hackers take down the most wired country in Europe.' *WIRED Magazine, 15*(09). Retrieved February 12, 2011, from http://www.wired.com/politics/security/magazine/15-09/ff_estonia

Dobson, I., Carreras, B. A., Lynch, V. E. & Newman, D. E. (2007). 'Complex systems analysis of series of blackouts: Cascading failure, critical points, and self-organization.' *Chaos, 17*(2). Retrieved February 12, 2011, from http://citeseerx.ist.psu.edu/viewdoc/download?doi=10.1.1.142.6082&rep=rep1&type=pdf

Eck, J. E., Clarke, R. V. & Guerette, R. T. (2007). 'Risky facilities: Crime concentration in homogeneous sets of establishments and facilities.' *Crime Prevention Studies, 21*, 225–264.

Faber, D. (2009). *And Then The Roof Caved In: How Wall Street's Greed and Stupidity Brought Capitalism to its Knees*. Hoboken, NJ, John Wiley & Sons.

Fischhoff, B., Slovic, P., Lichtenstein, S., Read, S. & Combs, B. (1978). 'How safe is enough? A psychometric study of attitudes towards technological risks and benefits.' *Policy Sciences, 9*(2), 127-152.

Garrett, B. L. & Tetlow, T. (2006). 'Criminal justice collapse: The constitution after Hurricane Katrina.' *University of Virginia Law School Public Law and Legal Theory Working Paper Series #44* (2006). Retrieved February 12, 2011, from http://law.bepress.com/cgi/viewcontent.cgi?article=1080&context=uvalwps

Gladwell, M. (2000). *The Tipping Point: How Little Things Can Make a Big Difference*. New York, Little, Brown & Company.

Grassberger, P. (2002). 'Critical behaviour of the Drossel-Schwabl forest fire model.' *New Journal of Physics, 4*(17).

Grossi, P. & Kunreuther, H. (2005). *Catastrophe Modeling: A New Approach to Managing Risk*. New York, Springer.

Helbing, D., Farkas, I. & Vicsek, T. (2000). 'Simulating dynamical features of escape panic.' *Nature, 407*, 487-490.

Hanson, R. (2007). 'Catastrophe, social collapse, and human extinction.' In Rees, M., Bostrom, N. & Cirkovic, M. (Eds). *Global Catastrophic Risks*. Oxford, Oxford University Press, 363-377.

Harris, S. (2009, November 13). 'The cyberwar plan, not just a defensive game.' *National Journal*, Retrieved February 12, 2011, from http://www.nextgov.com/nextgov/ng_20091113_1728.php

Hu, Y., Luo, D., Xu, X., Han, Z. & Di, Z. (2010). 'Effects of Levy flights mobility pattern on epidemic spreading under limited energy constraint.' *Physics and Society*. (Submitted February 5, 2010). Retrieved February 12, 2011, from http://arxiv.org/abs/1002.1332

Johnson, N. F., Spagat, M., Restrepo, J., Bohorquez, J., Suarez, N., Restrepo, E. & Zarama, R. (2005). 'From old wars to new wars and global terrorism.' *Physics and Society*. (Submitted June 29, 2005). Retrieved February 12, 2011, from http://arxiv.org/physics/0506213

Johnson, N. F., Spagat, M., Restrepo, J. A., Becerra, O., Bohorquez, J. C., Suarez, N., et al. (2006). 'Universal patterns underlying ongoing wars and terrorism.' *Physics and Society*. (Submitted May 3, 2006). Retrieved February 12, 2011, from http://arxiv.org/abs/physics/0605035

Kendall, G. (2001). 'Power outages during market deregulation.' *IEEE Control Systems Magazine* (December), 33-39.

Kermack, W. O. & McKendrick, A. G. (1927). 'A contribution to the mathematical theory of epidemics.' *Proceedings of the Royal Society, London* (August), 115, 700-721.

Kinney, R., Crucitti, P., Albert, R. & Latora, V. (2005). 'Modeling cascading failures in the North American power grid.' *European Physical Journal B, 46*(1).

Kleiber, M. (1932). 'Body size and metabolism.' *Hilgardia, 6,* 315–353.

Krebs, V. E. (2002, April) 'Uncloaking terrorist networks.' *First Monday, 7*(4).

Kuhn, R. (1997). 'Sources of failure in the public switched telephone network.' *IEEE COMPUTER, 30*(4).

La, C-A. & Pietro, M. (2008). 'Characterizing user mobility in Second Life.' *WOSP '08: Proceedings of the First Workshop on Online Social Networks (2008)*, 79-84.

Lewis, T. G. (2006). *Critical Infrastructure Protection: Defending a Networked Nation.* Hoboken, NJ, John Wiley & Sons.

Lewis, T. G. (2009). *Network Science: Theory and Applications.* Hoboken, NJ, John Wiley & Sons.

Lewis, T. G. (2010). 'Cause-and-effect or fooled by randomness?' *Homeland Security Affairs, 6*(1), 1-12. Retrieved February 12, 2011, from http://www.hsaj.org/?article=6.1.6

Liu, Y., Gopikrishnan, P., Cizeau, P., Meyer, M., Peng, C. & Stanley, H. E. (1999). 'Statistical properties of the volatility of price fluctuations.' *Physical Review E, 60*(2), 1390-1400.

Malamud, B., Morein, G. & Turcotte, D. (1998). 'Forest fires: An example of self-organized critical behavior.' *Science, 281*, 1840-1842.

Malamud, B. D. & Turcotte, D. L. (2006). 'The applicability of power-law frequency statistics to floods.' *Journal of Hydrology, 322*, 168-180.

Massie, D. L., Campbell, K. L. & Williams, A. F. (1995). 'Traffic accident involvement rates by driver age and gender.' *Accident Analysis & Prevention, 27*(1), 73-87.

Mayo, J. R., Minnich, R. G., Rudish, D. W. & Armstrong, R. C. (2009). 'Approaches for scalable modeling and emulation of cyber systems: LDRD final report.' *SANDIA Report: SAND2009-6068.* Albuquerque, NM, Sandia National Laboratories. Retrieved February 12, 2011, from http://prod.sandia. gov/techlib/access-control.cgi/2009/096068.pdf

Mignan, A., Grossi, P. & Muir-Wood, R. (2010). 'Risk assessment of Tunguska-type airbursts.' *Natural Hazards, Online First* (August 16).

Miscamble, W. D. (2007). *From Roosevelt to Truman: Potsdam, Hiroshima, and the Cold War.* Cambridge, UK, Cambridge University Press.

Tikk, E., Kaska, K., Runnimeri, K., Kert, M., Taliharm, A-M. & Vihul, L. (2008). *Cyber Attacks Against Georgia: Legal Lessons Identified.* Tallinn, Estonia, Cooperative Cyber Defense Center of Excellence. Retrieved February 12, 2011, from www.carlisle.army.mil/DIME/documents/ Georgia%201%200.pdf

Newman, D. E., Carreras, B. A., Lynch, V. E. & Dobson, I. (2008). 'Evaluating the effect of upgrade, control and development strategies on robustness and failure risk of the Power Transmission Grid.' *Proceedings of the 41st Annual Hawaii International Conference on System Sciences (HICSS '08), 1-5.*

NIPP. (2006). *The National Infrastructure Protection Plan.* Washington, DC, U.S. Department of Homeland Security.

NIPP. (2009). The *National Infrastructure Protection Plan.* Washington, DC, U.S. Department of Homeland Security. Retrieved February 12, 2011, from www.dhs.gov/xlibrary/assets/NIPP_Plan.pdf

National Security Telecommunications Advisory Committee. (2003). *Vulnerabilities Task Force Report, Concentration of Assets: Telecom Hotels.* Washington, DC. Retrieved February 12, 2011, from www.ncs.gov/nstac/reports/2003/Telecom%20Hotels.pdf

Perrow, C. (1999). *Normal Accidents: Living with High Risk Technologies.* Princeton, NJ, Princeton University Press. (First Ed. 1984).

Petraeus, D. H. (2007, September 10-11). *Report to Congress on the Situation in Iraq, General David H. Petraeus, Commander, Multi-National Force-Iraq.* Retrieved February 12, 2011, from www.defense.gov/pubs/pdfs/Petraeus-Testimony20070910.pdf

Pruessner, G. & Jensen, H. J. (2002). 'The Oslo rice pile model is a quenched Edwards-Wilkinson equation.' *Physical Review E, 65*(5).

Ramo, J. C. (2009). *The Age of the Unthinkable: Why the New World Disorder Constantly Surprises Us and What We Can Do About It.* New York, Little, Brown & Company.

Ren, H., Dobson, I. & Carreras, B. A. (2008). Long-term effect of the n-1 criterion on cascade line outages in an evolving power transmission grid.' *IEEE Transactions on Power Systems, 23*(3), 1217-1225.

Reynolds, C. (1987). 'Flocks, herds and schools: A distributed behavioral model.' *SIGGRAPH '87: Proceedings of the 14th Annual Conference on Computer Graphics and Interactive Techniques.* Association for Computing Machinery. 25-34.

Resnick, M. (1994). *Turtles, Termites, and Traffic Jams: Explorations in Massively Parallel Microworlds*. Cambridge, MA, MIT Press.

Rhee, I., Shin, M., Hong, S., Lee, K. & Chong, S. (2008). 'On the Levy-walk nature of human mobility.' *Proceedings of the 27th Annual Joint Conference of the IEEE Computer and Communications Societies (INFOCOM) (April 2008)*, 924–932. Retrieved February 12, 2011, from netsrv.csc.ncsu.edu/export/infocom2008_mobility_final.pdf

Schumpeter, J. A. (1942). *Capitalism, Socialism and Democracy*. New York, Harper & Brothers Publishers.

Slovic, P. (1987). 'Perception of risk.' *Science, 236*, 280-285.

Song, W., Weicheng, F., Binghong, W. & Jianjun, Z. (2001). 'Self-organized criticality of forest fires in China.' *Ecological Modelling, 145*, 61-68.

Song, W. G., Zhang, H. P., Chen, T., Fan, W. C. (2003). 'Power-law distribution of city fires.' *Fire Safety Journal, 38*, 453–465.

Starr, C. (1969, Sept 19). 'Social benefit versus technological risk.' *Science, 165*, 1232-1238.

Taleb, N. N. (2004). *Fooled by Randomness: The Hidden Role of Chance in Life and in the Markets*. New York, Random House (Second Rev. Ed.).

Taleb, N. N. (2007). *The Black Swan: The Impact of the Highly Improbable.* New York, Random House.

Taleb, N. N. 'Fooled by rationalism: Lecturing birds how to fly.' *Notebook.* Taleb's blog. Retrieved February 12, 2011, from http://www.fooledbyrandomness.com/notebook.htm

Tang, C., Wiesenfeld, K., Bak, P., Coppersmith, S. & Littlewood, P. (1987). 'Phase organization.' *Physical Review Letters, 58,* 1161.

Theraulaz, G. & Bonabeau, E. (1999). 'A brief history of stigmergy.' *Artificial Life,* 5(2), 97-116.

Tseng, J., Lee, M. & Li, S. (2009). 'Heavy-tailed distributions in fatal traffic accidents: role of human activities.' *IEEE Computer, 30,* 419. Retrieved February 12, 2011, from http://www.arxiv.org/abs/0901.3183v1

Turcotte, D. L. (1999). 'Self-organized criticality.' *Reports on Progress in Physics, 62,* 1377-1429.

Turcotte, D. L., Smalley, R. F. & Solla, S. A. (1985). 'Collapse of loaded fractal trees.' *Nature, 313,* 6004.

Wang, Z., Chakrabarti, D., Wang, C. & Faloutsos, C. (2003). 'Epidemic spreading in real networks: an eigenvalue viewpoint.' *Proceedings of the 22nd International Symposium on Reliable Distributed Systems.* (October 6-18), 25-34.

Williams, J. T. & Hyde, A. C. (2009, October). *The mega-fire phenomenon: Observations from a coarse-scale assessment with implications for foresters, land managers, and policy-makers.* Paper presented at the Society of American Foresters' National Convention, Orlando, Fl.

Wingert, P. (2010, June 14). 'The (somewhat) good and (mostly) bad news about high-school dropout rates.' *Newsweek*. Retrieved February 12, 2011, from http://www.newsweek.com/blogs/the-gaggle/2010/06/14/the-somewhat-good-and-mostly-bad-news-about-high-school-dropout-rates.html

Xu, R-H., He, J-F., Evans, M. R., Peng, G-W., Field, H. E., Yu, D-W. et al. (2004). 'Epidemiologic clues to SARS origin in China.' *Emerging Infectious Diseases Journal, 10*(6), *1030-1037*. Retrieved February 12, 2011, from http://www.cdc.gov/ncidod/EID/vol10no6/03-0852.htm

Zimmerman, F. M. (2001). *Trends in Manufacturing*. Retrieved February 12, 2011, from http://courseweb.stthomas.edu/fmzimmerman/books/TrendsinMfg.pdf

Zipf, G. K. (1949). *Human Behavior and the Principle of Least Effort*. Cambridge, MA, Addison-Wesley.

GLOSSARY

Attractor – a terminal state that emerges from a complex system as it self-organizes. Once in an attractor state, called a fixed point, the system remains there forever or until changed by some outside force.

Average cluster coefficient – the average over all nodes of node cluster coefficients.

Bak's paradox – contradiction between efficiency and optimal operation of a complex system and its inevitable collapse.

Betweeness – the number of paths running through a node from all other nodes to all other nodes reachable from the node.

Black Swan – the outlier; the rare, impressive, unpredictable event.

Boids – artificial life forms proposed by Craig Reynolds that move through space via a combination of flocking and random displacements.

Bond percolation – process of adding links to a network, e.g. adding relationships between pairs of people in a social network.

Chaos – property of a system with high entropy.

Chaotic – disorganized, non-linear, high entropy.

Cluster coefficient – the percentage of neighboring nodes that are also connected to one another, e.g. the percentage of triangular sub-networks formed around a node by its neighboring nodes.

Clustered network – a network with high average cluster coefficient, i.e. a network with a high number of clusters surrounding nodes.

Complex system – a system with behaviors not entirely explained by the behaviors of its individual parts.

Complexity – property of a system with many parts in an intricate arrangement.

Connectivity – the degree of dependency among nodes in a network, e.g. the density of links in a network.

Critical point – state of a complex system near its point of breakdown, collapse, or catastrophic disruption.

Duopoly – a competitive system dominated by two players.

Emergence – global properties of a complex system appear as a result of local changes to a system's individual parts. The global property does not seem to be explainable by observing the local changes.

Entropy – disorganized, random, without structure.

Exceedence probability - the likelihood of an event such as an avalanche, earthquake, airplane accident, or terrorist attack with an associated damage of a certainsize or larger.

Exceedence probability – the probability that an event equals or exceeds a certain value.

Extremistan – Taleb's metaphorical place where Black Swan events happen and the laws of unpredictable events obey the power law.

Flocking – movement through space or time by a complex system whereby the positions of its individual parts are determined by nearest neighbors.

Gross Domestic Product (GDP) - a measure of the goods and services produced by a country in a year.

Levy flight – movement through space or time whereby the lengths of waypoints obey a power law distribution.

Linear – change is proportional to the force applied.

Link – an abstract relationship between a pair of nodes representing anything of interest

Mediocristan – Taleb's metaphorical place where the expected happens; the laws of unpredictable events obey the Bell curve.

Network – a collection of nodes and links and a mapping function that defines how nodes are connected via links; an abstract representation of connected things

Node – an abstract entity representing anything of interest

Non-linear – change is out of proportion to the force applied.

Normal accident – major disruptive event caused by a series of seemingly insignificant incidents that magnify and snowball as subsequent incidents spread to other parts of a system.

Oligopoly – a competitive system containing many players of roughly equal weight.

Percolation – process of adding parts (nodes, links) to a complex system.

Power law – An L-shaped curve for modeling frequency, exceedence probability, and other phenomenon that do not obey the Bell curve.

Preferential attachment – An emergence process whereby a node in a network is more likely to connect to preferred nodes, because they already have more links, higher betweeness, etc.

Probability distribution - the range of possible values that a random variable can take and the probability that the value of the random variable is within any (measurable) subset of that range.

Punctuated equilibrium – Per Bak's phrase for the behavior of a complex system that is in equilibrium most of the time but is rarely and briefly rendered unstable because of some catastrophic event.

Punctuated reality – application of Bak's theory of punctuated equilibrium to reality.

Random network – a network containing links that are connected to randomly chosen node-pairs.

Random process – a process whereby all events are equally likely to occur.

Randomness – the result of a random process.

Sand pile – metaphor for a complex system susceptible to unpredictable collapse.

Scale-free network – a network containing links that are connected to node-pairs such that the pattern of node connectivity obeys a power law, whereby the most-highly connected node – called the hub - is rare.

Self-organization – an emergent process whereby a system organizes itself into some form of structure, e. g., connectivity, betweeness, and hubness are examples of self-organization.

Self-organized criticality, SOC - a fundamental property of many complex systems that tend to self-organize into a critical state and once in this state any change to the system results in chain reactions that may impact a varying number of elements in the system.

Simple system – a system with a linear or predictable relationship between its inputs and its outputs.

Site percolation – process of adding nodes to a network, e.g. adding trees in a forest.

Stigmergy – a form of self-organization whereby the next state and the rules applied to form the next state of a system are determined by the previous state of the system.

System – a collection of interrelated parts or components.

INDEX

ABOUT THE AUTHOR

Ted G. Lewis is currently Professor of Computer Science and Executive Director of the Center for Homeland Defense and Security at the Naval Postgraduate School, Monterey, California. He has previously held a variety of positions within the IEEE Computer Society (EIC of IEEE Software, EIC of IEEE COMPUTER), industry (CEO of DaimlerChrysler Research and Technology NA, Senior Vice President of Eastman Kodak), and academia (University of Louisiana, Oregon State University, Naval Postgraduate School). Lewis is the author of over 30 books and 100 papers on computing, critical infrastructure, and complexity.